The Dreyfus Affair

The Dreyfus Affair

'J'accuse' and Other Writings

Emile Zola

Edited by Alain Pagès
Translated by Eleanor Levieux

Yale University Press
New Haven & London

Copyright © 1996 by Yale University
First published in paperback 1998

English language translation © by Eleanor Levieux 1996

Much of the material in this edition is from *L'affaire Dreyfus: Lettres et entretiens inédits*, edited by Alain Pagès © 1994 CNRS Editions

Set in Photina by Best-set Typesetter Ltd, Hong Kong
Printed and bound in Great Britain by Biddles Ltd, Guildford and Kings Lynn

Library of Congress Cataloging-in-Publication Data

Zola, Emile, 1840–1902.
    [Affaire Dreyfus.   English]
    The Dreyfus Affair: J'accuse and other writings/Emile Zola; edited by Alain Pagès; translated by Eleanor Levieux.
    Includes bibliographical references and index.
    ISBN 0–300–06689–9 (hbk: alk. paper)
    ISBN 0–300–07367–4 (pbk.)
    1. Dreyfus, Alfred, 1859–1935—Trials, litigation, etc.—Sources.   2. Trials (Treason)—France—Sources.   3. Zola, Emile, 1840–1902—Correspondence. 4. Antisemitism—France.   5. Press and politics—France.   I. Pagès, Alain. II. Levieux, Eleanor.   III. Title.
DC354.8.Z6513   1996
944'.0812'092—dc20   96–1735
                                                                                        CIP

A catalogue record for this book is available from the British Library.

*With warmest thanks to my husband, Michel,
and to Bill Calin, Howard Greenfeld, Michael Riccioli,
George Sheridan, Mark Sholl and Barbara Shuey
for their knowledge, advice and encouragement.*

Eleanor Levieux

Contents

Part One: *For Humanity, Truth and Justice*

Part Two: *Beset by Uncertainty*

Part Three: *Waiting for Victory*

Illustrations

Translator's Preface

Everyone has heard of 'J'accuse' – but how many people have actually read it? How many know that it was not the only open letter Zola published during the Dreyfus Affair but in fact the sixth? That it was followed by seven more over the next three years? That some were dashed off in the white heat of outrage and others proceeded from cooler reflection? That all were written in response to specific developments as the case unfolded, at a time when memories of the French army's humiliation by Prussia one generation earlier nurtured systematic espionage, and the collapse of the Panama Canal scheme nurtured anti-Semitism? That Zola himself paid dearly for his unflinching involvement in what soon became a crusade?

Nowhere could I find a translation of his entire series of articles, or of 'Pour les Juifs' which preceded it by eighteen months and to which the other articles now appear as a sadly predictable sequel. Books on the Affair or studies of Zola sometimes included brief excerpts, rarely exceeding two or three paragraphs, from a handful of the articles; 'J'accuse' was of course the most widely quoted of the articles, but even it was generally not complete. Bibliographical research confirmed that today's English-speaking reader simply did not have access to the entirety of Zola's contribution to the monumental campaign which transformed French history and still echoes down the decades.

I began translating the published articles. Then Yale University Press encouraged me and greatly enhanced my original purpose by suggesting that the translation could also include much of the material contained in *Emile Zola: L'affaire Dreyfus: Lettres et entretiens inédits*, edited by Alain Pagès and published jointly in 1994 by the CNRS in France and Les Presses de l'Université de Montréal. Accordingly, the most significant letters from Zola's private correspondence were selected from that volume, along with the interviews; thus, this Yale publication constitutes the most comprehensive collection of Zola's writings on and during the Dreyfus Affair available in English. The reader will be able to hear both the public Zola who thunders fearlessly with Biblical wrath and ardent republicanism and the private Zola who fretfully lies low in exile and who, in order to learn that developments across the Channel in France have at last reached a critical turning point (Colonel Henry's confession and death), must bicycle to the nearest town, incognito, to buy the British newspapers and decipher them with the help of a dictionary!

It has been my aim to render Zola's impassioned late nineteenth-century cadences as faithfully as possible, yet in language that will not sound archaic or stilted to late twentieth-century ears. When we hear Zola warn that reactionary thinking, excessive nationalism and abuse of power lead directly to dictatorship, it is never too late to remember events a few scant decades later, never too late to heed his words.

Eleanor Levieux, Paris, November 1995

Introduction

Each successive degree of Zola's involvement in the Dreyfus Affair during its three most critical years, beginning at the time of Scheurer-Kestner's campaign in the autumn of 1897 to have the Jewish captain rehabilitated, and ending with the trial in Rennes and the pardon in the autumn of 1899, then the amnesty in 1900, emerges clearly from this volume. It comprises numerous letters,[1] an article published in 1896 and the entire contents of *La Vérité en marche* (*The Truth is on the March*), which Zola published in 1901 in order to bring together the pamphlets and all of the articles he had published in the press throughout the Affair, including the famous 'J'accuse'; for the most part, they had explicitly taken the form of 'open letters' to individual or collective addressees. Lastly, a number of interviews, hitherto unpublished in book form, are included because they enable us to hear another type of discourse, in counterpoint, yet preserve the same tone, that of thought expressed through dialogue. They therefore fit perfectly into the unity of this volume.

Taken in chronological order, these writings blend Zola's public texts and excerpts from the private correspondence including letters to the people nearest him – Alexandrine, his wife; Fernand Desmoulin, his most faithful companion; Fernand Labori, his lawyer; and Jeanne Rozerot. Threats sometimes hung over this correspondence. Again and again the police attempted to intercept or copy it. Beginning in January 1898, Zola's mail was opened by a special department (*cabinet noir*) at the prefecture of police, and when he went into exile in England the hunt was intensified. Zola had to conceal his name and address; he had to rely on other individuals to whom he sent his messages, each in an envelope placed inside another envelope. But any reader who leafs through this volume in the hope of discovering secrets that have lain buried for the past century will be disappointed. These texts were not meant to conceal anything. They were intended to illustrate an ideological struggle, or to bring opposing

---

1   The letters are taken from Volume IX of Zola's *Correspondance*, devoted to the Dreyfus Affair, which was edited by Alain Pagès and published by the CNRS in France and the Presses de l'Université de Montréal in 1994. Readers wishing for further information can refer to the notes provided in that scholarly edition.

points of view closer together. Above all, they sought to convince. Between the letters belonging to the private correspondence but opened for the purposes of this volume, and the genuine open letters, intended as such in the manner and at the time they were written, there is no gap. On the contrary, there is a surprising unity of tone and content. Zola's activity as a polemicist was rooted in the reflections made possible by the intimacy of his private relationships.

Zola in fact never looked upon the activity of letter-writing as the place for clandestine intrigues. Very early on he decided that he would turn over to posterity the dossiers he compiled for each of his novels, and he constructed them with that in mind. And with the same straight-forwardness, he explicitly authorized the reading of his correspondence. When Henry Céard, his disciple, warned him that some of his autograph letters were going to be put up for sale, Zola proudly replied in these words in June 1884: 'I have no secrets; the keys are in the cupboard doors. They can publish my letters some day. They will not give the lie to a single one of my friendships, or a single one of the positions I have taken.'[2] By January 1898, when he published 'J'accuse' in *L'Aurore*, he had not changed his mind. Despite the turmoil of the Dreyfus Affair in which he was caught up, despite the hatred and the insults, he still wished his correspondence to be an open book where everything would be perfectly clear and readable for all.

At the beginning of November 1897, Zola was living alone in Paris, in his home in the rue de Bruxelles. A few weeks earlier he had returned to the city from his country house at Médan, near Poissy, west of Paris, where he had spent the spring and summer. Alexandrine had left for Italy for a long stay on 10 October. Every autumn for the past two years she had travelled to Italy. The couple had surmounted the crises of the previous years and relations between them had become normal again, or nearly normal. Ulti-mately Alexandrine had resigned herself to Zola's liaison with Jeanne Rozerot, even if she hadn't forgiven him for it.[3] All sides involved made the best they could of the compromise that had been reached concerning the way their existence was to be shared, the hours that could be given over to Jeanne and the children. The children had grown; Denise was now eight and Jacques was six. And one of Zola's great joys, on these early November days, was to take them to the Tuileries gardens on Sunday afternoons.

It was all the easier for him at this time to enjoy the pleasures of father-hood because he felt free of commitments; his mind was not taken up with any major project. In fact, he had just completed a new stage in his work

---

2 Letter of 14 June 1884 to Henry Céard, *Correspondance*, Presses de l'Université de Montréal and Editions du CNRS, 1985, vol. V, p. 125.
3 See 'Leading Figures Involved in the Dreyfus Affair', at the end of this volume.

by finishing *Paris*, the last novel in his trilogy, *Trois villes*, at the end of the summer, and the first instalment had appeared in *Le Journal* on 23 October. Several of the themes Zola had already explored in *Les Rougon-Macquart* come together in the character of Pierre Froment, the priest who has lost his faith and will discover happiness thanks to young Marie's love. Through this priest, Zola brings in every social class in the capital, from the most wretched slum dwellers to the debauched and corrupt grande bourgeoisie. In the plot of *Paris*, Zola combines the separate worlds of *La Curée*, *Nana* and *L'Assommoir*. But the novel's chief interest is that it offers a modern historical setting. The France that Zola talks about in *Paris* is the France of 1892–4, marked by parliamentary scandals and anarchist attempts to overthrow the government. And that France is already, in advance, so to speak, the France of the Dreyfus Affair. *La Libre Parole*, the real-life newspaper of the anti-Semite, Edouard Drumont (transposed as *La Voix du peuple*, the newspaper of the fictional Sanier), comes into its own amid the disorderly climate of parliamentary intrigues. As Edmond Lepelletier, the critic, rather shrewdly observed, 'Although *Paris* was written and published long before the clamour over the Affair broke out, it was premonitory; it anticipated the struggle that was about to take place. The Dreyfus Affair was the battle that Zola depicted in the novel, translated into reality.'[4]

Zola's well-regulated life was to be thoroughly upset by the Dreyfus Affair. He was totally absorbed in his work and nothing, it would seem, predisposed him to make such a choice.

He did not look upon the world of politics with any fondness. Again and again he had vituperated against the mediocrity of the Third Republic's parliamentary figures, denouncing their low morals and their taste for intrigue. His public statements of opinion, ranging from the positions he upheld in 'La République et la littérature' in 1879 to those appearing in 'L'élite et la politique' during the campaign conducted in *Le Figaro* in 1896, had always been unambiguous.[5] Yet he could also see the value of serious political action aimed at effective reform. He had mulled over the careers of Maurice Barrès, a member of the Chamber of Deputies between 1889 and 1893, and Gabriele D'Annunzio in Italy. And he had occasionally daydreamed of a different destiny. In August 1893, in an interview he granted to Jules Huret, Zola confessed that if overtures were made to him, he too might become a Deputy.[6] He had some idea of what his political influence might be, because of his experience as president of the Société des gens de lettres (virtually without interruption from 1891 to 1896), and because

---

4   E. Lepelletier, *Emile Zola. Sa vie. Son oeuvre*, Mercure de France, 1908, p. 419.
5   The first of these articles was included in *Le Roman expérimental* (1880) and the second in *Nouvelle Campagne* (1897).
6   J. Huret, *Interviews de littérature et d'art*, Ed. Thot, 1984, pp. 43–4. Zola, it will be recalled, wrote the parliamentary chronicle for the *Sémaphore de Marseille* and *La Cloche* in 1871.

during his visits to England (September 1893) and Italy (October to December 1894) he had been feted and honoured as the outstanding representative of French literature.

A series of encounters drew Zola into the Dreyfus Affair.[7] The first was with Bernard-Lazare, a young Symbolist poet, who came to see him on 6 November 1897. Ever since February 1895, Bernard-Lazare had been supporting Mathieu Dreyfus's efforts to defend his brother, and in November 1896 he had already approached Zola but to no avail. This time he had more arguments at his disposal; he was about to publish his second pamphlet, which would contain detailed analyses of the bordereau by a number of international experts.[8] Then, Louis Leblois, Picquart's lawyer and friend, came to see Zola at his Paris home. He came twice, first on 8 November and again on the 10th. He went into the story of the whole Affair from the beginning, described the intrigues going on in military circles and showed Zola some of the documents in his possession. And he urged Zola to attend a luncheon on 13 November at the home of Auguste Scheurer-Kestner, vice-president of the Senate.

That encounter proved decisive, and thanks to the journal Scheurer-Kestner kept, we know what transpired in the course of it. With a view to leading a campaign in the press, Scheurer wished to 'gather about him a council of men accustomed to speaking to the masses'.[9] To this luncheon he had invited another novelist as well, Marcel Prévost. At the end of the meal, Scheurer-Kestner, aided by Leblois, outlined every episode of the Affair. The two novelists listened closely. Scheurer-Kestner observed their reactions and compared them in his journal: 'What a difference between [Zola] and Marcel Prévost, who has an attractive and fine-featured head, the dark head of a man from the Midi; his eyes are searching and the mouth is sensual and sceptical, but what [Prévost] lacks is forcefulness. I can see it; I can feel it in what he says. I have the impression that [Zola] will do "something" whereas [Prévost], though he calls it regrettable, will not do a thing.'[10]

Zola came away from this gathering deeply stirred by all he had learned. The possibility of his intervening had been raised. He had tried to keep his distance. But in spite of himself he was drawn to what he felt was an 'extraordinary' and 'thrilling' story. He poured out his hesitations in long

---

7 For the sequence of events during the Dreyfus Affair, see the detailed Chronology. Readers may also wish to consult J.-D. Bredin, *L'Affaire* (new reworked edition, Fayard/Julliard, 1993), which achieves an excellent synthesis of events. (*The Affair*, trans. J. Mehlman, Geo. Braziller, NY, 1986; Sidgwick and Jackson, London, 1987.)

8 The pamphlet was put on sale on 12 November 1897. It was reissued in 1993 by Editions Allia (Ph. Oriol, ed.). See also J-D. Bredin, *Bernard-Lazare*, Ed. de Fallois, 1992.

9 A. Scheurer-Kestner, *Mémoires d'un sénateur dreyfusard* (A. Roumieux, ed.), Strasbourg, Bueb et Reumaux, 1988, p. 179.

10 *Ibid.*, p. 180.

letters to Alexandrine which, unfortunately, we have not been able to publish in this volume.[11] Scheurer-Kestner's courageous attitude had made a deep impression on him. Fernand de Rodays, the director of *Le Figaro*, whom Zola had known for a long time, promised to give his support. So Zola made up his mind. On 25 November, *Le Figaro* published his first article on the Affair, 'M. Scheurer-Kestner', in defence of the campaign launched by the vice-president of the Senate. Zola had clearly taken sides.

Let us stop for a moment to evaluate the significance of his decision. Was Zola's involvement in the Affair somewhat belated? It has been pointed out that he was not among the very first Dreyfusards, and that Bernard-Lazare's initial visit to him, in 1896, had left him unconvinced. But these criticisms stem from reconstructions after the fact that do not pay enough heed to the finer points of chronology. At the beginning of November 1897 there was not as yet any Dreyfus Affair, although the idea that Dreyfus might be innocent had begun to gain some ground since 14 July, when Scheurer-Kestner had informed his fellow Senators that he intended to campaign for a revision of Dreyfus's trial. But aside from Scheurer-Kestner and Leblois, who were both sworn to secrecy, no one as yet knew the name of the guilty man; not even Mathieu Dreyfus, who for three years had been striving desperately to solve the mystery. He did not discover the truth until 9 November. Only then, when it became possible to bring Esterhazy's name into play, was there any real hope of proving that Alfred Dreyfus was innocent. With encouragement from Scheurer-Kestner, Mathieu Dreyfus publicly denounced Esterhazy on the evening of 15 November, in a letter to the Minister of War; it appeared in the papers the next day. Thus, 16 November was the day on which the Dreyfus Affair burst upon the general public. Implicated in the affair, the government decided to conduct an inquiry and placed General de Pellieux in charge of it. The inquiry was relayed by a second one, judicial this time, with Major Ravary in charge, and led to Esterhazy's trial, on 10 and 11 January 1898.

Zola was informed very early on and was involved in the discussions during which, in the first half of November, the Dreyfusard group gradually took shape around Scheurer-Kestner and Leblois. Thus, from the beginning, Zola was among those in the front lines, and immediately he demonstrated his commitment with the campaign he conducted in *Le Figaro*, while the investigation led by de Pellieux was going on.

The three articles he published between 25 November and 5 December ('M. Scheurer-Kestner', 'The Syndicate' and 'The Minutes') strive to spell out the circumstances of the Affair and to describe its ideological and political nature. Irony – which he uses in an attempt to combat the lasting

11   They are kept in family archives and are as yet unpublished.

legend of a Jewish 'syndicate' – is followed, in the 'Minutes', by a denunciation of anti-Semitism and the 'base exploitation of patriotism' in which the press was indulging. This was too much for *Le Figaro*'s conservative readership; indignant, the readers threatened to cancel their subscriptions. Forced to cease his campaign in the press, Zola turned to his publisher, Eugène Fasquelle, suggesting that he publish his 'open letters' in pamphlet form. Zola strove to place himself above the events of the day and adopted a more lyrical tone. Both his *Letter to the Young People*, which Fasquelle published on 14 December, and the *Letter to France* on 7 January 1898, launched an appeal to reason and expressed hope. In fact they were hoping against hope that justice might yet be done. But the outcome of Esterhazy's trial on 11 January made a mockery of that hope.

The result was 'J'accuse', which blazed across *L'Aurore*'s front page on the morning of 13 January. It was not some hotheaded, spur-of-the-moment affair. Instead, it was the culmination of the reflection that had begun in early November, combining the historical analysis that characterized the articles in *Le Figaro* with the vehement pleas contained in the pamphlets. By writing this open letter to Félix Faure, President of the French Republic, Zola was deliberately exposing himself to legal action. He states this unequivocally at the end of his peroration, after he has finished accusing the highest authorities in the land: 'I have but one goal: that light be shed, in the name of mankind which has suffered so much and has the right to happiness. My ardent protest is merely a cry from my very soul. Let them dare to summon me before a court of law! Let the inquiry be held in broad daylight! I am waiting.' Clearly, his aim was to bring about a new trial.

The effect of this bold stroke was tremendous. 'There was a burst of indignation,' writes Charles Péguy. 'The battle could be joined again. All day long, the street vendors in Paris shouted "*L'Aurore*" at the top of their lungs, ran about with huge bundles of *L'Aurore* under their arms, and thrust copies of *L'Aurore* at eager buyers. In hoarse but triumphant voices, the fine name of this newspaper rose above the feverish activity in the streets. The impact was so stunning that Paris was nearly turned upside down.'[12] *L'Aurore* sold between 200,000 and 300,000 copies, ten times the normal number. Léon Blum was to recall, in his *Souvenirs*, '"J'accuse" overwhelmed Paris in a single day. The Dreyfus cause was given a new lease of life. We regained confidence; we could feel it flooding through us, while our furious adversaries staggered under the blow.'[13] And Henri Barbusse, another witness, commented,

---

12 *Les Cahiers de la Quinzaine*, 4 December 1902, p. 31; *Oeuvres en prose complètes*, Gallimard, coll. 'Bibl. de la Pléiade', 1987, vol. I, p. 244.
13 L. Blum, *Souvenirs sur l'Affaire*, Gallimard, coll. 'Folio', 1993 (1st edn. 1935), p. 120.

We must admire the valour of this man who was plunging wholeheartedly into the campaign for justice at the risk of sinking forever, with his bundles of books and his glory, and we must admire even more the perfect clearsightedness with which he summed up the entire situation. . . . Many of his contemporaries who had the best possible intentions with regard to just causes were shaken, beset by doubt, still seeking clues, still awaiting confirmation, whereas he – who did not have any more proof at his disposal than they did – he had become convinced through and through, with a flawless grasp of the situation.[14]

The work of a journalist, 'J'accuse' was part of a collective action. Clemenceau and Vaughan were associated with the plans to publish it, since *L'Aurore* was legally liable. It was Clemenceau, as we know, who came up with the title 'J'accuse', taken from the challenge reiterated in the final paragraphs. He foresaw the battle that would ensue and lucidly, even ardently, prepared for it. Reinach later claimed that when Clemenceau (who 'would be an incurable dilettante until the end of his days') read Zola's article hot off the presses, he declared, 'Now the child can walk unaided.'[15] The government soon reacted; somewhat hesitantly, but urged on by the Deputies of the majority, it accepted the challenge. Both Zola and Perrenx, the manager of *L'Aurore*, were sued for libel and summoned to appear before the Assize Court of the Seine.

The trial lasted two weeks, from 7 February to 23 February, and caused heated debate. The first hearings were taken up with statements by the most important figures of the Affair, who told what they knew about it. The Dreyfusards gave as many details as possible; the army's witnesses provided a good deal of information even though they employed various tactics to conceal what they could. The high point occurred with Picquart's testimony; on 12 February, his face-to-face encounter with Henry became a direct challenge. Then the experts paraded one by one before the court. Those who had appeared before the courts martial of December 1894 and January 1895 (Bertillon, Teysonnières, Charavay, Pelletier and Gobert, then Couard, Belhomme and Varinard) were followed by the counter-experts whom the defence thrust into the spotlight, including Paul Meyer, Director of the Ecole des Chartes, Edouard Grimaux, who taught at the Ecole Polytechnique, and Louis Havet, professor at the Collège de France. The proceedings took a new turn on the ninth day, 16 February. De Pellieux had made some inadvertent revelations; he appealed to the testimony of General de Boisdeffre, Chief of the General Staff. De Boisdeffre appeared in dress uniform. Standing at the bar, he issued this threat: 'You are the jury; you are the nation. If the nation has no confidence in the chiefs of its army, in the men who are responsible for the nation's defence, those men are prepared to hand over that grave task to others. . . .'[16] From that moment on, the outcome of the trial was clear.

The next day, Zola read his statement to the jury with fervour. He was thoroughly convinced: 'Dreyfus is innocent, I swear he is. I stake my life on that. I stake my honour on it.' Labori's impassioned plea lasted three days, 21 to 23 February; Clemenceau's briefer plea came last. On the evening of 23 February the verdict was announced: Perrenx was sentenced to four months in prison and a fine of three thousand francs, while the author of 'J'accuse!' was sentenced to one year in prison and a fine of three thousand francs.

For the next several weeks, Zola attempted to forget some of the terrible strain he had just been through by withdrawing to his country house in Médan. Besides, his circle of friends shrank rapidly, and in Paris literary circles he was assiduously avoided. It was not healthy to be seen with him. On 27 March, at the general assembly of the Société des gens de lettres, when Paul Alexis, his steadfast friend, proposed a motion of support for Zola, half the members present called the motion scandalous and a terrific brouhaha ensued. Alexis was denied the floor and his motion was harshly rejected.[17] The reaction was the same, although more subtly expressed, on 26 May, at the Académie française, where elections were held to fill the two seats left vacant by the Duc d'Aumale and Henri Meilhac. Zola received not a single vote, not even from his few isolated supporters of previous years.

Meanwhile, the legal twists and turns of the Affair were far from over. On 2 April, the Supreme Court of Appeal overturned the verdict of the lower court; new proceedings became inevitable. On 23 May, the case came up again before the Assize Court of Versailles; the government had decided to remove the case from Paris and chosen Versailles, which was considered to be in less of an uproar. Judges with a reputation for firmness were appointed, and it was hoped that the case would be handled expeditiously. But the lawyers for the defence used delaying tactics in the hope that the other investigations being carried out at the same time (particularly the one concerning Esterhazy) would produce new evidence. Labori introduced a claim of lack of jurisdiction, on the grounds that only a Paris jury had authority to judge the facts as stated. When his claim was rejected, he lodged an appeal, knowing that this ploy would have the effect of suspending the proceedings.

The case had to be heard all over again. On 18 July the parties appeared in court in Versailles, where the same tactic was used. But this time it failed;

16 *Le Procès Zola*, P. V. Stock, 1898, vol. II. p. 127.
17 'A la Société des gens de lettres', *L'Aurore* of 28 March 1898.

the appeal did not cause proceedings to be suspended. Accordingly, the defendants withdrew, thus defaulting. In absentia, they received the maximum sentence: one year in prison and a fine of three thousand francs, just as on 23 February. It appeared that they were right back where they had started. But Labori and Clemenceau believed it was still possible to gain time: if Zola went into exile, the verdict which had just been reached could not be notified to him in the prescribed legal manner and become effective. That very evening Zola took the boat-train for London.

It had not been his wish to leave France; the departure was imposed upon him, but by leaving he avoided becoming bogged down in legal skirmishes and, in a sense, put himself out of harm's way. At the very least he was safe from the hatred of his most enraged enemies: the absurd hatred of the anti-Semitic demonstrators who pursued him around the Palais de Justice in Paris and again in Versailles; the imbecilic hatred of the soldiers who attacked him in Médan, on 10 April, while he was riding his bicycle; and the calculated hatred of Ernest Judet, editor-in-chief of *Le Petit Journal*, who had begun a libellous campaign to discredit Zola's father. The campaign was well orchestrated: Judet's first article, 'Zola père et fils', appeared on 23 May, the day on which the trial in Versailles began. The second appeared on 25 May, and a third on 18 July, when the trial resumed in Versailles. In order to cast doubts on François Zola's military record and make him out to be a thief, Judet used documents taken from the archives of the Ministry of War. Emile Zola retorted in *L'Aurore* on 28 May, recalling his father's career as civil engineer and vowing to defend his good name. And so it was that a new 'affair' suddenly appeared, grafted onto the first and complicating it with a plot of secondary importance. Zola's dream of purity and truth vanished amid sordid machinations. How remote victory seemed to be, at this point!

On 19 July, when Zola reached Victoria Station, in London, a page was turned. He was stepping into the unknown, in an unfamiliar country where he did not speak the language. Throughout his exile he was to feel extremely lonely, sometimes abandoned; but he was also able to use the experience to reaffirm his identity and find within himself a new moral strength.

First, he stayed at the Grosvenor Hotel near Victoria Station. Then, on 22 July, with the help of the faithful Desmoulin, who had come over from France, he left the centre of London and went to the village of Weybridge in Surrey, where he took board and lodging at the Oatlands Park Hotel. He was using the name of Jean Beauchamp, for it was essential that no one be able to trace him. Was he in danger from the French courts? Could French law be enforced against him on English soil? None of his advisers at this time – whether Labori in Paris or Wareham, an English solicitor to whom he had been introduced by Ernest Vizetelly, his translator – really knew what to say. Accordingly, he took all kinds of precautions although, deep down, he did not have much faith in them. The situation sometimes verged on the comical. His attempt to pass incognito fooled no one, but the individuals who recognized him were very discreet. And in the end, all went well. The legendary national character of England – reserved and puritanical – proved to be the best of shelters.

On 24 July, Desmoulin returned to France to make preparations for Alexandrine's voyage to England; she was to join her husband as quickly as possible. A few days later he was back in England with a trunk containing some clothing, a camera and Zola's preparatory notes for *Fécondité*, the novel he had begun after completing *Paris*. On 1 August, Zola moved from the Oatlands Park Hotel to a modest house, 'Penn', that he had rented for four weeks. Desmoulin left him there alone and returned to Paris, this time to stay. During this period young Violette Vizetelly, the translator's daughter, was to be Zola's interpreter and governess. He was able to resume his regular rhythm of work at last and recover his peace of mind. In the diary he kept during his exile, he assessed the events that had just taken place. 'It is now eleven months since I finished my last novel, *Paris*. Almost a year already that the monstrous Affair has taken out of my life and my work. I do not regret a thing; I would begin my struggle for truth and justice all over again. But even so, what an astonishing adventure this is, at my age, after a methodical and home-loving existence as a writer and nothing but a writer!' And he added, 'Now that I am at the mercy of events, nothing should come as a surprise to me, and all I ask is the strength to continue this new work and to complete it, even amidst the turmoil. It will be a great comfort to me, or so I hope. As it has so many times already, amidst the most unbearable moral suffering, my work will keep me on my feet.'[18]

An unhoped-for interlude of happiness was soon to be granted him. Because Alexandrine was obliged to stay on in Paris to look after practical matters, she encouraged Zola to send for Jeanne and the children, his 'other affections', as she called them, with understatement. The unexpected turn that the Affair had taken had brought Zola and his wife closer together, and now it was Alexandrine who chose to step aside. On 11 August, Jeanne and the children arrived in England, where they remained until 15 October. On 27 August, all four of them moved to 'Summerfield', in Addlestone. It was a more spacious house, and its 'large garden, half overgrown with tall grasses', as *Pages d'exil* describes it,[19] was soon filled with games and laughter. All of a sudden, exile seemed to give way to a peaceful English summer.

Zola had no intention, however, of spending the winter in London. He made plans to go to Genoa after 15 October; there Alexandrine would at

18   *Pages d'exil*, in *Oeuvres complètes*, Cercle du Livre Précieux, 1970, vol. XIV, p. 1151.
19   *Ibid.*, p. 1159.

last be able to join him. Then suddenly, on 31 August, came a dramatic turn of events: Colonel Henry, who had been arrested and imprisoned at the Mont-Valérien, committed suicide. 'A moment of the intensest joy,' wrote Zola in the diary he kept during his exile;[20] he believed the Affair was over and he would be able to return to France. But these hopes were soon dashed. Henri Brisson, the Prime Minister, procrastinated, as usual; the nationalist press, momentarily taken aback, now howled more loudly than ever and made Henry a hero; and the new Minister of War, General Zurlinden, was vigorously opposed to a revision of any kind.

Once again a long period of waiting set in; it was made even harder to bear by these recent events. Zola gave up his plans of leaving for Italy – why move from one exile to another? On 15 October, using the name of Richard, he settled at the Queen's Hotel in Upper Norwood, in the suburbs south of London, close to the famous Crystal Palace, built for the 1851 World Fair. And it was there, in the comfort of one of those grand British hotels which possess the art – unknown anywhere else – of welcoming their guests discreetly yet with the warmth of a family seat, that Zola spent the remaining months of his exile. His hopes of returning to France revived in late October, when the Criminal Chamber of the Supreme Court of Appeal began its inquiry. But in Paris, the Dreyfusard leaders, concerned by the legal action being taken against Picquart, rejected the idea of Zola's return. It was better to wait, they said again. Labori repeatedly advised caution. 'Let the procedure in the Supreme Court follow its course,' he wrote, 'as long as it acts in accordance with justice; and when you do come back, your triumph will be made all the more dazzling by the extent of your sacrifice, and the gratitude and the admiration of all France will be immense.'

Matters did not improve, however. Quesnay de Beaurepaire, president of the Civil Chamber, accused his colleagues in the Criminal Chamber of lacking impartiality. The government's reaction was to introduce a bill (la loi du dessaisissement) withdrawing jurisdiction from the Criminal Chamber. It seemed to Zola that France had gone 'utterly mad' when he learned that the Chamber of Deputies had passed this law on 10 February, for it entrusted the revision procedure to all three Chambers of the Supreme Court of Appeal ruling together, thus making a revision even more unlikely than before. Just as it looked as though all was lost for the Dreyfusards, their second miracle occurred: on 16 February, Félix Faure, President of the French Republic and a fierce adversary of revision, died in the arms of the beautiful Madame Steinheil. The course of fate seemed to have been reversed. Emile Loubet, who was in favour of a revision, was elected President of the Republic. And the failure of Déroulède's attempted coup

20   *Ibid.*, p. 1160.

d'état, during the ceremonies attending Félix Faure's funeral, put an end to nationalist hopes, at least for the time being.

The final period which now began was again one of waiting – but this time with confidence in the likely outcome. Now and again Zola was disturbed by the personality of Ballot-Beaupré, rapporteur of the Supreme Court of Appeal, but Alexis and Reinach gave him information which reassured him on this score. The last months of his London exile were enlivened by visits from several Paris friends. And work was still important, for Zola was determined to have finished *Fécondité* by the time he returned to France, so as to be as free as possible. At last, on 3 June, he received a telegram from Alexandrine: 'Cheque delayed. Invoice received. All goes well.' This coded message meant that the three Chambers had jointly quashed the 1894 verdict and that Alfred Dreyfus was to appear before another court martial. On 4 June, accompanied by Eugène Fasquelle, his publisher, Zola took the 9 p.m. train from London. He was in Paris by 5:38 the next morning. His return was not triumphant, not that of a victor acclaimed by the crowds, but discreet, the return of a clear-sighted participant well aware that the last act of the Affair still lay far in the future.

Zola explained his position in an article headed 'Justice' which *L'Aurore* published that same day. 'It is almost eleven months since I left France. For eleven months I forced myself to live a life of total exile and observe total silence, and kept my whereabouts strictly secret. I deliberately lay in the depths of the tomb as if dead, and awaited truth and justice. Today, the truth has won, justice reigns at last, and I am reborn. I have come back to resume my place on French soil.' And he ended with these words: 'I am at home. Thus, whenever it may please the public prosecutor, he can officially notify to me the decision of the Assize Court in Versailles which sentenced me, in absentia, to one year in prison and a fine of three thousand francs. And once again we shall come before the jury.'[21] Zola waited in vain. The authorities did summon him to appear at the end of August but thereafter they regularly postponed the trial from one session to the next, until the amnesty law was passed in December 1900.

Dreyfus's second trial began in Rennes on 7 August and, for the Dreyfusards, this meant another period of waiting. Zola chose to remain in exile, so to speak, during the retrial. He withdrew to Médan and kept out of the spotlight, informing the journalists of his decision not to testify before the court martial and, above all, not to attend the hearings. But he kept very closely in touch with developments throughout those long days of summer 1899, eagerly scanning *L'Aurore* every morning, reading between the lines of each item, seeking reasons to hope in spite of the pessimistic letters he received from his friends. When Labori was wounded in an

21 *La Vérité en marche*, in *Oeuvres complètes*, vol. XIV, p. 949 and p. 956.

assassination attempt on 14 August, Zola felt anguish as keen as any he had felt in exile. And when Dreyfus was sentenced for the second time, on 9 September, Zola was dumbfounded. He protested vigorously in 'The Fifth Act', published in *L'Aurore* a few days later. 'I am terrified. What I feel is no longer anger, no longer indignation and the craving to avenge it, no longer the need to denounce a crime and demand its punishment in the name of truth and justice. I am terrified, filled with the sacred awe of a man who witnesses the supernatural: rivers flowing backwards towards their sources and the earth toppling over under the sun. I cry out with consternation, for our noble and generous France has fallen to the bottom of the abyss.' Describing the trial in Rennes, he uses the same tone as in 'J'accuse':

> It proved to be the most extraordinary set of manoeuvres to undermine truth and justice. A band of witnesses steering the debates, meeting every evening to plot the next day's dubious ambush, using lies to interrogate in place and instead of the public prosecutor, terrifying and insulting anyone who contradicted them, throwing around the weight of their rank, their ribbons and braid. Superior officers invading the courtroom and judges overwhelmed by their presence, clearly suffering at seeing them in a criminal role, obedient to an entire and very special set of mind which would have to be analysed at length in order to judge the judges. A ludicrous public prosecutor, raising idiocy to new heights, bequeathing to future historians a final summing up so vapid, so silly and so lethal that it will forever be a source of wonderment, of such senile and stubborn cruelty that it seems senseless, the brainchild of some human animal that has never yet been classified. As for the lawyers for the defence – first they try to assassinate them; then they force them to be seated every time they begin to get in the way and then, when those lawyers wish to bring in the only witnesses who know the facts, they refuse them that opportunity to introduce crucial evidence.[22]

But Waldeck-Rousseau's government was eager to avoid clashes and soothe troubled spirits. General de Galliffet (who had put down the Commune in 1871) was chosen as Minister of War, with the task of making the army listen to reason. President Loubet signed Alfred Dreyfus's pardon on 19 September. That same day, Scheurer-Kestner died of exhaustion, after a long illness. And on 21 September, General de Galliffet, fulfilling his role, issued his famous orders to the army, beginning 'The incident is closed.'

Dreyfus accepted the pardon that was offered to him. Zola realized that this was a political compromise and that, with it, the grandeur of the

---

22   'The Fifth Act', *L'Aurore* of 12 September 1899, and *La Vérité en marche*, in *Oeuvres complètes*, vol. XIV, p. 959.

struggle begun in November 1897 came to an end. But unlike the most die-hard Dreyfusards (including Clemenceau, Labori and Picquart), he refused to criticize Dreyfus.[23] In his magnificent open letter to Lucie Dreyfus, Zola expressed his joy at seeing the father reunited with his children and, reflecting on the exemplary campaign led thus far, he promised to pursue it until acquittal was finally achieved. He developed this theme the following year in his last two open letters about the Affair, the 'Letter to the Senate', protesting against the proposed amnesty law, and the 'Letter to Emile Loubet', which looked back on 'J'accuse' and observed, in an ironical tone, how well justified its accusations had been. Despite the disillusionment caused by the realities of political life, a message of hope remained, confident in the lessons that mankind would learn from the ordeals it had undergone.

The letters making up this volume are organized around the date which forms a caesura: 18 July 1898, when Zola went into exile in England. Prior to that date, the man we hear in these letters is the man of action, buffeted by the turmoil he had unleashed, struggling to assume the choices he had made and preserve their ideological orientations. But starting from mid-summer 1898, we hear a much more internalized discourse; he is still attentive to the echoes of events in the outside world but personal feelings predominate. In normal circumstances, Zola's correspondence had to manage a complex network of relations with the public and was therefore very reserved, loath to confide in anyone; but exile altered his circuit of communication, and this trying experience opened him up to the language of feelings, making him step outside his customary boundaries.

How did this change come about? The instant Zola threw himself into the Dreyfusard battle, in November 1897, his energy never flagged; on the contrary, it grew. As his indignation swelled and, along with it, his commitment and his moral certainties, his public campaign gradually changed character, moving from the three articles published in *Le Figaro*, to the pamphlets published with Fasquelle's help, and finally to 'J'accuse'. The trial in no way undermined his determination. The interviews included in this volume show a man who enters into combat with the law confidently, with gusto almost. At the first session of the trial, *Le Figaro*'s reporter portrayed Zola in these terms: 'He is wearing a black morning coat and a light-coloured waistcoat with starched shirtfront. He appears altogether happy, jaunty even: thanks to the slimming diet he has been following as obstinately as he has the revision of Dreyfus's trial, he is once again as

---

23   Along with Waldeck-Rousseau, Joseph Reinach was responsible for engineering the pardon; concerning this outstandingly political solution, see P. Vidal-Naquet, *Les Juifs, la mémoire et le présent*, II, La Découverte, 1991, pp. 88–158. Also concerning this problem and the ensuing quarrel over the amnesty, see the remarks by J.-C. Cassaing in 'Vive la République!', *Les Cahiers naturalistes*, no. 54, 1980.

slender as he was at 20.'[24] As the witnesses took the stand, one after the other, Zola did show some signs of increasing nervousness, but he withstood the pressure well. Octave Mirbeau, who described him one morning as he was about to leave for another session at the Palais de Justice, emphasized how serene Zola was: 'As he finishes his breakfast, he is perfectly calm; the long, excruciating sessions have not succeeded in tiring him. Those howls and shouts demanding his death which pursue him every time he enters or leaves the Palais have not even got on his nerves. The sight of civilian justice prostituting itself to military justice, the judge's hat being carried by the soldier's sabre, has not discouraged him in the least; quite the contrary. His face is rested and smiling; it expresses a joyous tranquillity.' And Mirbeau added: 'When I see this strong and simple man who has not once flinched throughout these tragic hours, whose soul has become greater and greater with every insult, every threat, my heart overflows with emotion. . . . Now I know what the word "heroic" means. . . .'[25]

'Heroic' – is it an exaggeration to say that Zola was heroic? Certainly it took courage to face the nationalists' rowdy demonstrations in front of the Palais de Justice, the crowds waiting to rough him up at the end of each session, the death threats and the implacable hatred on people's faces while the police were apparently in no hurry to protect him from the mob. The painful memory of those days of struggle inside and outside the courtroom stayed with the Dreyfusards for a long time. 'Over two weeks of disgust, shame and anguish every evening,' cried Pierre Quillard, 'of anxious shudders, of fear that blood might be shed amid this dismal spectacle – and the loathsome participants, mercenaries in the pay of the anti-Semites, did not even have the excuse of sincere and spontaneous hatred.'[26] Later, in one of his speeches to the Senate, Clemenceau offered this striking testimony to the atmosphere that prevailed during the trial. 'I know what I am saying. I saw Zola close up during those dreadful hours. I was with him at the end of each session before the Assize Court, each time he had to flee from the abominable crowds; they were hurling stones, hissing, booing, shrieking for his death. I was there when he was sentenced – there were twelve of us – and I must admit I had not expected such a ferocious display of hatred. If Zola had been acquitted that day, not one of us would have left the courtroom alive. That is what this man did. He braved his times. He braved his countrymen.'[27]

24   A. Bataille, 'La cour d'assises', *Le Figaro* of 8 February 1898.
25   *Livre d'hommage des Lettres françaises*, Société libre d'édition des Gens de lettres/G. Balat, 1898, first part, pp. 72–3.
26   P. Quillard, 'Impressions d'un témoin', *La Revue blanche*, 1 March 1898, p. 342.
27   Speech to the Senate on 12 December 1906, quoted in Louis Leblois, *L'Affaire Dreyfus*, Quillet, 1929, p. 696.

The almost unbearable tension of those February days was followed by months of relative introspection. Zola had imagined what his trial might be like, but he had not foreseen the sequence of legal procedures that followed it: the appeal to a higher court, the abortive hearings before the Assize Court in Versailles, the tactical manoeuvres that came to override all other considerations. Because now he was no longer making decisions alone. Labori, his lawyer, was there to guide him, and the Dreyfusards, led by Clemenceau and Reinach, formed a circle around him. Of course he could still put up resistance, still express his opinions and try to shape the course of events. He took a very determined attitude, for instance, during the negotiations which ultimately led to the publication of his open letter to Prime Minister Brisson in *L'Aurore* on 16 July. But whether he liked it or not, he was imprisoned within a logical pattern whose origin was external to him. All things considered, he would have preferred a prison sentence (although his vision of it was somewhat naive and idealistic, blending his wish to be left alone and his determination to get on with his work). But the other members of the circle, using legal arguments, convinced him that it would be wiser to flee and go into exile. The decision was reached in a matter of hours, late in the afternoon of 18 July. Suddenly everything happened very fast: the hasty note he scribbled to Jeanne that evening, just before 9 o'clock; Alexandrine's tearful face, a few minutes later, at the railway station; the train for Calais, then the boat for Dover. . . . Later, in his notes for *Pages d'exil*, he recalled those hours he had experienced so intensely.

At last, I was on board the boat, and it was moving away from the pier. It was done: I was no longer in France. I looked at my watch; it was half past one in the morning. The sky was clear but moonless and the night was very dark. There were no more than about thirty passengers, all of them English. And I stayed on deck, watching the lights of Calais disappear in the night. I confess that tears sprang to my eyes, that never before had my poor soul felt so distressed. Of course I did not believe that I was leaving my own country forever; I knew that I would be coming back in a few months, that my departure was only a tactical necessity. But even so, what a monstrous thing it was! All I had wanted were truth and justice; all I had dreamt of was to see France's good name, as a free and generous country, re-established in the eyes of the other nations – and yet here I was, forced to flee, with a nightshirt folded up in a newspaper! And that very same France had been so poisoned and led astray by the foul press that it seemed to me I could still hear it hissing me – I, who had never striven for anything else but France's glory! I, whose only ambition was to be the humble soldier fighting for France's true grandeur among the peoples of the earth! And I had had to sneak away! To flee all alone with not one kindly soul to accompany me, not one friend to whom I could express the terrible resentment I felt rising in my throat like a

bitter flood! I had already known much suffering in my life, but never had
my heart had to bear pangs as sharp as those.[28]

Here was a man who for years had compelled himself to observe other
people and had always reserved his comments not for his own feelings but
for the creative process that gave birth to his works. Suddenly he was
turning his gaze upon himself, and with indulgence. Suddenly Zola, the
'experimental novelist', had become the subject of the experiment himself.
His exile acted like a developer upon a roll of film. The tone of his correspondence changed abruptly. It was limited to the few people closest
to him: Alexandrine and Jeanne, first of all; then his most faithful com-
panions – Fernand Desmoulin, Paul Alexis, Alfred Bruneau; then Labori
and Reinach; and finally, the 'political' friends who represented the
Dreyfusards. In this constellation, Octave Mirbeau and his wife Alice held
an intermediate position, halfway between the second circle and the third.
All of these letters were sent and received via intermediaries. In Paris, they
included Dr Jules Larat and Isidore Paquin, the fashion designer (for
Labori); in London, Wareham, the solicitor. Proper names were abbrevi-
ated or reduced to initials, or were changed completely. Alexandrine
became 'Alexandre' and Jeanne was 'Jean'; Zola was first 'Pascal', then
'Beauchamp', and finally 'Richard'. (None of these metamorphoses fooled
anyone, but never mind!) Whereas the author of *L'Assommoir* and *Germi-
nal* had been used to communicating and handling his literary affairs
within a far-flung realm which covered all of Europe and sometimes the
entire world, now, suddenly, he had to function *à huis clos*, a stifling
situation that bred anxiety and an atmosphere of crisis.

The feeling of isolation was accentuated by the country itself; England
was radically foreign. Twenty years earlier, Jules Vallès had undergone the
same experience of exile; his book, *La Rue à Londres*, conveys the extent to
which England seemed hostile to a Frenchman at the end of the nineteenth
century. Vallès found London's streets mournful, unenlivened by the
minor trades and crafts that formed such a picturesque spectacle in Paris,
and turned towards the interior of those hermetically sealed houses. He
complained that English women were horrible; they looked either childish
or else old before their time. 'One day we see a gazelle and the next day we
see a giraffe; and any Frenchman who scours the streets will only find
infants that have sprouted too tall or grey-haired, yellow-toothed carica-
tures.'[29] Everything seemed dark and lugubrious to Vallès. 'Anyone who
has lived the life of an exile', he wrote in one of his letters, 'will bear an
indelible mark – an anger or a melancholy that nothing can remedy. It's
dreadful! England is a prison ship whose convicts are neither jolly nor

---

28   *Pages d'exil*, in *Oeuvres complètes*, vol. XIV, p. 1139.
29   Jules Vallès, *La Rue à Londres*, Gallimard, coll. 'Bibl. de la Pléiade', 1990, vol. II, p. 1136.

rebellious.'[30] Zola, too, felt lost in a universe that deprived him of all his familiar landmarks; he thought the cooking detestable and could not understand how sash windows worked. But he was far from sharing Vallès's excessive gloom. He was charmed by the English countryside ('a dream of infinite melancholy and gentleness', he noted in the journal which provided the basis for his *Pages d'exil*) and admired the women, especially the cyclists; there were far more women cyclists than in France, and he found them elegant and distinguished.[31]

Throughout these letters one theme was predominant: the pain of being separated. It was momentarily assuaged when he resumed work (on 4 August he began writing his new novel, *Fécondité*) and again when Jeanne arrived, then, after Jeanne's departure, when Alexandrine joined him. But the same suffering resurfaced again and again. Sometimes it was the dominant note, overriding all other feelings; sometimes it was more insidious, a persistent weight at the back of his mind. His entire correspondence became an ongoing effort to seek company and overcome the separation. Oddly enough, Zola was constantly negotiating, not with a view to writing a treatise or publishing a novel, as usual, but with a view to bringing other people nearer. With the utmost care he organized Jeanne's trip to London with their children. Alexandrine had remained in Paris and for a brief moment (as a compensation?) he dreamed of going to Italy with her.

The toughest of all these emotional negotiations were of course those that concerned him personally, the instant he expressed the wish to return to France. In relation to his 'Paris friends', as he called them, he was in an awkward and sometimes humiliating position, halfway between begging them and reasoning with them. His requests were turned down again and again. Each time his friends repeated that he must remain in exile, that the time was not yet ripe, that his return to the native country would be all the more glorious for occurring later. Each time, he gave in. Was he being too conciliatory? Alexis warned him, 'As for those "Paris friends" of yours . . . , your political friends – Clemenceau, Labori, Mirbeau, etc. . . . , well, while we play politics today, we must be on our guard; don't take political friendship for any more than what it is.'[32] Alexandrine too was irritated: 'I'm not at all surprised to see how scared Lab[ori] is; it's as overdone as those triumphal airs he used to put on. . . . I think it would be wiser if you just relied on your own intuition without taking other people's advice, or if you just took advice that corresponded to your own ideas. All your life long you have always done things your own way. [Why] don't you continue now?'[33] But Zola agreed to bow to the wishes of the group; he told himself that he

30 Letter to Hector Malot, August 1877, *ibid.*, p. 1981.
31 *Pages d'exil*, in *Oeuvres complètes*, vol. XIV, p. 1154.
32 Letter dated 18 December 1898, in *Lettres inédites de Paul Alexis à Emile Zola, 1871–1900* (ed. B. Bakker), University of Toronto Press, pp. 423–4.
33 Letter dated 30 March 1899, *Correspondance*, vol. IX, p. 452.

couldn't think only of his own interests. He thought of Dreyfus's fate and Picquart's courage and, as if to reassure himself, Zola made Picquart out to be a bigger-than-life-size hero. It was the prospect of going to prison that had forced Zola into exile; and now he chose, strangely enough, to feel that exile was itself a prison.

Love could have played a very large part in these letters; instead it is expressed in half-tones, and lurks just beneath the surface, barely discernible through the fabric of events. This is partly due to Zola's sense of propriety; he was not generally one to let his feelings well over. But there is also another reason. This correspondence is written in order to talk about separation and distress, not to comment on moments of happiness. In fact it must *conceal* happiness when it does occur. We do not need to dwell on his mirror-image situation, the life he lived between two women – his 'two wives' – whom he loved and respected equally. To each one in turn he must take care not to express his feelings; this was the only way to manage the compromise that both had been obliged to accept whether they liked it or not. Hence, his long letters to Alexandrine during the month of August 1898 – when Jeanne and the children are with him in England – are rich in details but draw a veil over the essential. On 18 August he writes, 'I think of you when I kiss the children.' And again, on 25 August, 'The children are well. The boy is slightly disorientated and his general state of health reflects that a little, but nothing serious.' A casual reader skimming through these letters might assume that this was an allusion to the ideal trio: father, mother and children. And yet, how much is left unsaid in those few sentences! Here, Alexandrine takes the place of Jeanne; the mere fact of writing these letters compels him to remove Jeanne by a stroke of the pen. It is true that Alexandrine too loved the children; for some years she had seen them frequently, taken an active interest in them and inquired regularly about their health. So, the words neither lie nor cheat – Zola would detest doing either – but there is a borderline which they cannot cross.

Throughout his exile Zola wrote an approximately equal number of letters to Alexandrine and to Jeanne. Generally, he chose Thursdays and Sundays to tell each of them about the happenings in his life from day to day; with Alexandrine he commented in detail on the repercussions of the Dreyfus Affair and with Jeanne he talked at length about the children. This volume would have liked to reconstruct that surprising dual love life, courageously lived in spite of all the difficulties. However, while some of the finest letters to Alexandrine are included here, the archives belonging to Zola's descendants did not make it possible to include more than four letters addressed to Jeanne.[34] This is regrettable. Jeanne was already absent from

---

34 The other letters remain unpublished.

Pages d'exil; now she disappears still more from the testimony these documents afford. For today's reader, she is elusive and shadowy; the only clues are the admirable but uncaptioned photographs that Zola took on sunny days at Penn and Summerfield. But after all, perhaps this silence is in line with what Zola himself would have wished.

The intimacy created by exile contrasted with Zola's public actions as a polemicist. All the while he lived in England, Zola did not publish anything in the press, even though the English papers urged him to do so. In France, however, Zola made skilful use of the media, as is clear from Parts One and Three of this volume, where the resounding open letters of the Dreyfusard campaign are reproduced side by side with a number of interviews which complement them.

The open letters[35] fall into two categories. The first is made up of lyrical addresses which appeal to collective feelings and play on the reader's 'pathos'; among these are the *Letter to the Young People* published in December 1897 and the *Letter to France* published at the beginning of January 1898, as well as the 'Letter to Mme Alfred Dreyfus' published in September 1899. The second category consists of political interpellations which challenge the public authorities and at the same time implicate the writer's personality ('ethos'). The most striking example is 'J'accuse', published in mid-January 1898. The 'Letter to Brisson', in July of that year, and the 'Letter to the Senate' and the 'Letter to Emile Loubet', both dating from 1900, are constructed along similar principles. The dramatic tension is of course greater in 'J'accuse' and 'Letter to Brisson', which are exhortations launched before the legal battle takes place, and in 'The Fifth Act', voicing consternation at Dreyfus's second conviction, whereas, in the letters to the Senate and to Emile Loubet, which come after the battle, it declines and takes on the tone of an epilogue.

These texts must be read in relation to the historical facts on which they comment. Each time, some very recent development had aroused the polemicist's ire and made him react; each such development dates the text very precisely. For 'M. Scheurer-Kestner', Zola's first skirmish, the catalyst was the way events fascinated him as a novelist; as Zola noted with hindsight, in 1901, 'Pity, faith and the passionate search for truth and justice came later.'[36] For 'The Syndicate' and 'The Minutes', published at one-week intervals in the same newspaper, it was the momentum created by *Le*

35 We have not included here the two letters written to General de Gallifet and Waldeck-Rousseau in December 1899 or the letter to Labori in March 1901 ('They can keep the money'), as they are rather brief, occasional texts relating to the lawsuit with Judet. (Zola did not include them in his *La Vérité en marche*.) As for the reply to the summons to appear in court, addressed to the Minister of War and published in *L'Aurore* on 22 January 1898, although it carries Zola's signature, it was actually written by Clemenceau, as was the article entitled 'Pour la preuve' which appeared on 20 July 1898.
36 *La Vérité en marche*, Editions Complexe, Brussels, Henri Guillemin, ed., 1988 and 1991.

Figaro's willingness to air the campaign. For the *Letter to the Young People*, it was the Senate session on 7 December 1897, during which Scheurer-Kestner had explained his position, but in vain; for *Letter to France*, the end of de Pellieux's investigation and the decision to bring Esterhazy before a court martial; for 'J'accuse', Esterhazy's acquittal on 11 January; for 'Statement to the Jury', Zola's trial in February; for the 'Letter to Brisson', the Chamber's session of 7 July, in which Cavaignac attempted to demonstrate that Dreyfus was guilty, and the imminent prospect of Zola's second trial. For 'Justice', the catalyst was Zola's return from exile. For 'The Fifth Act', it was Dreyfus's second conviction, and for 'Letter to Mme Alfred Dreyfus', it was the pardon granted to Dreyfus ten days later. For the 'Letter to the Senate' and 'Letter to Emile Loubet', the catalyst was the passing of the amnesty law. In 1901, gathering all of these pieces together in *La Vérité en marche*, Zola frankly states in the Preface, 'Naturally I have altered not one word. I have let the repetitions stand; I have left as is the harsh, rough-and-ready tone of pages that were often dashed off in one feverish burst.'[37]

Parliamentary debates are central to Zola's analyses; they provide both the principal theme and the rhetorical model for their content. When Zola writes in *L'Aurore*, he is interpellating the government just as a Deputy would do in the *hémicycle* of the Chamber. In order to grasp fully the theatrical impact of the scenes which have made such an impression on Zola's mind, we would need to be able to read the minutes of those debates. Those of the Senate's session on 7 December 1897, for instance, show the elderly Scheurer-Kestner, 'tall, straight, pale, a white beard with yellowish locks, looking as severe as a sixteenth-century Huguenot',[38] stiffly mounting the steps to the rostrum and beginning to speak amid laughter and catcalls. At one point he refers to Zola's support; this gives rise to still more exclamations on all the benches. Voices howl 'Pot-Bouille!' Or those of the session on 7 July the following year when, in order to reassure the Deputies, Cavaignac reveals the contents of the three key pieces in the secret file, including the 'Henry forgery'. Virtually unanimously, the enthusiastic Chamber voted to have his speech posted up officially in every French town; only a few cautious souls abstained, as if they were waiting to see what would happen next. Cavaignac did not realize that by opening the secret file, he handed his opponents the arguments that would make a revision inevitable two months later.

The themes aired in these open letters sometimes reflect a relatively

---

37 *Ibid.*, Author's Preface, p. 34.
38 As described by Romain Rolland (quoted by A. Roumieux in A. Scheurer-Kestner, *Mémoires d'un sénateur dreyfusard* (A. Roumieux, ed.), Strasbourg, Bueb et Reumaux, 1988, p. 305). See also the record of the debates reproduced in the book by Louis Leblois, *L'Affaire Dreyfus*, Quillet, 1929, pp. 517–28.

recent awareness on Zola's part, as in his 'A Plea for the Jews', his first denunciation of anti-Semitism, which appeared in *Le Figaro* in May 1896. In most cases, their roots already go deep into his work; this was the case with his analysis of the power of the press and the idea of making an appeal to the younger generation, both of which went back to the late 1880s when *Le Roman expérimental* was written. But in either case, once these principles have been posed and justified, they take on an astonishingly sturdy quality which enables them to withstand any and all objections. Gathered together into a coherent doctrine, they can stand close scrutiny and open out onto a vision of history.

'J'accuse' is the best example of this kind of discursive synthesis, combining fundamental ideas affirmed like a credo with a very close observation of reality, examined in its chronological sequence. The analysis of events in 'J'accuse' has since been subject to a great deal of criticism. Its accuracy has been challenged and its origin has even been thought suspect; the hidden influence of Bernard-Lazare is supposed to be perceptible between the lines. There can be no doubt that the pamphlets Bernard-Lazare had written did provide material for 'J'accuse'; up until its publication, in January 1898, they had constituted the most complete file on the events marking the Affair. Among the so-called errors in Zola's historical exposé are the excessive role attributed to du Paty de Clam, whereas Henry is not mentioned, and the unduly heavy accusations levelled at de Pellieux and the handwriting experts. But such charges do not take account of the rhetorical necessities involved in pamphleteering. As for Colonel Henry's role, the kind of information available to the Dreyfusards at that time did not enable Zola to be aware of it; he cannot be held responsible for the oversight. But that is not what matters most. The great merit of 'J'accuse' lies, obviously, in the fact that it drew clear conclusions from a particularly unclear and entangled set of facts, that it raised decisive questions and made it possible for the answers to them to emerge publicly. When Zola's first trial had ended, Léon Blum noted, 'It is possible that M. Zola made mistakes in interpreting the facts. But as for the facts themselves, as a whole – who can deny that they have now been verified and proven by the hearings?'[39] For that matter, what historian would not encounter similar difficulties if he or she had to improvise a historical narrative, reconstructing it one day at a time? Certain details in Zola's demonstration may be relatively weak, but the line he followed was unswerving, insistent, even obstinate. With amazing prophetic power, it anticipated a future phase which Zola's own determination helped to bring forth from error and chaos.

Was Zola the novelist, author of the *Rougon-Macquart* series, submerged

---

39   L. Blum, 'Le Procès', *La Revue blanche*, 15 March 1898, p. 414.

as the political controversy swelled? Zola had initially reacted to the Affair as a writer; this is clear from the very first lines of his article on Scheurer-Kestner in *Le Figaro* on 25 November 1897: 'What a poignant drama, and what superb characters! Life has brought these documents to our attention, and they are of such tragic beauty that, as a novelist, my heart leaps with admiration and excitement. I know of nothing that is of loftier psychological interest.'[40] Zola was very soon tempted by the idea of writing a history of the Affair some day; he stated this to the Russian journalist Eugen Semenov in the interview published in *Le Matin* on 4 December 1897, and included in this volume. Expressed in various forms, the idea recurs in many of his letters. 'I am excited about it, because later it may lead to an admirable book,' he wrote to Alexandrine on 16 November 1897. 'For eighteen months, History has been working for us novelists,' he wrote to Paul Alexis on 12 March 1899. 'Quite aside from any role I may have played in the events now taking place, they excite the writer in me. They provide me with the material for the last works I would like to write, where I could express my thoughts in a sort of last will and testament of truth and justice,' he said to Théodore Duret on 26 March 1899. As we can see, the project seems to have gathered strength from the loneliness of his exile. But as soon as Zola returned to France, he explicitly and energetically abandoned the idea, in the interview granted to Philippe Dubois in late July 1899: 'It would be base and ugly on my part to exploit the Dreyfus Affair.' And in February 1901, the preface to *La Vérité en marche* confirmed this decision, leaving room only for his intention of simply testifying one day to the events he had lived through.

Yet at that time, the drama of the Dreyfus Affair was already inscribed in Zola's work, perhaps without his being fully aware of the fact. The drama was linked to the one word 'truth', *vérité*. It constituted the last title added to his projected *Evangiles* (*Gospels*), originally conceived of as a trilogy of novels: *Fécondité*, *Travail* and *Justice* (*Fertility*, *Work* and *Justice*). The addition of *Vérité* dates from December 1897. *Fécondité* was written during the exile in England. *Travail* followed, in 1900. And in April 1901, when Zola opened the dossier of *Vérité*, in which he planned to describe the struggles of the public, non-denominational schools and create a sort of 'ode to the schoolmaster', suddenly he was carried away by memories.[41] The moments of extreme tension that he had lived through surged into his mind and the people who had played parts in the Affair stood before him, ready to lend their features to the fictional characters he was about to bring to life. Why resist the temptation? *Vérité* proved to be a double creation, a novel about school life and at the same time a novel about the Affair. It told

---

40 *La Vérité en marche*, in *Oeuvres complètes*, vol. XIV, p. 885.
41 *Vérité* is available in the new edition established by A. Pagès and published by C. Pirot (1993, two volumes, 351 and 359 pp.).

how a Jewish schoolmaster, Simon, was unjustly accused of murdering his nephew and was convicted. In it, Zola transposed all the events of the period from 1897 to 1899 – his own trial, the combat to win recognition of the convicted man's innocence, the expectations and disappointments, the endless succession of sudden new developments, the interaction of political compromises, the farcical trial in Rennes. . . .

In so doing, was Zola contradicting himself? Was he exploiting the Affair after all? In fact, no; he constructed a fictional tale set in a different universe and, above all, he was anticipating future events. In *Vérité*, Simon-Dreyfus is rehabilitated after several years of unyielding struggle. For Dreyfus, rehabilitation really did come in 1906; Zola died too early to know of it but he had had the intellectual power to imagine it, to anticipate the future once again, as he had done in 'J'accuse'. Thus, while *Vérité* does not exploit the Affair, it does pursue the ideological combat begun in 1897, but transposed to the level of Utopian thinking. This was the aim of Zola's *Evangiles* – to accomplish the dream that arose out of the events of the Dreyfus Affair, accelerate time and substitute for 'the religion of Christ' another religion, that of 'the innocent man', as Zola stated in his 'Letter to Mme Alfred Dreyfus': 'Four centuries were needed before the religion of Christ found its formulation and won over certain nations, but the religion of the innocent man, sentenced once and then twice, instantly spread around the globe, uniting all the civilized nations in one vast human race.'

Vérité, which appeared in the bookstores a few weeks after Zola's death, completed the epic adventure that had begun with 'J'accuse'. The novel reviews its different episodes, one by one, like a film projected in slow motion towards the end of a lifetime. But the final images do not brood bitterly on the past. They are luminous with hope. They maintain that a philosophy of the universal is possible, and describe its radiant influence. The battle is still to be fought. It is our battle, today.

Alain Pagès
with additional
material by
Eleanor Levieux

Part One
For Humanity, Truth and Justice

This article was published in May 1896, and thus preceded Zola's involvement in the Dreyfusard campaign as such by a year and a half.

A Plea for the Jews[1]

For several years, with growing surprise and disgust, I have been following the campaign that people in France are trying to mount against the Jews. It seems to me a monstrosity; by that I mean something that is altogether beyond the bounds of common sense, truth and justice, a blind and stupid thing that would drag us back centuries in time, ultimately a thing that would lead to religious persecution, which is the worst of abominations and would bathe every country in blood.

And I am determined to say this.

*

First of all, what are the Jews accused of? What are they reproached with?

Some people, even friends of mine, say that they cannot bear them, that they cannot touch their hands without their skin crawling with revulsion. It is a matter of physical horror, the repulsion of one race for another, of the white man for the yellow man, of the red man for the black man. I do not ask whether part of this revulsion doesn't stem from the ancient anger of the Christian against the Jew who crucified his God, a centuries-old atavism of scorn and vengeance. In short, physical repugnance is a good reason, in fact the only reason, because there is nothing to be said in reply to people who declare, 'I abhor them because I abhor them, because merely at the sight of their noses I am beside myself, because my very flesh rebels when I feel how different and other they are.'

But if the truth be told, that reason – the hostility of one race towards another – is not sufficient. We might as well revert to the depths of the forest; we might as well recommence the barbarous war that pits one species against another; we might as well devour one another because we do not utter the same cries and our fur does not grow in the same way. What civilizations strive for is precisely to erase that savage need to hurl ourselves at our fellow creature, when he does not resemble us exactly. Down through the centuries, the history of the peoples of this earth is nothing other than a lesson in mutual tolerance, and indeed the final dream will be to induce them all to engage in universal brotherhood, to blend them all into one common tenderness so as to save them all, as much

---

1   In Emile Zola, *L'Affaire Dreyfus: La Vérité en marche*, Colette Becker, ed., Garnier-Flammarion, Paris, 1969.

as possible, from their common anguish. And in our own times, hating and biting one another because we don't all have skulls quite the same shape becomes sheer, monstrous folly.

Now I come to the real reproach, the serious one, which is essentially a social matter. I shall merely sum up the arguments of the prosecution, merely outline them. The Jews are accused of being a nation within the nation, of separately leading the life of a religious caste and thus of transcending borders, of being a sort of international sect which has no real mother country and which, if it were to triumph one day, would be capable of dominating the world. The Jews marry among themselves; they maintain extremely close family ties, unlike the loosened ties that prevail in the modern world; they support and encourage one another and, in their very isolation, demonstrate an extraordinary power of resistance and gradual conquest. But above all, they are a wise and practical race; in their blood they carry a need for lucre, a love of money, a prodigious business sense which, in less than a hundred years, has enabled them to gather vast fortunes into their hands and, in a day and age when money is king, seems to ensure that the kingdom is theirs.

And all of this is true. But while we may observe the fact, we must also explain it. What we must add is that the Jews, as they exist today, are our creation, the result of our eighteen hundred years of idiotic persecution. Since we have penned them up in revolting districts like so many lepers, it is not in the least surprising if they have lived apart, preserved all of their traditions and tightened the family bonds, remaining the vanquished among the victors. Since we have struck them and insulted them and heaped injustice and violence upon them, it is not in the least surprising if deep down in their hearts, even unconsciously, they nurture the hope of revenge in some distant future, the will to resist, to stay alive and to vanquish. Above all, because we scorned money, we disdainfully abandoned the realm of money to them and thus made them play the role of dealers and usurers in our society; so it is not in the least surprising that, once brute force had ceased to hold sway and had given way to domination through intelligence and work, we found that, with their supple brains, trained by centuries of heredity, they had become the masters of capital and were all ready for empire.

And what is happening today? Terrified by this creation of sheer blindness, a-tremble at discovering what the sectarian faith of the Middle Ages has made of the Jews, you can think of nothing better than to revert to the year 1000, to revive the old persecutions, preach a holy war once again so that the Jews will be hounded, despoiled, and forced to huddle together again, consumed by fury, treated as a vanquished nation by a victorious nation!

Oh yes, you're fine intelligent fellows, indeed you are, and what a lovely conception of society you have!

What? There are over two hundred million of you Catholics and barely five million Jews, and yet you tremble, you call the gendarmes, you cry out in terror and make the most appalling din, as if hordes of vandals had swarmed over the country! Now, that's courage for you!

The conditions in which the struggle is waged seem acceptable to me. Where business is concerned, why not be as intelligent and as good at it as they are? For a month I went to the Stock Exchange to try to understand something about the way it works; a Catholic banker, talking about the Jews, said to me, 'Oh, they're better at it than we are, sir; they will always beat us.' If that were true, it would really be humiliating. But why should it be true? Some people may be gifted; all right, but even so, hard work and intelligence can overcome everything. Already I know certain Christians who are very distinguished Jews. The field is wide open. If they have had centuries in which to love money and learn how to make it, then all you need do is follow them on their own ground and, there, learn to take on their own qualities and fight them with their own weapons. Stop insulting them pointlessly, for heaven's sake! Defeat them by being superior to them. Nothing could be simpler. It is the basic law of life itself.

How proud and gratified they must feel when they hear your howls of distress! To be such a tiny minority and yet arouse such a lavish deployment of weapons! Each and every morning you hurl your thunderbolts at them and issue desperate calls to arms, as if the entire city were in danger of falling to the enemy. If you had your way we would reinstate the ghetto; once again we would have the Jewish quarter and place chains across its streets each night. Wouldn't that be a pretty sight, a quarantine like that, in our free and open cities! No wonder they are not upset! No wonder they continue to triumph in all our financial markets; for an insult is like the legendary arrow: it whizzes back to strike the wicked archer in the eye! If you want them to keep on winning, just keep on persecuting them!

Persecution! Really, are you still at that stage! Do you still cling to that wonderful delusion – doing away with people by persecuting them! No, no, it's quite the opposite: never has a cause grown bigger without being watered by the blood of its martyrs. If there are still Jews today, it is your fault. They would have disappeared, would have blended into the rest of the population if they had not been compelled to defend themselves, group together and stubbornly cling to their race. And even today, their most genuine source of power is you, who make their power perceptible by exaggerating it. By warning of danger every morning at the top of your lungs, ultimately you make that danger exist. By showing the people a scarecrow, you create a real monster. You must stop talking. The day the Jews are merely people like ourselves, they will be our brothers.

The tactic to be used is obvious; it is the opposite of the one used until now. Let us open our arms wide, take the equality that our legal Code has acknowledged and make it a social reality. Let us embrace the Jews so as to absorb them and blend them into our ranks. Let us enrich ourselves with their virtues, since virtues they have. Let us put an end to war between the races by intermingling the races. Let us encourage intermarriages and leave it to the children to reconcile the fathers. This and this alone will achieve unity. This will be the great humanitarian and liberating achievement.

Anti-Semitism, in those countries where it is a major force, is never anything but the weapon of a political party or the result of a grave economic situation.

But in France, where it is not true that the Jews are the absolute masters of power and money, as some people try to convince us they are, anti-Semitism has no roots in the people; it is not attached to anything. It took the inflamed passions of a few fuzzy minds to create the illusion of a real movement. (In fact, it is nothing but noise.) By a sort of literary trick, the suspect and sectarian Catholicism that preys on those minds hounds even the Rothschilds as the descendants of a Judas who betrayed and crucified its God. I might add that the need to have a pretext for rowdiness, the ungovernable craving to be read and to acquire resounding fame, have certainly not been unrelated to the urge to designate victims and publicly fan the sacrificial flames. Fortunately those flames are merely a stage set.

What a pitiful failure it is, as a result! All these long months, these insults and denunciations, with Jews being informed on every single day like thieves and murderers, even Christians being called Jews when the aim is to sully them, the whole Jewish world hounded, insulted, condemned have only generated noise, nasty words, and a display of contemptible feelings, but not one single action, not one crowd turned into a mob, not one skull split, not one window smashed! Our humble people of France must be a good people indeed, and a wise and decent people, if they do not succumb to these daily calls to civil war, if they keep a clear head amidst these urgings and abominations, these daily demands for the blood of a Jew ! It used to be the priests that the papers attacked every morning for breakfast but now it's the Jews, the plumpest and most flourishing Jews they can find. This breakfast is no better than the first and is at least as stupid. At bottom, it is just a very ugly business, the most loathsome folly imaginable and happily the most useless as well, since the people going by in the street don't even turn their heads; they leave the troublemakers to twist and turn like devils caught in a baptismal font.

The most astonishing part is that the troublemakers claim to be carrying out a sound and indispensable mission. Ah, those poor people – how I pity them, if they are sincere! What an appalling record they will leave behind! What a daily accumulation of errors, lies, envious fury and demented exaggerations! If ever some critic tries to descend into this unsavoury quagmire, he will recoil in horror when he finds that all he can see there are inflamed religious passion and unbalanced intelligence. And those people will be nailed to the pillory of history for all the harm they will have done society, for crimes that have come to naught only because of the unbelievable blindness in which they were committed.

I am continually stunned to see that such a return to fanaticism, such an attempt to wage a holy war can have occurred in our day, in this great Paris of ours, amid the good people of France. And in this age of democracy and universal tolerance, just as a vast movement towards equality, fraternity and justice is taking shape on all sides! Just as we are doing away with borders, dreaming of a community of all peoples, convening congresses of religions so that priests of all faiths may embrace one another, realizing that suffering makes us all brothers, striving to rise above the misery of the human lot by erecting a single altar to human pity! And there in our midst is a handful of madmen, imbeciles or clever manipulators who bellow at us every morning, 'Let's kill the Jews! Let's eat the Jews! Let's massacre and exterminate, let's go back to burnings at the stake and dragonnades!' And of all times, this is the time they choose! Nothing could be more stupid. Worse, nothing could be more abominable.

That a distressing monopoly of wealth in the hands of a few Jews has come about is undeniable. But the same monopoly is to be found among Catholics and Protestants as well. Exploiting popular unrest by using it to further religious passions, serving up Jews to the demands of the disinherited on the grounds that Jews are in control of money – these are the doings of a lying, hypocritical socialism which must be denounced and treated with withering scorn. If, one day, work is rewarded in such a way that it furthers truth and happiness, it will re-create all of mankind; and little will it matter then whether one be Jew or Christian because all people will be governed by the same law of work, and all will have the same new rights and the same new duties.

The unity of mankind – that is what we must all strive to believe in if we want to have the courage to live and keep some hope alive in our hearts as we struggle! As yet, this belief is only a murmur; but soon it will become a swelling cry raised up by all peoples as they yearn for truth and justice and peace. Let us disarm our hatreds, let us love one another in our cities and beyond our borders, let us do our utmost to blend all races into a single family, a happy family at last! Though it may take us a thousand years, let us believe, even so, in the ultimate realization of love. Let us begin by loving one another today, at least as much as the misery of the times will allow us to love. Let the mad and the wicked, who believe justice can be done with the stabs of a knife, return to the barbaric existence of the primitive forests.

Let Jesus tell his bewildered believers that he has forgiven the Jews and that they are human too!

Le Figaro, 16 May 1896

Translator's note: This impassioned plea on behalf of the Jews stands out in a very special light if the reader remembers the terms used abundantly by Zola himself in *L'Argent* (1891): see pages 61, 131–2, 134, 136, 137, 138, 149, 160, etc. in the Garnier-Flammarion edition, 1974. In particular, the opening sentences of paragraph four in 'A Plea for the Jews' ('Some people, even friends . . .') borrow almost word for word from the description Zola gives, on pages 131–2 of *L'Argent*, of Saccard's revulsion towards Gundermann, his Jewish rival.

In 1892, Zola published *La Débâcle*, which proved to be his best-selling book. In one particularly grim, post-battle scene in Part Three, Chapter 1 (page 378 in the Livre de poche edition, 1985), he describes 'those prowlers who followed the German armies to rob the corpses, a pack of base, preying Jews'. Is this Zola himself speaking? Or one of his characters?

In both novels Zola was no doubt employing stereotyped phrases and a stereotyped description in use at that time to criticize Jews collectively. Did his use of those phrases and terms help, however, to propagate the views they expressed, the very views he was to denounce in this 'Plea for the Jews'? Where is the borderline between those two novels and this 'Plea', published four years later?

Early in November 1897, while public opinion was not yet very concerned over the Dreyfus Affair, Emile Zola was being mentioned in certain quarters as a possible candidate for the Chamber of Deputies. Although the rumour was denied in the interview we are about to read, it was not ungrounded. Certain people had in fact approached Zola privately, and very discreetly. It was out of the question for him to accept, of course. But this occasion gave him an opportunity to repeat the position he had always upheld, that of a man of letters anxious to stand aside from the realities of political life. It is curiously ironic, in the light of subsequent history, that Zola's defence of non-involvement, expressed on the eve of his involvement in the Dreyfus Affair, appeared in L'Aurore which, less than three months later, was to publish 'J'accuse'.

Zola Will Not Be A Deputy
The author of the 'Rougon-Macquart' series at home

False report in the Cologne Gazette *– The role of legislator judged by M. Zola –*
Men of letters in the Chamber – On the vanity of politics – Devoted to the social
issues – A word about Gabriele D'Annunzio.

'Is it true, M. Zola, that you intend to be a candidate in the next legislative elections?'

The author of the *Rougon-Macquart* series invited me to take a seat; then, raising the folds of the dressing gown he was wearing, he sat down opposite me.

'Who told you that?' he asked me.

I held out to him a newspaper in which the following dispatch was printed:

'The Cologne *Gazette* reports that Zola is said to be thinking seriously of standing for election as Deputy. Zola has many speeches to make and would take the floor frequently to outline anarchist theories.'

While M. Zola was reading, I ran my eye rapidly over the room in which he had just received me: a large, very high-ceilinged chamber, cluttered by countless knick-nacks, its walls completely covered with paintings and portraits, including two portraits of the master of the premises himself, among them one by Manet, facing a carved wooden bust of Zola signed Bloch.

'There is no truth in this item,' said Zola, with a slight shrug, once he had finished reading. 'I can easily guess how this rumour started. My new book, *Paris*, has been launched very successfully. The first instalments have been very widely published. As you know, they are about a worker named Salvat, who is planning an assassination attempt, and some Deputies to whom, I must add, I was not very kind. Noting that I introduced the reader into parliamentary circles, the Cologne *Gazette* must have concluded that I was planning to enter them myself so as to support Salvat's theories. That, in my opinion, is the origin of the absurd false report that you have shown me.

'No,' M. Zola continued, with downcast eyes, as if harking back to distant memories, 'I have long since ceased to think of being elected.'

'You had thought of it, then?'

'Why should I not admit it? At one time I did indeed have the intention of momentarily abandoning the unstinting labour which has already produced forty-five volumes and of devoting two or two and a half years of my life to the Chamber so as to bend all my efforts and all the weight of my word of honour to solving some of the social issues, that of old people's pensions, for instance.'

'Then you do believe in the effectiveness of the parliamentary system?'

'Not in the slightest. Politics leaves me completely indifferent. Little do I care whether such and such government is overturned and replaced by another. I detest the idea of Deputies submitting docilely to the discipline of interest groups and unable to take any initiative. I pity the men of letters, like Maurice Barrès and de Vogüé,[1] who get themselves nominated and, once they are elected, are content to remain quietly seated, then deposit their ballot in an urn after a debate in which they have taken no part.

'I had had a dream, a fine one. I dreamt of becoming a tribune who, through the power of his argumentation and the forcefulness of his eloquence, would succeed, if not in imposing some of his ideas on the Chamber, then at least in spreading them throughout the country, just as the sower broadcasts the seeds in the furrows of a fertile field.

'A book is a very powerful force. It interests and moves the reader; it charms and instructs him. The ideas it contains penetrate the masses slowly; they tunnel their way ahead just as moles do until one fine day the tunnel is finished and they emerge in broad daylight. A book accomplishes its task not rapidly but surely; for books remain, whereas words pass. Nonetheless, words too are potent weapons. And what a marvellous forum the Chamber would offer for anyone who knew how to make use of it.'

There was no need to encourage M. Zola to confide his secret thoughts. He was speaking volubly, with warmth and conviction. It was a real pleasure to listen to him.

'Dear Maître, why haven't you tried to make your dream come true?'

'Because I became convinced that I would never make a great speaker,' he replied. 'I am talking about the period when I was president of the Société des gens de lettres. Until then I had never done any public speaking. My new functions compelled me to make speeches in France, then in England. Later, during my travels in Italy, where I was gathering material for *Rome*, a number of banquets were given in my honour. I had to reply to toasts and offer toasts myself. That was how I realized that although I can prepare a speech and read it, just like anybody else, I am no orator. My nerves get the better of me when I am addressing a crowd, and I become almost helpless. No matter. I went back to my books. I began to write again, persevering, piling up page after page, concentrating exclusively on the task before me.'

Then I put my last question to M. Zola, insistently:

'So, in your opinion, there is no role for a man of letters to play in the legislature?'

---

1 Maurice Barrès was a member of the Chamber of Deputies between 1889 and 1893; Eugène de Vogüé, the novelist, was a member between 1893 and 1898.

'There may be one,' he repeated, 'but on two conditions: the man of letters must cease to write so as to be only a Deputy, and he must devote his great gift for using words to solving the major social issues. Politics is vanity, whereas social issues, on the contrary, should haunt the mind of every thinking man. Christianity abolished slavery and replaced it by wage-earning. And wage earners, in their turn, must disappear to be replaced by . . . I do not know what. One would have to be blind not to see that grave events will soon be taking place.'

I mentioned the name of Gabriele D'Annunzio.[2]

Zola said sharply, 'Anyone who travels in Italy is struck by the frightful poverty that prevails there. It is in Italy, perhaps, that the formidable problem appears more menacing than anywhere else. In such circumstances, D'Annunzio's electoral platform is surprising; he has had himself nominated not as a sociologist but as a writer and an artist. But what does the freedom of art weigh in the balance, compared with the happiness of mankind?'

It was noon. M. Zola had stood up. The conversation was over.

Ph. Dubois
L'Aurore, 4 November 1897

M. Scheurer-Kestner

What a poignant drama, and what superb characters! Life has brought these documents to our attention, and they are of such tragic beauty that, as a novelist, my heart leaps with admiration and excitement. I know of nothing that is of loftier psychological interest.

It is not my intention to talk about the Affair. Although circumstances have enabled me to examine it and reach a firm opinion concerning it, I cannot overlook the fact that an inquiry is under way, that the matter has been brought before the courts and that in all decency we must wait, without adding to the clutter of abominable gossip being used to obscure the Affair, which is so clear and simple in itself.

But already, the characters involved in this Affair belong to me; although I am merely a passer-by, my eyes are open, prepared to look at all that life has to offer. And while the man who was sentenced three years ago and the man who is a defendant today are still sacred to me, as long as the judicial system has not fulfilled its task, the third great character in this

---

2 Gabriele D'Annunzio, famous for his nationalist statements, had just been elected to the Italian Chamber of Deputies.

drama – the accuser – has nothing to fear from being talked about frankly and honestly.

What follows is what I have seen of M. Scheurer-Kestner, what I believe and what I assert. One day, perhaps, if circumstances allow it, I shall talk about the other two characters in the drama.

A life as clear as crystal, utterly clean and upright; not one blemish, not one flaw. A single and unwavering viewpoint, unwarped by any militant ambition, has led to an elevated political position, due solely to the respect and liking of his peers.

And he is no dreamy-eyed Utopian. He is an industrialist who has spent his life in his laboratory devoting himself to specialized research, in addition to the day-to-day cares of being responsible for a large commercial firm.

And I might add that he has a very considerable fortune. Wealth and honours and happinesses of every kind have crowned a pure life, devoted entirely to work and integrity. He has not one thing left to wish for except to end his life in the dignity and joy of his good name.

There you have it; that is what the man is like. Everyone knows him; no one can contradict me. And yet this is the man within whose breast the most tragic and absorbing of dramas is going to be played out. One day, a doubt enters his mind, for already there is some doubt in the air; already it has disturbed more than one conscience. A court martial has found a captain – who perhaps is innocent – guilty of treason. The punishment has been appalling: the captain has been stripped of his rank in public and imprisoned in a remote place; he is the target of an entire people's loathing; they trample on him as he lies defeated. But great God, what if he were innocent? What a measureless shudder of pity we feel! We break out in a cold sweat at the horrible thought that no amends can possibly make up for the wrong he has suffered.

Doubt did indeed enter M. Scheurer-Kestner's mind and from that instant, as he himself has explained, his torments began; he was haunted again and again as each new piece of information came to his attention. His intelligent, sturdy, logical mind was gradually overcome by the insatiable need for truth. Nothing could be nobler or more lofty, and what happened within this man is an astonishing spectacle. It arouses my enthusiasm, for it is my profession to examine men's consciences. There can be no more heroic combat than the struggle to determine the truth and see to it that justice is done.

To cut a long story short, M. Scheurer-Kestner at last feels certain. He knows where the truth lies; he will do what justice requires. This is the excruciating moment. For a mind such as his, I can well imagine how that moment of anguish must have felt. He fully realized what storms he was going to stir up, but truth and justice are sovereign over all else, for they alone make a nation great. Political interests may blot them out momentarily but any nation that did not base its sole *raison d'être* on truth and justice would today be a nation doomed.

*

Revealing the truth is a fine thing, but the revealer's ambition may be to derive glory from doing so. Some people sell the truth; others wish to derive some benefit, at least, from having spoken it.

What was M. Scheurer-Kestner's intention, however? To do his duty and, in so doing, to disappear. He had resolved to tell the government, 'Here is the situation. Take the Affair into your hands; if you choose to rectify the error, you will have the merit of being just. All acts of justice lead to triumph.' Because of circumstances which I do not wish to go into, his words were not heeded.

From that moment on, he began to suffer, and his martyrdom has continued for weeks. Rumour had it that he held the truth in his hands; and if a man knows the truth but does not shout it from the rooftops, then he must be a public enemy, isn't that so? Stoically at first, for two interminable weeks, he remained faithful to his promise to keep silent, hoping against hope that he would not be forced to take the action that certain other individuals should have taken. And we all know what a tide of invective and insult engulfed him for those two weeks. But amid that torrent of filthy accusations, he remained impassive and held his head high. Why did he keep silent? Why did he not open his file to anyone who asked to see it? Why did he not do what the others were doing, filling the newspapers with their gossip?

How great he was! How wise! He kept silent not only because of the promise he had made but precisely because he was responsible for the truth – the poor, naked, shivering truth that everyone was hissing and booing and seemed to have some interest in strangling to death. His only thought was to shield it from the passion and rage arrayed against it. He had vowed that no one would steal the truth from him and he intended to choose exactly when and how he would make the truth triumph. What could be more natural, more praiseworthy? I know of nothing more sublimely beautiful than M. Scheurer-Kestner's silence these past three weeks while an entire panic-stricken nation has suspected and insulted him. Novelists, there's an exceptional character for you! there's a hero!

His kindest critics aired doubts about his mental health: surely he was a feeble old man, who had fallen into a sort of infantile senility? Surely the onset of old age had made him helplessly gullible? And the other critics, a bunch of madmen and scoundrels, accused him outright of having been bought. It was very simple: the Jews had paid a million francs in exchange for his irresponsible behaviour. What an idiotic idea! It should have made people roar with laughter – and yet no one did.

On the one hand, you have M. Scheurer-Kestner and his crystal-clear life. On the other hand you have the people who are accusing and insulting him. You must judge. You must choose between him and them. Find what motivation he could possibly have, aside from his noble need for truth and justice. Covered with insults, his very soul bruised and rent, feeling his lofty and respected situation totter beneath him, yet prepared to sacrifice everything in order to accomplish his heroic task, he keeps silent. Calmly, he waits. The greatness of this man is exceptional.

*

I have said already that I do not wish to talk about the Affair itself. And yet, I must repeat, it is as clear and simple as you please once you see it as it really is.

A miscarriage of justice is a deplorable thing but it can always happen. Judges do make mistakes; army officers can make mistakes as well. What would that have to do with the honour of the army? If such a mistake has occurred, the only thing worth doing is to correct it. No wrongdoing has taken place – unless someone persists in refusing to acknowledge, even when confronted with indubitable proof, that a mistake has been made. At bottom, there is no other problem but that. All will be well once the people involved make up their minds to acknowledge that an error may have been made and that afterwards they hesitated because of the embarrassment of admitting it. Those who know will understand what I am talking about.

What about the diplomatic complications that might ensue? All that is merely a smokescreen. No foreign power has had anything to do with the Affair, and this must be stated loud and clear. The only thing we need be concerned with is French public opinion, which is exasperated and overwrought by the most odious of campaigns. The press is a necessary force; I believe that when all is said and done, it does more good than harm. Nonetheless, certain newspapers are the guilty parties, making some readers panic, terrifying others, feeding on scandals to treble their sales. Idiotic anti-Semitism has fanned this stupidity into flames. On all sides people are being denounced. Even the best and purest individuals no longer dare to do their duty, for fear of getting scorched.

And so we have come to this appalling mess where every type of statement is distorted and no one can plead in favour of justice without being called senile or a traitor. Lies spread wider and wider, the serious newspapers gravely print the silliest stories, the entire nation seems to have gone mad – and yet a little common sense is all it would take to bring everything back into proportion. I repeat: it will all be simplicity itself the day the people who are in power dare to behave like decent people, despite the mob!

One reason why M. Scheurer-Kestner has maintained a dignified silence before taking action is that he was waiting, I imagine, for each and every person to examine his own conscience. When he talked about his duty, when he said that even with everything in ruins all about him – his lofty position, his fortune and his happiness – his duty compelled him to speak the truth as soon as he became aware of it, he explained, 'Otherwise I could not have lived with myself.' Admirable words.

And that is exactly what all the decent people who are mixed up in this Affair must say. They will not be able to live with themselves if they do not see to it that justice is done.

*

If, for political considerations, justice were to be delayed, this would constitute an additional wrong that would merely delay the inevitable outcome and make it even more painful.

The truth is on the march, and nothing shall stop it.

Le Figaro, 25 November 1897

The Syndicate

We know what is behind it: a concept as low and as simple-minded as those who have dreamt it up.

Captain Dreyfus was convicted of the crime of treason by a court martial. From that instant he ceased to be a man and became The Traitor, an abstraction embodying the idea of the fatherland slain and delivered over to a conquering enemy. He stands not only for present treason and future treason but for past treason as well, for our old defeat is blamed on him by those who stubbornly cling to the notion that only because we were betrayed were we beaten.

Thus he is the damned soul, the abomination, the disgrace of the army, the felon who sold his brothers just as Judas sold his God. And since he is Jewish, the rest is simple: the Jews are rich and powerful, and they have no fatherland of their own; so millions and millions of them are going to work behind the scenes to get him out of trouble; they are going to silence people's consciences with bribes and entangle all France in a detestable plot until the guilty man is rehabilitated, even if it means putting an innocent man in his place. The convicted man's family, also Jewish, of course, comes into the Affair. For an affair it is. No expense will be spared in order to dishonour the system of justice, impose falsehoods, and sully an entire nation through the most insolent of campaigns. And all this in order to save a Jew from infamy and replace him by a Christian.

So, a syndicate is set up. Which means that bankers get together, pool their money and exploit the gullibility of the public. Somewhere there is a fund that pays for all the filth that gets stirred up. It is a vast and sinister undertaking: masked individuals, huge sums handed over at night to unknown characters lurking under bridges, prominent figures corrupted, and fantastic prices paid to undermine their longstanding integrity.

And little by little the syndicate spreads until it becomes an all-powerful organization working away in the shadows, one great shameless conspiracy to glorify the traitor and drown France in a flood of ignominy.

*

Let's take a closer look at this 'syndicate'.

The Jews have made money, and it is they who openly purchase the honour of their accomplices. Good heavens! I don't know how much they may have spent already, but even if it's only ten million or so, who can blame them for having spent it? These are French citizens, our equals and our brothers, who are being dragged through the mud every single day by such idiotic anti-Semitism. Captain Dreyfus has been used in an attempt to crush them; the crime of one among them has been called the crime of the entire race. Traitors, all of them! They've all sold out; they should all be convicted! And yet you expect these people not to fight back fiercely, not to try to clear themselves, not to give as good as they get? War has been declared on them, a war of extermination! Of course it is their passionate desire to see the innocence of their fellow Jew acknowledged; what could be more understandable? And if they think it is possible to achieve rehabilitation, how whole-heartedly they must be struggling for that goal!

What bothers me is that if there is some teller's window where people get their pay-offs, there aren't any inveterate scoundrels in this syndicate. Come now, you know very well the people I mean. How does it happen that this one, and that one, and that one too are not part of it? In fact, the most amazing thing is that the very people the Jews have supposedly bribed all have unimpeachable reputations for integrity. Maybe the Jews are very particular; maybe they want only the best and rarest merchandise and are willing to pay whatever it's worth. So, I have strong doubts about that teller's window, although at the same time I would be quite prepared to excuse the Jews if they were forced into such a tight corner that they used their millions to defend themselves. When you're being massacred, you fight back with whatever you've got. And I can speak of them impartially, for I neither love them nor hate them. I do not have among them any friend who is close to my heart. They are human beings, and that is all I need to know.

But when it comes to Captain Dreyfus's family, that is a different matter, and anybody who refuses to understand or acknowledge this must be completely heartless. Look here! His family has the right – the duty – to use all its money and its very blood if it believes its child is innocent. That is the sacred threshold that no one has the right to profane. We cannot enter that house where people weep, where a wife and brothers and parents mourn, unless we enter hat in hand; and only louts can think they are entitled to talk loudly and brazenly. 'Traitor's brother!' That is the insult they fling in the face of that brother! What moral standards are we living by, what God do we acknowledge, that it should be deemed right to blame an entire family for the wrongdoing of one of its members? Nothing could be more contemptible than that; nothing could be more unworthy of our culture and our generosity. The newspapers which insult Captain Dreyfus's brother because he is doing his duty are a disgrace to the French press.

Who else would have spoken up if he had not? He is playing his proper role. When his voice was heard, seeking justice, no one else needed to play that role any longer; everyone else stepped back. He alone was qualified to raise the formidable question of a possible miscarriage of justice, of the need for a dazzling revelation of the truth. You can heap insult upon injury but that will not alter one whit the notion that the defence of the absent man is in the hands of his own kin, who have maintained their hopes and their faith. And in fact the strongest moral proof of the convicted man's innocence is the unshakeable certainty of an entire honourable family, whose integrity and patriotism are irreproachable.

Then, after the Jews who founded the syndicate and after the family that is in charge of it, come the ordinary members of the syndicate, the ones who have been bribed. Two of the oldest members are M. Bernard-Lazare and Major Forzinetti. Then there were M. Scheurer-Kestner and M. Monod. Lately, they've discovered Colonel Picquart, not to mention M. Leblois. And I devoutly hope that since my first article I too have been considered part of the group. For that matter, anyone who is haunted by the dreadful suspicion that a miscarriage of justice may have occurred and who takes the liberty of wanting the truth to be revealed, for the sake of justice, is a member of the syndicate and is therefore convicted of being an evildoer and of having been bribed.

*

And who wished this syndicate into existence? Who created it? Why, all of you whose actions have led to this horrendous mess – you, the false patriots and the braying anti-Semites and the mere exploiters who thrive on the public debacle!

Isn't the proof there before our eyes? Isn't it complete, and plain as day? If there had been a syndicate there would have been an agreement – but where do you see any such agreement? What there is, is simply this: ever since the wretched man was convicted, certain consciences have felt uneasy and a doubt has arisen as he cries out his innocence to one and all. The dreadful crisis, the collective folly that we are witnessing surely stems from that, from the slight shudder our souls continue to feel. And Major

Forzinetti is the man behind this shudder that so many others have felt and that he has described to us in such a poignant way.

Then, there is M. Bernard-Lazare. He is gripped by doubt and he is striving to make things clear, conducting a solitary investigation; but he is groping in the dark. He published first one pamphlet and now a second, on the eve of today's revelations; and the proof that he was working alone, that he was not in contact with any of the other members of the syndicate, is that he knew nothing about the real truth of the matter and was unable to say a thing about it. What a peculiar syndicate, whose members do not even know each other!

And there was M. Scheurer-Kestner, tortured by his craving for truth and justice, and who was searching and trying to acquire a certainty beyond the shadow of a doubt, quite unaware of the official inquiry – I repeat, official – being conducted at the same time by Colonel Picquart, whose very functions at the War Ministry put him on the right track. It took a chance meeting, as was determined later, for these two men who did not know each other, who were both working towards the same goal but separately, to come together at the very last minute and to move ahead, side by side.

That is the whole story of the syndicate: men of good will, men devoted to truth and justice, starting from every different point on the horizon, working miles apart and unbeknownst to one another but all marching ahead along different trails towards the same goal, trudging ahead in silence, turning over every clod of earth until, one fine morning, they all converged at the same point. Inevitably, they all came together, hand in hand, at that crossroads of truth, that inevitable rendez-vous with justice.

Clearly it is you, is it not, who now bring these men together, you who force them to close ranks, to work towards the same goal of moral health and decency – these very men on whom you heap insults, whom you accuse of plotting in the most infamous way, when all they have tried to do is bring about the supreme act of reparation.

*

Incessantly, a dozen newspapers, a score of newspapers in which the most diverse passions and interests are interwoven, a whole foul swathe of the press that I cannot read without my heart bursting with indignation, has been convincing the public that a syndicate of Jews, paying fantastic bribes to corrupt decent men, was bent on carrying out the most loathsome plot. Their first aim was to save the traitor and replace him by an innocent man; then, it was the army itself that would be dishonoured and France that would be sold to the enemy, as it was in 1870. I will spare you the details, the flights of fancy concerning this sordid machination.

And I must admit that this view had become the view held by the vast majority of the public. How many ordinary people have come up to me in the past week to ask, dumbfounded, 'What? Are you trying to say that Scheurer-Kestner is not a scoundrel? And you're throwing in your lot with the likes of him? But don't you realize that those people have sold France down the river?'

My heart trembles with anxiety because I can see that leading the public astray like this will enable them to hide anything they wish. And the worst part is that precious few individuals are courageous enough to try swimming upstream, against the current. Any number of people will whisper in your ear that they are convinced Captain Dreyfus is innocent but that when it comes to fighting they don't care to find themselves in a tight corner!

Behind public opinion, and counting no doubt on its support, are the offices of the Ministry of War. I do not wish to speak about them today, for I still have hopes that justice will be done. But can anyone fail to realize that we are face to face with bad faith of the most obstinate kind? They refuse to admit that they have made mistakes – I was about to say, that they are guilty of misdeeds. Individuals have been compromised, and they persist in covering up for them. They will go to all lengths to dodge the broom that would make one gigantic clean sweep. Matters are so serious that the very people who hold the truth in their hands, who are being furiously urged to reveal it, are still hesitating, still reluctant to shout out the truth for all to hear, because they hope the truth will become obvious all by itself and they will be spared the embarrassment of telling it.

But there is at least one truth that I would like to announce throughout France this very minute: France – just and generous France – is being forced to commit a genuine crime. France cannot possibly be France any longer if it can be duped to this extent, whipped to a frenzy against a poor unfortunate man who for the past three years, and in the most atrocious conditions, has been expiating a crime he did not commit. Yes, far far away, on a remote island, under the glaring sun, there is a human being who has been separated from his fellow men. Not only does the vast ocean come between him and them but, in addition, he is enclosed night and day within a living wall formed by eleven guards. Eleven men have been immobilized to guard a single man. Never has any killer, any raving madman been walled up so closely. And what of the everlasting silence? the slow agony of being loathed by an entire people? Now, do you dare say that man is not guilty?

Yes, that is exactly what we say – we, the members of the syndicate. We say it to France, and we hope that France will hear us at last, for France is always ardent in support of just and righteous causes. We say to France that we are striving for the honour of the army and the greatness of the nation. A miscarriage of justice has been committed, and as long as it has not been corrected, France will be weak and sickly and will suffer as from a secret cancer gnawing at its flesh. If some of its limbs must be amputated in order to make France healthy again, then let them be amputated!

Ours is a syndicate to act on public opinion, to cure it of the frenzy into which the foul press has whipped it up, and restore it to its age-old dignity and generosity; a syndicate to repeat every morning that our diplomatic relations are not at stake, that the honour of the army is not in doubt, that only certain individuals may be compromised; a syndicate to demonstrate that any miscarriage of justice can be corrected; and that to perpetuate an error of that sort, on the grounds that a court martial cannot be wrong, is the most monstrous kind of obstinacy, the most blind and appalling belief in infallibility; a syndicate that will continue campaigning until the truth has been revealed, until justice has been rendered despite all the obstacles, even if years of struggle are required – of that syndicate I am a member, have no doubt about it! And I devoutly hope that every decent person in France will become a member!

Le Figaro, 1 December 1897

At the same time Zola granted an interview to a Russian journalist, Eugen Semenov, who published it in the St Petersburg Novosti *on 30 November. The editors of* Le Matin, *in Paris, always on the lookout for sensational items, managed to publish a translation of it a few days later.*

Conversation with M. Zola

Novosti – *A book about Dreyfus – Historical narrative.*

Mr E. Semenov, the Paris correspondent of the *Novosti*, has published an interview with M. Emile Zola, with this title, in the latest number of that journal. We reproduce it here as a matter of documentary interest.

'Your opinion with regard to the Dreyfus Affair is clearly conveyed in your article. I have come to see you, not to pry in the hope of eliciting sensational replies, but simply to ask you the following. Do you intend to make use of this exceptionally dramatic affair as subject matter for one of your forthcoming books?'

'If you were a French journalist, I would not tell you a thing, and you can immediately see why. But since you write in Russian and for a Russian readership, I will tell you this. Yes, once I have become familiar, thoroughly familiar, with this affair, I have made up my mind to use it, of course. But how and why, I do not know yet myself. So much passion is involved! So much human psychology! So many conflicting interests! Why not put it into dialogue form – certainly not for the stage, not for money, certainly not for its "scandal" value, but to create a work in which everything would hinge on the struggle for truth and justice. How interesting that would be – that was my first thought. But then I realized that dialogue would be an inconvenient form and began to look for others. The most satisfactory solution I have come up with, the one that is the most interesting, gripping and instructive, is the historical narrative.

'Yes,' the famous writer continued, warming to his subject, 'yes, I shall write the story of this affair because I know it so well; I know it inside out, exactly as it is. I know the truth, and history has nothing rarer or more moving to offer. At one point I had thought of writing the story of the Panama Affair but it is full of base actions and mudslinging, whereas here, in the Dreyfus Affair, we find the most intense passions, elements of extraordinary beauty, an extraordinary crime – I am not referring to espionage, which is an ordinary fact of international relations – and characters of a rare type in this day and age. Where could you find a better or more instructive story than the story of this affair with all of its details and all of the psychological motivations of the individuals who play a role in it? As a psychologist, I am in my element here. And the characters of those individuals! Especially the three central figures, the three main characters; you would have trouble finding anything to equal them. They embody three different character types: Scheurer-Kestner, whom I have already discussed; Dreyfus, the innocent man; and the man who is actually guilty.'

Zola's voice rang strong and clear in the midst of the deep silence that reigned throughout his house.

'And aside from those three,' Zola went on, 'how many characters we can see who are fighting against the truth, who have an interest in lying! and how many others who, on the contrary, are clamouring for the truth and working on its behalf! You wonder who those characters, those men, are. If you have read my article, if you listen closely to me, you will guess who they are; and if you can guess that, you will understand why I do not subscribe to the general assumption that the truth will not be long in coming to light and everything will be discovered. Yes, the affair is clear and simple; yet, precisely because the interests involved are too great and the men who wish to stifle the truth are too powerful, the truth will not be known for some time. But there is no doubt that ultimately every bit of it, without exception, will be divulged. It will be difficult; it will require a great

deal of effort, but the truth will be revealed. And the men in high positions who are combating the truth will find, to their dismay, that as the poet said:
  "*Quos vult perdere Jupiter dementat.*"[1]

When all is over

'Not of course until the Affair is all over will I write the story of it. First of all, it caught me, so to speak, while I was in the midst of my daily toil, writing instalments which have to be delivered on pre-arranged dates and which I cannot abandon; and second, the story must bide its time until the Affair is ended. It is following its course. I will not say or write anything more than what I have already said. The only reason I am talking to you is that you are Russian.

  'As for our press, here in France, you can see how, save for a few exceptions, feelings have got out of control, scandal has been unleashed and all human feelings have been perverted! Good heavens! as I talk with you and think of Russia, that great country, so different from us as to its customs and its moral disposition and in terms of race – yes, so different from us, no matter how you look at it – what does Russia think about this? What does it think of the excesses of the French press? In your capital, in St Petersburg, people know what is going on here in France; they can understand it and judge it; they are used to everything. But in the provinces? in the other cities? What can they be thinking of this Homeric lie? of such a smokescreen deliberately placed before what should be clear for the human mind and accessible for the human soul? In its own way, it is a terribly dramatic historical episode which may make some sense to us, here, but which, over there. . . . You must forgive me. You will readily understand that for the moment I cannot talk about the Affair in detail. I must keep silent, particularly as I am absorbed by my work and therefore, personally, I cannot do a thing.'

  'What are you working on now? What projects do you have?'

  'As you know, I do not like to talk about my books while they are germinating, so to speak. Right now, I don't know myself as yet which one I am going to start working on; but in a month or six weeks from now, once my novel has been printed,[2] I shall be able to talk to you about my projects and my plans.'

Le Matin, 4 December 1897

1 'Jupiter drives to madness those whose downfall he desires' (maxim by the Greek poet Euripides, translated into Latin by J. F. Boissonade, the French Hellenist).
2 Zola was referring to *Paris*, which was then appearing by instalments in the *Journal* and was to be published in book form by Charpentier in March 1898.

The Minutes

Ah, what a spectacle, these last three weeks! What tragic, unforgettable days we have just lived through! Never has any period aroused within me more humanity or anguish, or a more generous anger. I have been so exasperated, so filled with hatred for stupidity and bad faith, have thirsted so strongly for truth and justice, that I understand how the torments of the soul can drive a peaceful citizen to martyrdom.

The spectacle has been altogether unbelievable, truly it has. Its brutality, its effrontery, its ignoble episodes have gone beyond the basest instincts to which the human beast has ever confessed. Such an example of perversion, of a mob gone mad, is rare, and no doubt that is why I have been stirred to this extent: as a human being I feel outraged, but as a novelist and playwright I am overwhelmed with enthusiasm when confronted with a case of such horrendous beauty.

Now the Affair is entering its regular, logical phase, the one we have wished for and called for unceasingly. A court martial has the case before it and the truth will emerge from this new trial; we are confident that it will. We have never demanded anything but that. Now all we need do is keep silent and wait, for, once again, the truth should not come from us; it is the court martial which should reveal it, all of it. We will not speak out again unless the truth is not revealed in full – and that is a possibility which does not bear thinking about.

But since the first phase – the scandalous mess that was concocted and deliberately kept dark, all those ugly consciences that have now been stripped naked – has come to an end, the minutes of that process must be drawn up and the conclusions reached. They are inescapable and profoundly sad, but they do provide the manly lesson, the red hot iron which will cauterize our wounds. Let us all remember that. The excruciating spectacle that we have just put on for ourselves must be our salvation.

*

First of all, the press.

We have seen the gutter press in heat, making a profit out of sick minds, driving the public mad for the sake of selling its drivel, which ceases to find any customers the minute the nation becomes calm, healthy and strong. The hawkers for the evening rags, especially the tabloids, lure passersby with their huge headlines promising debauchery. The tabloids were merely exploiting their usual line of business but their insolence was significant.

One notch higher came the popular papers that sell for one *sou*; they write for the majority of the people and shape their opinions for them. We have seen these papers insinuate hideous passions, foam at the mouth in a campaign of frenzied bigotry, and stifle all generosity, all desire for truth and justice in our dear people of France. I am willing to believe in their sincerity, but what a sorry sight! those ageing pamphleteers, those demented agitators, those narrow-minded chauvinists becoming leaders of men and committing the worst of all crimes, that of clouding over the public's sense of values and leading an entire people astray! What makes their dirty tricks even more loathsome is that certain papers use such dastardly means, casually wielding lies, slander and denunciations that will go down in history as the disgrace of our times.

And lastly, we have seen the major newspapers – what are called the serious, decent papers – stand by and witness the whole thing so impassively (I was about to say, so serenely) that I find it staggering. These decent newspapers have merely recorded everything, truth and error alike, with scrupulous care. The pestilential flood has flowed through their columns without their omitting so much as a drop of it. Now, that shows impartiality, of course. But still! At best, a view, timidly expressed here and there, but not a single strong, noble voice has been raised – not one, do you hear me? – in that 'decent' press to protest that humanity was being mocked and justice flouted!

And above all, this is what we have seen – for among so many horrors, it should suffice to select the most revolting one of all – we have seen the press, the foul press, continue to defend a French officer who had insulted the army and spat upon the nation. Yes, that is what we have seen; some papers finding excuses for him, others criticizing him but only on restricted grounds. Where is the unanimous outcry of disgust and loathing? How is such a thing possible? What is going on? Here is a crime which at any other time would have kindled the public's fury and brought forth demands for instant punishment, and yet those very same newspapers which are so ticklish on matters of felony and treason have managed to find extenuating circumstances for it!

That is what we have witnessed. Now, I do not know how such a symptom has made the other spectators react, since no one says a thing, no one gets indignant. But I can tell you it has made me shudder because with unexpected violence it has revealed the disease from which we are suffering. The foul press has perverted the nation, and it is that moral deviance, that corruption which has just laid bare the running sore for all to see.

*

Next, anti-Semitism.

Anti-Semitism is the guilty party. I have already stated how this barbarous campaign, which drags us back a thousand years in time, goes against my craving for brotherhood and my passionate need for tolerance and the emancipation of the human mind. In this century of ours, this century of liberation, it strikes me as such utter nonsense to revert to the wars of religion – beginning religious persecutions all over again and urging one race to exterminate another – that I find any such attempt idiotic. It can only be the brainchild of some fuzzy-minded, unbalanced believer; it can only be motivated by the tremendous vanity of some obscure writer desperate to play a role, any role, even an odious one. And I still refuse to believe that any such movement will ever be of decisive importance in France, the country of open-minded inquiry, fraternal goodness and limpid rationalism.

And yet, look at its terrible deeds. I have to admit that very great harm has already been done. The entire nation may not have been poisoned, but the poison is at least present in the people. It is to anti-Semitism that we owe the dangerous virulence of the Panama scandals in this country. And this whole lamentable Dreyfus Affair is the work of anti-Semitism: it and it alone made the miscarriage of justice possible; it and it alone is driving the public to hysteria; it and it alone is preventing that miscarriage from being quietly, nobly acknowledged, in the interests of this country's health and good name. Could anything have been simpler or more natural than to seek out the truth as soon as the first serious doubts set in? Surely it is obvious that if we have come to this pass, to this degree of raging folly, it must be due to some concealed poison that is making us all delirious.

That poison is the rabid hatred of the Jews which has been spewed out for public consumption every morning for years. There is a band of these professional poison-distillers, and the worst part of it is that they do it in the name of morality, in the name of Christ; they claim to avenge Christ and do justice in His name. And who can say whether the atmosphere in which the court martial deliberated didn't influence its decision? A Jewish traitor, betraying his country: that goes without saying. But what if no human motive can be found for the crime? What if he is rich, of good conduct, hard-working, unswayed by any passion, leading an irreproachable life? Well, he's Jewish – isn't that enough?

Today, since we began demanding that the truth be brought to light, the anti-Semitism has become still more violent and instructive. It is anti-Semitism itself that is on trial – and if the innocence of a Jew were to be revealed, what a slap in the face that would be for the anti-Semites! Could there possibly be such a thing as an innocent Jew? The whole carefully constructed scheme of lies would collapse. A whiff of fresh air would be let in; good faith and fairness would then spell the ruin of a sect that only manages to hold sway over simple minds by brandishing the crudest insults and most bare-faced slander.

Furthermore, we have seen how furious these instruments of public malfeasance become at the thought that a little light was about to be shed. And alas! we have also seen how bewildered the people are – the people they have perverted and led astray, the dear general public made up of ordinary, humble people. Today, the people have been turned into Jew-baiters, but tomorrow they would bring about a revolution in order to rescue Captain Dreyfus if only some decent man could light the sacred flame of justice in their souls.

*

And finally, the spectators, the actors, you and me – all of us.

What a muddle! What an inextricable mess! And it is getting worse all the time. We have seen the tangle of interests and inflamed feelings grow more feverish with every passing day. We have heard inept tales, disgraceful gossip and the most galling denials. We have seen plain old common sense slapped in the face every morning; we have seen vice acclaimed and virtue hissed, the excruciating destruction of everything that goes to make up honour and the joy of living. And in the end we find all that hideous. Yes, of course – but who was it who wanted this state of affairs? Who has dragged it out? Our masters. Although they were alerted over a year ago, they dared not do a thing. We pleaded with them to take action; we prophesied the terrifying storm that was building up, phase by phase. They had conducted their inquiry; they had the file in their hands. And yet, up to the very last minute, and despite protestations of patriotism, they persisted in their inertia rather than taking the Affair into their own hands. That would have kept it from spreading, even if it meant sacrificing certain compromised individuals without delay. Now the river of mud has overflowed, as they had been warned it would, and it is their fault.

We have seen troublemakers triumph by demanding the truth of the people who claimed they knew it, whereas those same people were unable to tell the truth as long as an inquiry was being conducted. The truth was told to the general who was put in charge of the inquiry, and he alone was empowered to reveal the truth. The truth will be told again to the investigating judge and he alone will have the authority to hear it, in order to base his decision on it. The truth! What do you think the truth can be in an affair such as this, which is shaking an entire venerable organization to its very foundations? Do you suppose the truth is some simple object that you can carry about at will in the palm of your hand and casually place in other people's hands, like a little stone, or an apple? Evidence! Yes indeed, let's have the evidence right now, this very minute! That is what some people wanted, just as children want you to show them the wind as it blows. Be patient. The truth will be revealed, all right; but first, that will require a little intelligence and integrity.

We have seen the notion of patriotism basely exploited, the spectre of foreign governments waved about in a matter of honour that is strictly a family affair, strictly French. Revolutionaries of the worst kind have bawled that the army and its leaders were being insulted; yet the whole point is that those in the very highest ranks must not be out of reach. And in response to the ringleaders – the handful of newspapers that whip public opinion into a frenzy – terror has reigned. Not one Deputy in our successive National Assemblies has protested like a decent man. All of them have hesitated and kept quiet, prisoners of their political groups. All of them, worried about the next elections, no doubt, have kept a fearful eye on public opinion. Not one moderate, not one radical, not one socialist – not a single one of those who have responsibility for public liberties has yet risen to speak out as his conscience dictates. How can you expect the country to find its way amid this storm if the very people who call themselves its guides keep silent, either out of the narrowest political considerations or for fear of compromising their personal situations?

So cruel, so pathetic has this spectacle been, such a blow to our pride, that all around me I hear people saying, 'France must truly be sick if an outbreak of public madness such as this can occur.'

No, France has merely been debauched, turned away from its natural penchant and its genius. If only it could hear the language of humanity and justice once again, it would recover; it would come back to its true nature, its legendary generosity.

The first act has ended. The curtain has fallen on the appalling drama. Let us hope that tomorrow's spectacle will restore our courage and bring us consolation.

I have already said that the truth is on the march and nothing will stop it. The first step has been taken. Another will follow, then another, and then the final step will be taken. It is a mathematical certainty.

For the moment, until the court martial reaches its decision, my role is ended; and it is my ardent hope that once the truth has been brought to light and justice been done, I will no longer have to fight for them.

Le Figaro, 5 December 1897

On 4 December, following an interpellation by Albert de Mun, the Chamber of Deputies discussed the Dreyfus Affair at length. Overriding every objection, Jules Méline, the Prime Minister, repeated – to applause – 'There is no Dreyfus Affair. . . . There is not, at this time, and there cannot be, a Dreyfus Affair. . . .'And Billot, the Minister of War, added, 'Speaking as a soldier, as the commander of the army, I consider, in all conscience, that the verdict was sound and that M. Dreyfus is guilty.' In conclusion, the Chamber affirmed res judicata, the authority of the established verdict. In its final declaration, the Chamber 'joined the Minister of War in paying tribute to the army' and 'approved the government's statements'.

Such decisions could not leave Zola indifferent. In an interview he granted to L'Aurore, *he vehemently expressed his indignation.*

M. Zola and the Vote in the Chamber of Deputies
At the home of M. Emile Zola

'What is your reaction to the Chamber's vote on the Dreyfus Affair?' I asked M. Zola yesterday morning.

His face went red. The Maître clenched his fists and, with monumental wrath, replied,

'The infamous Chamber has just disgraced itself once again. That is my reaction. What it did yesterday was shameful. It committed an abomination. Ever since I got up this morning, I have been considering how to express my indignation to the Chamber. What sorry times we live in! What an unworthy spectacle! It is appalling.

'To think that not a single Deputy dared rise and address the Chamber, to utter a few words of sheer reason and common sense! Not one had the courage to shout, "You heap of petty little minds! Don't you realize that there are higher interests than the insignificant, fleeting considerations of your vain politicking? that far above your resentments and your hatreds there is humanity, there is justice, there is the honour of France? Can't you understand that you are doing a sordid thing, concocted in the smoke-filled back rooms of the parliamentary system? Don't you feel a general shudder? Don't you know that all Europe has its eyes on you? that all Europe is listening to you and passing judgement on you?"

'I receive a great many visitors, as you know. All of the foreigners I talk with ask me, "But where is the great France of the past, the just and generous France? What is happening in your country?" And I feel humiliated. An ardent patriot, I am saddened and bewildered, and all I can say in reply is, "Yes, alas, things have changed in France. Today, in our government, rot has set in and contaminates everything it touches. Those who govern us no longer hold convictions or principles. They only worship money and think of the next elections."

'That is how low we have fallen. How abject! There is not one man in the Chamber who heeds his conscience. Not one. If there had been one he would have understood where his duty lay and would have done it courageously, and let the fools howl as much as they liked.

'Ah, if only we had a Lamartine, a Louis Blanc, a Victor Hugo! If such an odious deed had been done in Hugo's time, he would have thundered with the voice of justice and defended the people's rights. His eloquent and generous words would have hit the target.

'Meanwhile our ministers, terrified at what tomorrow may bring, take refuge in clever lies and play on words. You have to read between the lines of their speeches. They have deliberately created an equivocal situation and hope they will be able to slip out the back door if things go wrong. No one could be more foolish, more brazen and more stupid than they are.

'For instance, they maintain that there is no connection between the Esterhazy affair and the Dreyfus Affair. The idiocy of it is staggering, since Esterhazy is accused of having written a bordereau on the strength of which Dreyfus was convicted.

'As for General Billot and M. Méline, when they invoke the honour of the army, they remind me of Rouher[1] brandishing the dread spectre of revolution, in the days of the Second Empire. All Rouher needed to do was talk about the "red spectre", and immediately the legislature became docile. Today, it is just the same: all you need do is talk about "the honour of the army" and every shade of opposition falls silent and all the Deputies prostrate themselves.

'Today, the army concerns everybody, since every Frenchman is a soldier. "Attacking the army" – what does that mean? It's a nonsensical expression. When Esterhazy was brought before the first court martial, did he represent the entire army? And does General Billot take the side of that individual? If Esterhazy is not a traitor, he has at least the makings of one.

'Such pathetic people! At any other time they would be laughable. Isn't it comical to see former revolutionaries who were once convicted by courts martial claim that courts martial are infallible?

'I can tell you about courts martial. I saw how they worked in 1871. On a number of occasions I tried to rescue friends who had fallen into their clutches. So I know how they arrive at their verdicts. And I assure you, it's worse than your wildest imaginings.

'No, there is no such thing as a court that is infallible. In fact, military judges, acting in good faith, are even more likely than all other judges to convict an innocent man.

'That is what the despicable politicians do not wish to acknowledge; that is why they are infamous. I cannot find words strong enough, do you see, to express the scorn and revulsion they make me feel. If you find one, use it. I shall be grateful to you.'

M. Zola stood up and accompanied me to the door.

'What consequences do you think yesterday's vote may have?'

'None whatsoever,' he replied as we went down the stairs. 'Our Deputies are mere puppets who bustle about in a void. Their words vanish on the wind. They will not prevent the truth from continuing its onward march any more than clouds that momentarily darken the sky can prevent the daylight from reaching us.'

A glass-paned door led to the vestibule. As M. Zola stood in the doorway, he added,

---

1 Eugène Rouher (1814–84) was an influential politician during the Second Empire. His rejection of liberalization led France into the conflict with Germany and the disastrous battle of Sedan.

'Those votes will have only one result: they will give an instant's satisfaction to the foul-smelling, scandal-mongering press that is concerned only with circulation figures, not with moral convictions. That press is making France lose its wits and fall apart.'

Ph. Dubois
L'Aurore, 6 December 1897

Letter to the Young People

Where are you going, you young men, you bands of students who dash through the streets, demonstrating angrily or enthusiastically, obeying the irresistible urge to express in public what your indignant consciences feel?

Are you going to protest against some abuse of power? Has someone thwarted the craving for truth and justice that is still so ardent in those fresh young souls of yours, as yet unaware of political compromises and the cowardly renouncements of daily life?

Are you going to right some social wrong, to place your protests – the vibrant protests of youth – on the uneven scales where the fates of the fortunate and the unfortunate of this world are so unfairly weighed?

Are you going to affirm the tolerance and the independence of the human race by hissing some bigoted, sectarian spirit who has attempted to drag your liberated minds back to age-old error by proclaiming the failure of science?

Are you going to stand beneath the windows of some shifty, hypocritical character and shout out your invincible faith in the future, your faith in the coming century that you will usher in, the century that is to bring peace in the world, in the name of justice and love?

'Oh no, we're going to boo an old man who has lived a long life filled with integrity and hard work and has got it into his head that he could support a generous cause with impunity! that he could urge that the truth be brought to light and an error be corrected, for the sake of France's sacred honour!'

*

Oh, when I was young myself, the Latin Quarter I knew throbbed with the proud passions of youth, with love of freedom and hatred of the brute strength that crushes minds and wrings souls dry. In the days of the Second Empire, I watched the Latin Quarter play its courageous role of opposition, unjustly sometimes but always out of an excess of unfettered human freedom. The Latin Quarter hissed the authors whom the Tuileries Palace smiled upon, jeered teachers whose courses it found suspect, and rose up against anyone who was visibly on the side of darkness and despotism. In that Quarter burned the sacred flame, the splendid folly that inhabits twenty-year-olds, so certain that all hopes will be realized and that tomorrow will bring the triumph of the ideal City.

And if we delve further into the history of the noble passions that have made the young people of our great schools rise up, we will find that injustice has always aroused their indignation, that they have always opposed the fierce and the powerful on behalf of the humble, the abandoned and the persecuted. Our young people have demonstrated in favour of the oppressed peoples, they have been on Poland's side and Greece's side, they have defended whoever was suffering and dying from the brutality of a mob or a despot. Whenever the Latin Quarter was reported to be ablaze with passion, you could be sure of what was behind that: an outburst of some juvenile love of justice, scorning compromise, spurred by heartfelt enthusiasm. And how spontaneous it all was! how they flowed through the streets, like a river at the flood!

Oh, I'm well aware of what the pretext is, even today: France is in danger, the country has been handed over to a victorious enemy by a gang of traitors. But I ask you: where will we ever find a clear intuition of things, an instinctive feel for what is true and just, if not in these fresh new souls, in these young people who are just entering political life, whose good and upright reasoning should not yet be obscured by anything? That politicians, sullied by years of intriguing, or journalists, unbalanced by all the compromises inherent in their profession, should swallow the most impudent lies and close their eyes to what is blindingly obvious – that is understandable, that we can grasp. But the young people! The gangrene must be in an advanced stage already if the purity and natural frankness of youth do not cry out in the midst of the unacceptable errors, if they do not point straight to what is obvious and limpid in the full and honest light of day!

The story could not be simpler. An officer was found guilty, and no one would dream of impugning the judges' good faith. They sentenced him as their consciences dictated, on the basis of evidence they believed unshakeable. And then, one day, a man, several men, had doubts and ultimately became convinced that one of the pieces of evidence – the most important one, at any rate the only piece on which the judges publicly based their decision – had been wrongly attributed to the condemned man, that beyond all doubt that piece of evidence was in another man's handwriting. So they speak up, and that other man is denounced by the prisoner's brother, whose strictest duty it was to denounce him; and, inevitably, a new trial begins, which will lead to a revision of the first trial, if a sentence is handed out. Isn't all of that perfectly clear, just and reasonable? Is any part of that a machination, a dark plot to spare a traitor? That there has been a traitor, no one denies; the only thing anyone asks is that a guilty man and not an innocent one should expiate that crime. You'll have your traitor, all right; the only aim is to give you an authentic traitor.

Shouldn't a little common sense be enough? What could possibly be motivating the men who urge a revision of Dreyfus's trial? Forget the imbecilic anti-Semitism, the ferocious monomania which insists there is a Jewish plot, claiming that Jewish gold is determined to replace a Jew with a Christian in that infamous jail. It won't hold up; the improbabilities and impossibilities collapse on top of one another. All the gold in the world couldn't possibly buy certain men's consciences. In the end, we have to acknowledge reality, which is the natural, gradual, invincible expansion of any miscarriage of justice. It all boils down to that. A miscarriage of justice is an ongoing force; men with a moral sense are first won over, then haunted, and finally they dedicate themselves ever more stubbornly at the risk of their fortunes and their lives until justice is done. There is no other conceivable explanation for what is happening today; all the rest is but a magma of inflamed feelings, political and religious, an overflowing torrent of calumny and insults.

But what excuse would youth have if its concepts of humanity and justice were to be clouded over even for an instant! During its session on 4 December, a French Chamber covered itself with shame by voting a motion 'harshly condemning the ringleaders of the odious campaign which is disturbing the public's peace of mind'. I firmly declare – for the benefit of the future which will, I hope, read these words – that such a vote is unworthy of our generous country and will remain an ineradicable blot on our honour. 'The ringleaders' are men of conscience and courage; certain that a miscarriage of justice has been committed, they have denounced it so that it can be made good, and have done so out of the patriotic conviction that any great nation in which an innocent man is left to writhe in torture is a nation doomed. 'The odious campaign' is those men's cry for truth and justice; it is their obstinate determination that in the gaze of other peoples, France will continue to be the compassionate nation which once brought the world liberty and will now bring justice. As you can clearly see, that Chamber has surely committed a crime since it has made even the young people of our great schools rotten to the core, and now those young people – deceived, misled, unleashed to run about our streets – are doing something we had never witnessed before: they are demonstrating against all that is proudest, bravest and most divine in the human soul!

*

After the Senate session on the 7th, it was noised about that M. Scheurer-Kestner had suffered a disaster. Oh yes, what a disaster, indeed, in his heart and soul! I can just imagine the anguish and torment he must have felt when he saw everything he loved about our Republic collapse about him, everything he had helped it to gain by fighting the good fight all his life long: liberty first of all, then the manly virtues of fairness, frankness and civic courage.

He is one of the last of his stalwart generation. In the days of the Second Empire, he knew what it meant for a people to be subject to the authority of a single man, to be devoured by feverish impatience, their mouths brutally gagged, unable to denounce injustice. He witnessed our defeats and his heart bled; he knew what had caused them all – blindness, despotic imbecility. Later, he was one of those who laboured most wisely and most ardently to raise up the country again from its ruins and restore its rank among the nations of Europe. He dates back to the heroic days of our republican France, and I imagine he may have justifiably believed that he had done good, solid work, that despotism had been done away with forever and freedom won. By freedom I mean the human freedom that enables every single conscience to speak as its duty requires, secure in the tolerance of all other opinions.

Well, it was true! All of that had been won! But now it all lies in shambles once again. Within him and all around him are nothing but ruins. Now it is a crime to have been obsessed by the need for truth. It is a crime to have striven for justice. Despotism has come back in all its horror; mouths are harshly gagged once again. This time it is not the boot of a Caesar stamping out the public conscience; no, this time an entire Chamber castigates those who are inflamed by a passion for justice. No speaking out! Fists crush lips that try to defend truth; crowds are whipped up into mobs to reduce isolated protesters to silence. Never has such monstrous oppression been organized and used to put down open discussion. Shameful terror reigns, the most courageous are cowed, no one dares any longer to say what he thinks, for fear of being denounced as a traitor or as someone who has sold out to traitors. The few newspapers that are still decent prostrate themselves before their readers, who ultimately lose their wits because of the stupid stories that have been fed to them. I do believe that no nation has ever known a darker, more troubled hour, a more disturbing one for its sanity and its dignity.

Yes, true enough, the whole of that great and fair-minded past must have collapsed about M. Scheurer-Kestner. If he is still able to believe in the goodness and fairness of men, his optimism must be unshakeable. Every day for the past three weeks he has been dragged through the mud because he has insisted on being just, jeopardizing, in the process, the honour and joy of his old age. For a decent man, no distress can be more painful than to be martyred for his decency. This man's faith in tomorrow has been slain, his hopes have been poisoned; and if he dies he will say, 'It is all over, there is nothing left, every good thing I have ever done will die with me, virtue is a mere word, the world is a black void!'

He is the very last representative of Alsace-Lorraine in our legislature – and yet this is the man they have singled out in their wish to slap patriotism in the face! They dare to say he has sold out, they dare to label him a traitor, an insulter of the army, when his name should have been enough to reassure the most suspicious doubters. No doubt it was naive of him to believe that his status as an Alsatian and his renown as an ardent patriot would suffice to guarantee his good faith in playing the difficult role of dispenser of justice. The very fact that he was involved in this Affair should have clearly signified that he felt its prompt conclusion was essential to the honour of the army and the honour of our country. Let it drag on for weeks more, try to stifle the truth and turn a blind eye to justice, and you'll soon see that you've become the laughing stock of all Europe and you've relegated France to the lowest rank among all nations!

But no, no, the simple-minded political and religious passions will not listen to anything, and the students of France offer the whole world a dismal spectacle: they go and hiss M. Scheurer-Kestner, the 'traitor', the man who has 'sold out', the man who 'insults our army and compromises our country'!

*

I am well aware that the few young people who are demonstrating are not the entire younger generation. I know that one hundred rowdies out in the street make more noise than ten thousand workers, studiously staying home. But those one hundred rowdies are one hundred too many. And what a dismal symptom it is that such a movement, no matter how limited it may be, can take place in our Latin Quarter today!

Can young people be anti-Semites? Is that possible? Can it be that their fresh new brains and souls have already been deranged by that idiotic poison? How very sad, how disturbing a prospect for the twentieth century that is about to begin! One hundred years after the Declaration of the Rights of Man, one hundred years after that supreme act of tolerance and emancipation, we are reverting to wars of religion, to the most obnoxious and inane type of fanaticism! It may be understandable in certain men who have their role to play, an attitude to keep up and an all-devouring ambition to satisfy. But in the young! in those who are born and who grow so that all the rights and freedoms we dreamt the coming century would be resplendent with can flourish! They are the long-awaited architects of that dream – and what do they do but proclaim their anti-Semitism! They will begin the century by massacring all the Jews, their fellow citizens, because they are of a different race and a different faith! Is this the way to take possession of the City of our dreams, the City of equality and fraternity? If youth had really come to that, it would be enough to make a man weep, enough to make him deny all hope and all human happiness.

Oh youth, I beg of you, think of the great task that awaits you. You are the workmen of the future. You will lay the foundations of the next century which, we firmly believe, will resolve the problems of fairness and truth that this waning century raises. We old people, we elders bequeath our investigation to you; a tremendous heap of contradictions and obscure findings it may be, but also the most heartfelt effort any century has ever made to reach the light, comprising the most honest and unattackable documents, the very foundations of that vast edifice of knowledge which you, youth, must continue to build for the sake of your honour and your happiness. All we ask is this: be even more generous, more open-minded; outdo us by striving for a life lived normally, devoting all of your efforts to the fecund work of man and earth until it culminates at last in an abundant harvest of joy, bathed in the dazzling glow of the sun. We will hand over our place to you, our brothers; we will be happy to disappear, to sleep the good sleep of death and rest from doing our share of the task, if we know that you are continuing and carrying out our dreams.

Youth! Remember the sufferings your fathers endured, the terrible battles they had to win in order to secure the freedom you enjoy today. If you feel independent, if you can come and go as you please, say what you like in the press, have an opinion and express it publicly, it is because your fathers paid the price with their intelligence and their blood. You were not born in a reign of tyranny; you do not know what it is to wake up each morning and feel the weight of a master's boot crushing your chest; you have not had to fight to escape the sword of a dictator or the unfair scales of a corrupt judge. Thank your fathers, and do not commit the crime of acclaiming falsehood, campaigning beside the brute force and intolerance of the fanatics and the greed of the ambitious. That way lies dictatorship.

Youth! Be always on the side of justice. If ever the idea of justice should grow dim within you, you would be a prey to every peril. I am not talking about the justice prescribed by our Codes of law; that justice merely guarantees our social relationships. It must be respected, of course; but the justice I mean is a loftier notion. It lays down as a principle that all human judgement is fallible and deems it no insult to the judges to believe that a man found guilty may in fact be innocent. Isn't that an undertaking that should sustain your ardent passion for what is right? Who will stand up and demand that justice be done – if not you? you who are not embroiled in our selfish quarrels and personal feuds, you who are not yet involved or compromised in any dubious affair, you who can speak up in all purity and all good faith?

Youth! Be humane! Be generous! Even if we are mistaken, be on our side when we affirm that an innocent man is serving an appalling sentence and that our rebellious hearts burst with indignation. Just for one second, allow yourselves to think that a mistake may have been made and that the punishment is appallingly disproportionate – and you will begin to choke; tears will flow from your eyes. Oh, the self-appointed watch-dogs remain unmoved, oh yes; but you, Youth! What about you? you who can still weep, you who are receptive to every form of woe, capable of the utmost pity! What has happened to your sense of chivalry? Wherever there is a martyr crushed by hatred, is it not your dream to defend his cause and set him free? If you do not take the most sublime of risks, if you do not launch into a superb and perilous cause, if you do not stand up to an entire nation, in the name of ideal justice, then who will? Don't you feel ashamed to see your elders, the old people, take up this cause today with ardour, carrying out the task of generous folly that should be yours?

*

Where are you going, you young men, you students, you twenty-year-olds who dash about the streets, demonstrating, voicing your gallantry and hope in the midst of our discord?

'We're going to the aid of humanity, truth and justice!'

14 December 1897

Letter to France

We are going through a frightful time of moral confusion; the public's conscience appears to be clouding over. At this time, France, it is to you that I must speak, to the nation, to the mother country.

Every morning, France, when I read in the papers what you seem to think of this lamentable Dreyfus Affair, my stupefaction increases, my reason rebels still more. Is it possible that you, France, have come to this? Have you really been convinced by the most blatant lies? Are you really siding with the evildoers and their muck, against a few decent individuals? Are you really losing your head on the asinine pretext that your army has been insulted and there is a plot to sell you to the enemy? Why, the wisest and most loyal of your children have in fact but one desire: that, as all Europe turns its eyes attentively towards you, you should remain the nation of honour, of humanity, truth and justice.

Indeed, the general public has come to that, especially the ordinary people, the humblest people in the towns and almost everywhere in the provinces and in the country, that great majority of the people who accept what their newspapers or their neighbours tell them, who have no way of gathering information for themselves, no way of stopping to think for themselves. France, what has happened? How have your goodhearted, common-sensical people let fear make them so ferocious and intolerance plunge them into such darkness? Your people are told that a man who may be innocent is being tortured in the most appalling way; there is moral and material evidence that a revision of his trial is indispensable – and yet your people flatly refuse to see the light, they hide behind the scoundrels and the sectarians who find it in their interest to let the body stay buried. Are these the same people who not long ago would have torn down the Bastille all over again to rescue a single prisoner from it?

What anguish, what sadness in the souls of all those who love you, France, who strive for your honour and your grandeur! With what distress I behold these rough and stormy seas and try to discern the causes of the tempest that threatens to make your greatest glory founder. Nothing could be more deadly serious; no symptoms could be more alarming. I will dare to speak out, for all my life I have had but one passion: the truth, and I am merely continuing my life's work.

Don't you realize that the danger lies precisely in the wilful obscurantism of public opinion? Day after day a hundred different newspapers repeat again and again that public opinion does not want Dreyfus to be innocent, that his guilt is essential to the country's salvation. But France, don't you realize how very guilty you would be if your leaders allowed themselves to use such a sophism to stifle the truth? It would be the fault of France itself for having insisted on finding a crime, and then what a responsibility France would bear one day! That is why those of your sons who love you and honour you, France, have but one ardent duty in this gravest hour: to act powerfully on public opinion; to enlighten it and rescue it from the error towards which blind passions are steering it. There is no more useful, more sacrosanct task than this.

*

Oh, I'll speak to them, all right – with all my might, I'll speak to the ordinary people, the humble people who are being poisoned and forced into delirium. That and that alone is the mission I assign myself. I will cry out to them, tell them where the country's soul and its invincible energy and its undoubted triumph really spring from.

Let's see where things stand. A new step has just been taken: Major Esterhazy has been summoned before a court martial. As I have been saying from the very first day, the truth is on the march and nothing shall stop it. Despite the attempts to stand in its way, every step forward will be taken, mathematically, in due time. The truth carries a power within it that sweeps away all obstacles. And whenever its way is barred, whenever someone does succeed in burying it for any time at all, it builds up underground, gathering such explosive violence that the day it bursts out at last it blows up everything with it. Just try to keep it walled up a few months longer behind lies or behind closed doors, and ultimately you'll see that you have paved the way for the most shattering disaster.

But as truth moves forward the lies pile up, denying that truth is on the march. Nothing could be more significant. When General de Pellieux, in charge of the preliminary inquiry, submitted his report which came to the conclusion that Major Esterhazy might be guilty, the foul press made up the following story: that at Esterhazy's express wish, General Saussier – hesitating, convinced of Esterhazy's innocence – agreed to turn him over to military justice, in order to keep him happy. Today the papers are doing better still. They are saying that since three experts have again recognized the bordereau as having been beyond any doubt written by Dreyfus, Major Ravary, in the course of his investigation, concluded that the case must be dismissed and that the reason why Major Esterhazy is to appear before a court martial is that he had once again forced General Saussier's hand, demanding to be judged after all.

Isn't all this intensely comical! Isn't it all utterly stupid! Can you picture this defendant leading the whole case, dictating the decrees? Can you believe that whereas two investigations have concluded that the man is innocent, they are now going to the tremendous trouble of holding a court session for his benefit, for the sole purpose of producing a decorative comedy, a sort of judicial apotheosis? This would merely be a mockery of justice, since they declare that he is certain to be acquitted; after all, justice is not intended to judge the innocent, and the least we can ask is that the court's ruling will not be written off-stage, in the wings, before the session even begins. Since Major Esterhazy is summoned before a court martial, let us hope for the sake of our nation's honour that this is a serious business and not just some sham to keep the idle onlookers amused. Poor, poor France, they must take you for a fool, if they try to palm off such nonsense on you.

And similarly, those reports that the foul press publishes – aren't they all a heap of lies? They should be enough to open your eyes. Personally, I flatly refuse to believe that those three experts failed to recognize, at their very first glance, that Major Esterhazy's handwriting and the writing of the bordereau were absolutely identical. Take any small child going by in the street, bring him upstairs, place both pieces of writing in front of him and he will tell you, 'These two pages were written by the same gentleman.' You don't need any experts; anyone will do; the resemblance between certain words is that obvious. So true is it, in fact, that the Major has recognized this frightening resemblance and, to explain it away, he claims that tracings were made of several of his letters and launches into a whole laboriously complicated and thoroughly childish story that the press has been busy with for weeks. And yet they come and tell us that three experts have been found who declare once again that the bordereau is indeed in Dreyfus's writing! No no, it's too much! Such audacity becomes suspect in the end, and decent people are going to get angry, I hope!

Some papers go so far as to say that the bordereau will be omitted, that it won't even be mentioned in court. Then what *will* be mentioned? and why will the court bother to sit? That's the crux of the Affair: if Dreyfus was sentenced on the strength of a piece of evidence written by another person and if that piece of evidence is enough to prove that other person guilty, then a revision of the trial is indispensable – the logic requiring it is undeniable, for it is not possible to declare two people guilty of the same crime. Maître Demange has repeated, officially, that the only piece of evidence communicated to him was the bordereau; Dreyfus was legally found guilty only on the strength of that bordereau, and, even supposing that in defiance of all the rules of legal proceedings there are pieces of evidence that have been kept secret (personally, I cannot believe that), who would dare to refuse a revision once it was proven that the bordereau – the only known, acknowledged piece of evidence – is in another man's handwriting? And that is why there has been such an accumulation of lies concerning that bordereau, for it is at the very heart of the entire Affair.

Here, then, is the first point to be noted: to a large extent public opinion is arrived at on the basis of those lies, those idiotic and extraordinary tales the press prints every morning. The time will come when responsibilities will have to be taken and accounts will have to be settled with the foul press that dishonours us in the eyes of the whole world. Some of those newspapers are perfectly at home in that role; they've never done anything else but sling mud. But how astonishing and sad it is to find that among them is *L'Echo de Paris*, a literary sheet that is so often in the vanguard of ideas and yet here it is playing such a nasty role in this Dreyfus Affair! Its articles are scandalously violent and prejudiced – and unsigned. It is said that the people behind them are the very ones who were so disastrously clumsy as to have Dreyfus found guilty. Does M. Valentin Simond realize that they cover his paper with shame? And there is another paper whose attitude should smite the conscience of all decent people; I refer to *Le Petit Journal*. If the insidious broadsheets that have a circulation of only a few thousand howl and lie in order to boost their circulation, that is understandable, and besides it does only limited harm. But when *Le Petit Journal*, with a circulation of over one million, which speaks to the ordinary people and reaches everywhere, disseminates error and leads public opinion astray, then matters are exceptionally grave. When a newspaper has such a moral responsibility, when it is the spiritual leader of such a large flock, it must be of the most scrupulous intellectual integrity lest it commit crimes against the public good.

And that, France, is the first thing I find in the madness that is sweeping you away: the lies in the press, the diet of inept farce, low insults and moral depravity that it feeds you every morning. How could you possibly demand truth and justice when they are doing so much to denature your legendary virtues, the clarity of your intelligence and the sturdiness of your reasoning?

*

But there are facts that are more serious still, a whole set of symptoms which turn the crisis you are going through into a terrifying lesson, for anyone who knows how to see and judge. The Dreyfus Affair is merely a deplorable incident. The terrible thing that must be admitted is the way you are behaving throughout this business. You look healthy enough – but suddenly little blotches appear on the skin: death is there, inside you. All the political and social poison you have absorbed suddenly breaks out on your face.

Why did you let them get away with it when they shouted that your army was being insulted? (and why did you ultimately shout it too?) whereas all that the ardent patriots wanted was to defend the army's dignity and honour. What is your army, after all? Why, today, it is you, it is all of France. The army is not just a certain chief, not just a certain officers' corps, not just the bemedalled higher ranks. The army is all of your children, ready to defend France's soil. Ask yourself frankly: was it really your army you were rushing to defend when no one was attacking it? What you suddenly needed to cheer on was the sabre itself – isn't that the truth? We're told that the chiefs were insulted, but personally, what I hear, in the noisy ovation they are given, is the reawakening (unconscious, no doubt) of the latent Boulangism you are still infected with. The blood that flows in your veins is not yet republican blood. Whenever any plumes and ribbons go parading by, your heart beats faster! Whenever a king comes along, you fall in love with him! You're not thinking of your army at all – you just want to go to bed with its general! How very remote the Dreyfus Affair is from all that! While General Billot was being cheered in the Chamber, I could see the shadow of the sabre taking shape on the wall. France, if you're not careful, you're heading straight for dictatorship.

And do you know where else you're headed, France? To the Church. You're going back to the past, the past filled with intolerance and theocracy that your most illustrious children wrestled with and thought they had slain by sacrificing their intelligence and their blood. Today, the tactics of anti-Semitism are very simple. In vain did Catholicism try to influence the people by creating workers' associations and calling for pilgrimage after pilgrimage; it failed to win over the people and bring them to kneel before the altar again. It was all over; the churches remained empty, the people no longer believed. And now what has happened? Circumstances have made it possible to breathe the anti-Semitic madness into the people; they are being poisoned with this fanaticism, hurled into the streets howling, 'Down with the Jews! Death to the Jews!' What a triumph it would be if a religious war could be unleashed! No, no, the people are not believers any more; but isn't this the first step towards making believers of them – starting the old medieval intolerance all over again, burning Jews in public? Anyhow, the poison has been found; and once the people of France have been turned into fanatics and executioners, once their generosity and their love for the hard-won rights of man have been wrenched out of their hearts, God no doubt will do the rest.

They have the nerve to deny the reactionary clericalism. Yet it's everywhere you look – in politics, in the arts, in the press, in the streets! Today it's Jews who are being persecuted, tomorrow it will be Protestants; already the campaign is beginning. The Republic is overrun by reactionaries of every stripe; they adore it with a harsh and terrifying love, they stifle it with kisses. All you hear, on all sides, is that the idea of freedom is bankrupt. And when the Dreyfus Affair broke out, it supplied the growing hatred of freedom with an astonishing opportunity; passions began to blaze, even in the most oblivious people. Can't you see why they hurled themselves so furiously at M. Scheurer-Kestner? Because he is of a generation that believed in freedom and strove for freedom. Today, people shrug their shoulders and laugh mockingly: obsolete old fuddy-duddies, they call them. If M. Scheurer-Kestner is defeated, that will complete the ruin of the Republic's founders, the ruin of all who are dead and whom they've tried to bury in the mud. Those founders spurned the sabre and left the Church, and that is why Scheurer-Kestner, that great and decent man, is vilified today. They have to drown him in shame so that the Republic itself will be sullied and washed away.

And in addition, this Dreyfus Affair reveals in broad daylight all the nasty politicking that goes on in smoke-filled back rooms; it besmirches the parliamentary system and will do it in. Unfortunately for the Affair, it comes towards the end of the legislative session, when there are only three or four months left in which to rig the next session. Naturally, the government that is currently in power wants to hold elections, and the Deputies are just as determined to get themselves re-elected. So, rather than let portfolios out of their grasp, rather than compromise their chances of election, they are determined to take the most extreme steps. A drowning man could not cling more convulsively to his lifebuoy. That is the crux, that's what explains everything. First of all, the government's extraordinary attitude in this Dreyfus Affair, its silence, its hesitation, the wicked deed it is doing by letting the country agonize amid imposture, when it was the government itself that was responsible for establishing the truth; and then the limp and cowardly lack of interest shown by the Deputies, who pretend they don't know what's going on. They are afraid of only one thing: compromising their re-election by alienating the people, whom they believe to be anti-Semitic. They keep telling you over and over again, 'Ah, if only you would hold elections! you'd see how the government and the parliament would settle the Dreyfus Affair in twenty-four hours!' And that's how the smoke-filled-room politicking of the parliamentary system brings low a great people!

So that, France, is how your public opinion is still determined: by a need for sabres and reactionary clericalism dragging you several centuries backward, by the overweening ambition of those who govern you, gobble you up and refuse to stop gorging on you!

*

France, I beg of you, come to your senses, be yourself again, be that great country, France.

Singlehanded, anti-Semitism has perpetrated two sensational affairs that have done so much harm to France: the Panama Canal Affair and the Dreyfus Affair. Do you remember how the foul press used denunciations, spread abominable gossip and published false or stolen documents until the Panama business became a hideous ulcer that ate away at the country for years, making it weaker and weaker? The press drove public opinion wild; the entire nation was perverted, intoxicated; the entire nation saw red, demanded figures, decreed that the Parliament was rotten to the core and clamoured for a mass execution of all its members. Ah, if only Arton would come back! if only Arton would speak up! Well, come back he did, and speak up he did. Then all the lies spread by the foul press were revealed as hollow fabrications. And in fact public opinion abruptly swung to the opposite extreme, refusing so much as to suspect a single guilty person and insisting on a mass acquittal! Now, I don't suppose that everyone actually had a clear conscience, for what had happened was what happens in every Parliament in the world when big companies are handling millions and millions. But ultimately the public was nauseated by all the filth; too many people had been smeared, too many had been denounced, and finally the public felt an overriding need to wash it all away and breathe pure air. It needed to believe that everyone was innocent.

Well, I predict that this is what will happen with the Dreyfus Affair, the other crime against society perpetrated by anti-Semitism. Once again, the foul press is saturating the public too heavily with lies and calumny. The press is over determined to turn decent people into knaves, and knaves into decent people. It is spreading so many idiotic stories that finally even children stop believing them. It is arousing too many denials, going too much against the grain of sheer common sense and integrity. One of these days the public will suddenly gag on all the filth it has been fed. It is bound to happen. And just as in the Panama Canal scandal, you'll see that in this Dreyfus Affair as well, the public will bring its weight to bear. In an outpouring of sovereign generosity, the public will decide there are to be no more traitors; it will call for truth and justice. Thus, anti-Semitism will be tried and sentenced for its evil deeds, for the two mortally dangerous follies it has led this country into and for the loss of dignity and health this country has suffered as a result.

France, that is why I beseech you, come back to your senses now; do not wait any longer. The truth cannot be told to you now, since the matter is before the courts and we have no choice but to believe they will reveal the truth. At this point only the judges have the floor. No one else will have a duty to speak out unless the judges fail to reveal the whole truth, the simple truth. But don't you already suspect what that truth is? First there was a mistake; then came all the misdeeds for the sake of hiding that mistake. The facts have been so eloquent that every phase of the investigation has been an admission: Major Esterhazy given the benefit of inexplicable protection again and again; Colonel Picquart treated as if he were the guilty party and suffering outrageous insults, the Ministers playing on words, the unofficial newspapers lying in their teeth, the initial inquiry merely groping about with desperate slowness. Don't you agree there's a rotten stench? Doesn't it reek of dead bodies? Don't you agree they must really have a great many things to hide since they openly let themselves be defended by all the scoundrels in Paris, while decent people are clamouring for a ray of light, even though their doing so prevents them from leading peaceful lives?

France, awaken! Think of your glory! Is it possible that your liberal middle class and your emancipated people do not realize what a senseless scandal they have been tricked into? I cannot believe they are accomplices to it. They must have been fooled, since they are not aware that two things lie behind it: military dictatorship and reactionary clericalism. France, is that what you want? Do you want to jeopardize all that you have paid for so dearly: religious tolerance, equality of justice for all, fraternal solidarity among all of your citizens? If there is the slightest doubt about Dreyfus's guilt and if in spite of that doubt you leave him to languish as an outcast, that is enough to compromise your glorious conquest of law and liberty forever. Will there really be only a handful of us to say these things out loud? Won't we be joined by all of your children, all the decent individuals, all the free spirits, all the generous souls who founded the Republic and should be trembling to see it in such frightful danger?

*

France, those are the people I appeal to! They must group together! They must write; they must speak up. They must work with us to enlighten the little people, the humble people who are being poisoned and forced into delirium. The nation's soul and energy cannot be triumphant except in a climate of fairness and generosity.

I worry about one thing only: that light may not be shed in full, and may not be shed immediately. A judgement behind closed doors, following on a secret investigation, would not put an end to anything. Only then would the Affair truly begin; for people would have to speak up, since keeping silent would make them accomplices. What folly it is, to think that one can prevent History from being written! Well, the history of this affair *shall* be written, and not one person with any responsibility in it, no matter how slight, will go unpunished.

And ultimately, France, this will enhance your glory. At heart, I do not fear for you; they will try to undermine your sanity and your health, but in vain. You are the future. You will always reawaken, you will always triumph amid truth and justice!

7 January 1898

Letter to M. Félix Faure, President of the Republic ('J'accuse')

Monsieur le Président,
Will you allow me, out of my gratitude for the gracious manner in which you once granted me an audience, to express my concern for your well-deserved glory? Will you allow me to tell you that although your star has been in the ascendant hitherto, it is now in danger of being dimmed by the most shameful and indelible of stains?

You have emerged unscathed from libellous slurs,[1] you have won the people's hearts. You are the radiant centre of our apotheosis, for the Russian alliance has been indeed, for France, a patriotic celebration. And now you are about to preside over our World Fair. What a solemn triumph it will be, the crowning touch on our grand century of diligent labour, truth and liberty. But what a blot on your name (I was about to say, on your reign) this abominable Dreyfus Affair is! A court martial, acting on orders, has just dared to acquit such a man as Esterhazy. Truth itself and justice itself have been slapped in the face. And now it is too late, France's cheek has been sullied by that supreme insult, and History will record that it was during your Presidency that such a crime against society was committed.

They have dared to do this. Very well, then, I shall dare too. I shall tell the truth, for I pledged that I would tell it, if our judicial system, once the matter was brought before it through the normal channels, did not tell the truth, the whole truth. It is my duty to speak up; I will not be an accessory to the fact. If I were, my nights would be haunted by the spectre of that innocent man so far away, suffering the worst kind of torture as he pays for a crime he did not commit.

And it is to you, M. le Président, that I will shout out the truth with all the revulsion of a decent man. To your credit, I am convinced that you are unaware of the truth. And to whom should I denounce the evil

---

1 In December 1895 Drumont, in his *Libre Parole*, had unleashed a campaign aimed at Faure's father-in-law.

machinations of those who are truly guilty if not to you, the First Magistrate in the land?

*

First of all, the truth about the trial and the verdict against Dreyfus.

One wicked man has led it all, done it all: Lt-Col du Paty de Clam. At the time he was only a Major. He *is* the entire Dreyfus Affair. Not until a fair inquiry has clearly established his actions and his responsibilities will we understand the Dreyfus Affair. He appears to have an unbelievably fuzzy and complicated mind, haunted by implausible plots and indulging in the methods that litter cheap novels – stolen papers, anonymous letters, rendez-vous in deserted places, mysterious women who flit about at night to peddle damaging proof. It was his idea to dictate the bordereau to Dreyfus; it was his idea to examine it in a room entirely lined with mirrors; it was du Paty de Clam, Major Forzinetti tells us, who went out with a dark lantern intending to slip into the cell where the accused man was sleeping and flash the light on his face all of a sudden so that he would be taken by surprise and blurt out a confession. And there is more to reveal, but it is not up to me to reveal it all; let them look, let them find what there is to be found. I shall simply say that Major du Paty de Clam, in charge of investigating the Dreyfus Affair, in his capacity as a criminal police officer, bears the greatest burden of guilt – in terms of chronological order and rank – in the appalling miscarriage of justice that has been committed.

For some time already, the bordereau had been in the possession of Colonel Sandherr, head of the Intelligence Bureau, who has since died of total paralysis. There were 'leaks', papers disappeared, just as papers continue to disappear today; and efforts were being made to find out who had written the bordereau when a conviction slowly grew up that that person could only be an officer from the General Staff, and an artillery officer at that. This was a glaring double error, which shows how superficially the bordereau had been examined, since a close and rational scrutiny of it proves that it could only have been written by an infantry officer.

Accordingly, they searched throughout the premises; they examined handwriting samples as if it were a family matter; a traitor was to be caught by surprise in the offices themselves and expelled from them. Now, the story is partly familiar to us and I do not wish to repeat it all over again; but this is where Major du Paty de Clam comes into it, as soon as the first suspicion falls on Dreyfus. From that moment on, it was du Paty de Clam who invented Dreyfus. The Affair became *his* affair. He was sure that he could confound the traitor and wring a complete confession from him. Of course, there is the War Minister, General Mercier, whose intelligence seems to be on a mediocre level; and of course there is the Chief of the General Staff, General de Boisdeffre, who appears to have been swayed by his intense clericalism, and there is the Deputy Chief, General Gonse, whose conscience managed to make room for a good many things. But to begin with, there was really only Major du Paty de Clam. He led those men by the nose. He hypnotized them. Yes indeed, he also dabbles in spiritism and occultism; he converses with spirits. The experiments to which he subjected the unfortunate Dreyfus and the whole demented system of torture – the traps he attempted to make him fall into, the foolish investigations, the monstrous fabrications – are beyond belief.

Ah, for anyone who knows the true details of the first affair, what a nightmare it is! Major du Paty de Clam arrests Dreyfus and has him placed in solitary confinement. He rushes to the home of Madame Dreyfus and terrifies her, saying that if she speaks up, her husband is lost. Meanwhile the unfortunate man is tearing out his hair, clamouring his innocence. And that is how the investigation proceeded, as in some fifteenth-century chronicle, shrouded in mystery and a wealth of the wildest expedients, and all on the basis of a single, childish accusation, that idiotic bordereau, which was not only a very ordinary kind of treason but also the most impudent kind of swindle, since almost all of the so-called secrets that had supposedly been turned over to the enemy were of no value. I dwell on this point because this is the egg from which the real crime – the dreadful denial of justice which has laid France low – was later to hatch. I would like to make it perfectly clear how the miscarriage of justice came about, how it is the product of Major du Paty de Clam's machinations, how General Mercier and Generals de Boisdeffre and Gonse came to be taken in by it and gradually became responsible for this error and how it is that later they felt they had a duty to impose it as the sacred truth, a truth that will not admit of even the slightest discussion. At the beginning, all they contributed was negligence and lack of intelligence. The worst we can say is that they gave in to the religious passions of the circles they move in and the prejudices wrought by esprit de corps. They let stupidity have its way.

But now, here is Dreyfus summoned before the court martial. The most utter secrecy is demanded. They could not have imposed stricter silence and been more rigorous and mysterious if a traitor had actually opened our borders to the enemy and led the German Emperor straight to Notre Dame. The entire nation is flabbergasted. Terrible deeds are whispered about, monstrous betrayals that scandalize History itself, and of course the nation bows to these rumours. No punishment can be too severe; the nation will applaud the traitor's public humiliation; the nation is adamant: the guilty man shall remain on the remote rock where infamy has placed him and he shall be devoured by remorse. But then, those unspeakable accusations, those dangerous accusations that might inflame all of Europe and had to be so carefully concealed behind the closed doors of a secret session – are they true? No, they are not! There is nothing behind all that but the extravagant, demented flights of fancy of Major du Paty de Clam. It's all a smokescreen with just one purpose: to conceal a cheap novel of the most

outlandish sort. And to be convinced of this, one need only examine the
formal indictment that was read before the court martial.

How hollow that indictment is! Is it possible a man has been found guilty
on the strength of it? Such iniquity is staggering. I challenge decent people
to read it: their hearts will leap with indignation and rebellion when they
think of the disproportionate price Dreyfus is paying so far away on
Devil's Island. So Dreyfus speaks several languages, does he? This is a
crime. Not one compromising paper was found in his home? A crime.
He occasionally pays a visit to the region he hails from? A crime. He is a
hard-working man, eager to know everything? A crime. He does not
get flustered? A crime. He does get flustered? A crime. And how naively
it is worded! How baseless its claims are! They told us he was indicted
on fourteen different counts but in the end there is actually only one: that
famous bordereau; and we even find out that the experts did not all
agree, that one of them, M. Gobert, was subjected to some military pressure
because he dared to come to a different conclusion from the one they
wanted him to reach. We were also told that twenty-three officers had
come and testified against Dreyfus. We still do not know how they were
questioned, but what is certain is that not all of their testimony was negative. Besides, all of them, you will notice, came from the offices of the War
Department. This trial is a family conclave; they all *belong*. We must not
forget that. It is the General Staff who wanted this trial; it is they who
judged Dreyfus; and they have just judged him for the second time.

So all that was left was the bordereau, on which the experts had not
agreed. They say that in the council chambers, the judges were naturally
leaning towards acquittal. And if that is the case then you can understand
why, on the General Staff, they are so desperately insistent today on proclaiming, in order to justify the judgement, that there was a damning but
secret document; they cannot reveal it but it makes everything legitimate
and we must bow before it, as before an invisible and unknowable God! I
deny the existence of any such document, I deny it with all my strength!
Some ridiculous piece of paper, possibly; perhaps the one that talks about
easy women and mentions a man named D . . . who is becoming too
demanding; no doubt some husband or other who feels they're not paying
him enough for the use of his wife. But a document that concerns the
national defence, a document that would cause war to be declared
immediately if ever it was produced? No! No! It's a lie! And what makes the
whole business all the more odious and cynical is that they are lying with
impunity and there is no way to convict them. They turn France inside out,
they shelter behind the legitimate uproar they have caused, they seal
mouths by making hearts quake and perverting minds. I know of no
greater crime against society.

These, M. le Président, are the facts that explain how a miscarriage of
justice has come to be committed. And the evidence as to Dreyfus's char-

acter, his financial situation, his lack of motives, the fact that he has never
ceased to clamour his innocence – all these demonstrate that he has been
a victim of Major du Paty de Clam's overheated imagination, and of the
clericalism that prevails in the military circles in which he moves, and of
the hysterical hunt for 'dirty Jews' that disgraces our times.

*

Now we come to the Esterhazy affair. Three years have passed. Many
people's consciences are still profoundly uneasy; worried, they look
further, and ultimately they become convinced that Dreyfus is innocent.

I will not retrace the story of M. Scheurer-Kestner's doubts and then of
the certainty he came to feel. But while he was conducting his investigation, very serious events were taking place within the General Staff itself.
Colonel Sandherr had died and Lt-Col Picquart had succeeded him at the
head of the Intelligence Bureau. And it is in that capacity and in the exercise of his functions that Picquart one day held in his hands a special
delivery letter addressed to Major Esterhazy by an agent of a foreign
power. It was Picquart's strictest duty to launch an investigation. It is
clear that he never acted otherwise than with the consent of his superior
officers. So he outlined his suspicions to his hierarchical superiors –
General Gonse, then General de Boisdeffre, then General Billot, who had
succeeded General Mercier as Minister of War. The famous Picquart file
that has been talked about so much was never anything more nor less than
the Billot file, by which I mean the file that a subaltern prepared for his
Minister, the file that they must still have in the War Ministry. The inquiry
lasted from May to September 1896, and two things must be stated in no
uncertain terms: General Gonse was convinced that Esterhazy was guilty,
and neither General de Boisdeffre nor General Billot questioned the fact
that the bordereau was in Esterhazy's handwriting. Lt-Col Picquart's
investigation had led to that indubitable conclusion. But feeling ran very
high, for if Esterhazy was found guilty, then inevitably the Dreyfus verdict
would have to be revised, and that was what the General Staff was determined to avoid at all costs.

At that point there must have been an instant of the most intense
psychological anguish. Note that General Billot was not compromised in
any way; he had just come on stage; it was within his power to reveal the
truth. But he dared not do it – terrified of public opinion, no doubt, and
certainly afraid as well of handing over the entire General Staff, including
General de Boisdeffre and General Gonse, not to mention the subalterns.
Then there was but one minute of struggle between his conscience and
what he thought was in the best interests of the army. Once that
minute was over, it was already too late. He had made his choice; he was
compromised. And ever since then his share of responsibility has grown
and grown; he has taken the others' crime upon himself; he is as guilty as

the others; he is guiltier than the others, for he had the power to see that justice was done and he did nothing. Understand that if you can! For a year now, General Billot, General de Boisdeffre and General Gonse have known that Dreyfus is innocent, and they have kept this appalling knowledge to themselves! And people like that sleep soundly! And they have wives and children, and love them dearly!

Lt-Col Picquart had done his duty as a decent man. In the name of justice, he insisted to his superior officers. He even begged them; he told them how impolitic their dithering was, what a terrible storm was building up, how it was going to burst once the truth became known. Later on, M. Scheurer-Kestner used the same words to General Billot; out of patriotism, he implored him to get a grip on the Affair instead of letting it go from bad to worse until it became a public disaster. But no, the crime had been committed and the General Staff could no longer confess to it. And Lt-Col Picquart was sent away on mission; they sent him farther and farther away, all the way to Tunisia where one day they even tried to do his bravery the honour of assigning him to a mission that would assuredly have got him slaughtered, in the same region where the Marquis de Morès had been killed. Mind you, Picquart was not in disgrace; General Gonse had a friendly exchange of letters with him. Only, there are some secrets it is not wise to have discovered.

In Paris, the all-conquering truth was on the march, and we know how the predictable storm eventually burst. M. Mathieu Dreyfus denounced Major Esterhazy as the real author of the bordereau just as M. Scheurer-Kestner was about to place in the hands of the Minister of Justice a request for a revision of the Dreyfus trial. And this is where Major Esterhazy appears. Witnesses state that at first he panicked; he was on the verge of suicide or about to flee. Then suddenly he became boldness itself and grew so violent that all Paris was astonished. The reason is that help had suddenly materialized in the form of an anonymous letter warning him of his enemies' doings; a mysterious lady had even gone to the trouble one night of bringing him a document that had been stolen from the General Staff and was supposed to save him. And I cannot help suspecting Lt-Col du Paty de Clam, for I recognize the type of expedients in which his fertile imagination delights. His achievement – the decision that Dreyfus was guilty – was in danger, and no doubt he wished to defend his achievement. A revision of the verdict? Why, that would put an end to the far-fetched, tragic work of cheap fiction whose abominable last chapter is being written on Devil's Island! He could not allow that to happen. Henceforth, a duel was bound to take place between Lt-Col Picquart and Lt-Col du Paty de Clam. The one shows his face for all to see; the other is masked. Soon we will see them both in the civil courts. Behind it all is the General Staff, still defending itself, refusing to admit to its crime, which becomes more of an abomination with every passing hour.

In a daze, people wondered who Major Esterhazy's protectors could be. Behind the scenes there was Lt-Col du Paty de Clam, first of all; he cobbled it all together, led the whole thing. The means used were so preposterous that they give him away. Then, there are General de Boisdeffre and General Gonse and General Billot himself, who are obliged to get Esterhazy acquitted since they dare not let Dreyfus's innocence be acknowledged lest the War Office collapse as the public heaps scorn on it. It's a prodigious situation and the impressive result is that Lt-Col Picquart, the one decent man involved, the only one who has done his duty, is going to be the victim, the person they will ride rough-shod over and punish. Ah justice! what dreadful despair grips my heart! They are even claiming that Picquart is the forger, that he forged the letter-telegram purposely to cause Esterhazy's downfall. But in heaven's name, why? To what end? State one motive. Is he too paid by the Jews? The funniest thing about the whole story is that in fact he was anti-Semitic. Yes, we are witnessing an infamous sight: men heavily in debt and guilty of evil deeds but whose innocence is being proclaimed while the very honour of a man whose record is spotless is being dragged in the mud! When a society comes to that, it begins to rot away.

This, M. le Président, is the Esterhazy affair: a guilty man who had to be proved innocent. For almost two months now, we have been following every single episode of this pitiful business. I am simplifying, for by and large this is only a summary of the story, but one day every one of its turbulent pages will be written in full. So it is that we saw General de Pellieux, first of all, then Major Ravary, conduct a villainous investigation from which the scoundrels emerged transfigured while decent people were besmirched. Then, the court martial was convened.

*

Did anyone really hope that one court martial would undo what another court martial had done in the first place?

I am not even talking about the judges, who could have been chosen differently. Since these soldiers have a lofty idea of discipline in their blood, isn't that enough to disqualify them from arriving at an equitable judgement? Discipline means obedience. Once the Minister of War, the supreme commander, has publicly established the authority of the original verdict, and has done so to the acclamations of the nation's representatives, how can you expect a court martial to override his judgement officially? In hierarchical terms, that is impossible. General Billot, in his statement, planted certain ideas in the judges' minds, and they proceeded to judge the case in the same way as they would proceed to go into battle, that is, without stopping to think. The preconceived idea that they brought with them to the judges' bench was of course as follows: 'Dreyfus was sentenced for treason by a court martial, therefore he is guilty; and we, as a court martial, cannot find him innocent. Now, we know that if we recognize Esterhazy's guilt we will be proclaiming Dreyfus's innocence.' And nothing could make them budge from that line.

They reached an iniquitous verdict which will forever weigh heavy on all our future courts martial and forever make their future decisions suspect. There may be room for doubt as to whether the first court martial was intelligent but there is no doubt that the second has been criminal. Its excuse, I repeat, is that the commander in chief had spoken and declared the previous verdict unattackable, holy and superior to mere mortals – and how could his subordinates dare to contradict him? They talk to us about the honour of the army; they want us to love the army, respect the army. Oh yes, indeed, if you mean an army that would rise up at the very first hint of danger, that would defend French soil; that army is the French people themselves, and we have nothing but affection and respect for it. But the army that is involved here is not the dignified army that our need for justice calls out for. What we are faced with here is the sabre, the master that may be imposed on us tomorrow. Should we kiss the hilt of that sabre, that god, with pious devotion? No, we should not!

As I have already shown, the Dreyfus Affair was the affair of the War Office: an officer from the General Staff denounced by his fellow officers on the General Staff, sentenced under pressure from the Chiefs of the General Staff. And I repeat, he cannot emerge from his trial innocent without all of the General Staff being guilty. Which is why the War Office employed every means imaginable – campaigns in the press, statements and innuendoes, every type of influence – to cover Esterhazy, in order to convict Dreyfus a second time. The republican government should take a broom to that nest of Jesuits (General Billot calls them that himself) and make a clean sweep! Where, oh where is a strong and wisely patriotic ministry that will be bold enough to overhaul the whole system and make a fresh start? I know many people who tremble with alarm at the thought of a possible war, knowing what hands our national defence is in! and what a den of sneaking intrigue, rumour-mongering and back-biting that sacred chapel has become – yet that is where the fate of our country is decided! People take fright at the appalling light that has just been shed on it all by the Dreyfus Affair, that tale of human sacrifice! Yes, an unfortunate, a 'dirty Jew' has been sacrificed. Yes, what an accumulation of madness, stupidity, unbridled imagination, low police tactics, inquisitorial and tyrannical methods this handful of officers have got away with! They have crushed the nation under their boots, stuffing its calls for truth and justice down its throat on the fallacious and sacrilegious pretext that they are acting for the good of the country!

And they have committed other crimes. They have based their action on the foul press and let themselves be defended by all the rogues in Paris – and now the rogues are triumphant and insolent while law and integrity go down in defeat. It is a crime to have accused individuals of rending France apart when all those individuals ask for is a generous nation at the head of the procession of free, just nations – and all the while the people who committed that crime were hatching an insolent plot to make the entire world swallow a fabrication. It is a crime to lead public opinion astray, to manipulate it for a death-dealing purpose and pervert it to the point of delirium. It is a crime to poison the minds of the humble, ordinary people, to whip reactionary and intolerant passions into a frenzy while sheltering behind the odious bastion of anti-Semitism. France, the great and liberal cradle of the rights of man, will die of anti-Semitism if it is not cured of it. It is a crime to play on patriotism to further the aims of hatred. And it is a crime to worship the sabre as a modern god when all of human science is labouring to hasten the triumph of truth and justice.

Truth and justice – how ardently we have striven for them! And how distressing it is to see them slapped in the face, overlooked, forced to retreat! I can easily imagine the harrowing dismay that must be filling M. Scheurer-Kestner's soul, and one day, no doubt, he will wish that when he was questioned before the Senate he had taken the revolutionary step of revealing everything he knew, ripping away all pretence. He was your true good man, a man who could look back on an honest life. He assumed that truth alone would be enough – could not help but be enough, since it was plain as day to him. What was the point of upsetting everything, since the sun would soon be shining? He was serene and confident, and how cruelly he is being punished for that now! The same is true of Lt-Col Picquart: out of a lofty sense of dignity, he refrained from publishing General Gonse's letters. His scruples do him honour, particularly since while he was being respectful of discipline, his superior officers were busy slinging mud at him, conducting the investigation prior to his trial themselves, in the most outrageous and unbelievable way. There are two victims, two decent, stouthearted men, who stood back to let God have His way – and all the while the devil was doing his work. And where Lt-Col Picquart is concerned, we have even seen this ignoble thing: a French court first allowed the rapporteur to bring charges against a witness publicly, accuse him publicly of every wrong in the book, and then, when that witness was called to give an account of himself and speak in his own defence, that same court held its session behind closed doors. I say that that is still another crime, and I say that it will arouse the conscience of all mankind. Our military tribunals certainly do have a peculiar idea of justice.

That, M. le Président, is the plain truth. It is appalling. It will remain an indelible blot on your term as President. Oh, I know that you are powerless to deal with it, that you are the prisoner of the Constitution and of the people nearest to you. But as a man, your duty is clear, and you will not overlook it, and you will do your duty. Not for one minute do I despair that truth will triumph. I am confident and I repeat, more vehemently even than before, the truth is on the march and nothing shall stop it. The Affair is only just beginning, because only now have the positions become crystal clear: on the one hand, the guilty parties, who do not want the truth to be revealed; on the other, the defenders of justice, who will give their lives to see that justice is done. I have said it elsewhere and I repeat it here: if the truth is buried underground, it swells and grows and becomes so explosive that the day it bursts, it blows everything wide open along with it. Time will tell; we shall see whether we have not prepared, for some later date, the most resounding disaster.

*

But this letter has been a long one, M. le Président, and it is time to bring it to a close.

I accuse Lt-Col du Paty de Clam of having been the diabolical agent of a miscarriage of justice (though unwittingly, I am willing to believe) and then of having defended his evil deed for the past three years through the most preposterous and most blameworthy machinations.

I accuse General Mercier of having been an accomplice, at least by weak-mindedness, to one of the most iniquitous acts of this century.

I accuse General Billot of having had in his hands undeniable proof that Dreyfus was innocent and of having suppressed it, of having committed this crime against justice and against humanity for political purposes, so that the General Staff, which had been compromised, would not lose face.

I accuse Generals de Boisdeffre and Gonse of having been accomplices to this same crime, one out of intense clerical conviction, no doubt, and the other perhaps because of the esprit de corps which makes the War Office the Holy of Holies and hence unattackable.

I accuse General de Pellieux and Major Ravary of having led a villainous inquiry, by which I mean a most monstrously one-sided inquiry, the report on which, by Ravary, constitutes an imperishable monument of naive audacity.

I accuse the three handwriting experts, Messrs Belhomme, Varinard and Couard, of having submitted fraudulent and deceitful reports – unless a medical examination concludes that their eyesight and their judgement were impaired.

I accuse the War Office of having conducted an abominable campaign in the press (especially in *L'Eclair* and *L'Echo de Paris*) in order to cover up its misdeeds and lead public opinion astray.

Finally, I accuse the first court martial of having violated the law by sentencing a defendant on the basis of a document which remained secret, and I accuse the second court martial of having covered up that illegal action, on orders, by having, in its own turn, committed the judicial crime of knowingly acquitting a guilty man.

In making these accusations, I am fully aware that my action comes under Articles 30 and 31 of the law of 29 July 1881 on the press, which makes libel a punishable offence. I deliberately expose myself to that law.

As for the persons I have accused, I do not know them; I have never seen them; I feel no rancour or hatred towards them. To me, they are mere entities, mere embodiments of social malfeasance. And the action I am taking here is merely a revolutionary means to hasten the revelation of truth and justice.

I have but one goal: that light be shed, in the name of mankind which has suffered so much and has the right to happiness. My ardent protest is merely a cry from my very soul. Let them dare to summon me before a court of law! Let the inquiry be held in broad daylight!

I am waiting.

M. le Président, I beg you to accept the assurance of my profound respect.

L'Aurore, 13 January 1898

The three interviews that follow provide a dramatic backdrop to the trial before the Paris Assize Court. They enable us to assess what was at stake. The first two were given before the courtroom sessions began, on 7 February; the third was given after Zola had been convicted, on 23 February.

About Today's Trial
Interview with M. Emile Zola

M. Emile Zola is about to appear before the jury of the Seine. It is our good fortune to publish, below, a report on the brief interview which the eminent and courageous writer was kind enough to grant us yesterday, and the statements he was good enough to make to us, with a serenity which we hasten to applaud.

'As you can easily observe, the closer we come to that solemn moment when the hearing is to begin, the more unshakeable my ideas become and the more self-possessed I feel – as indeed I have always felt ever since this dreadful affair began.

'My first impulse is to say that the modesty and narrowness of any personal impressions I could express to you might involuntarily understate the resounding scope of a cause which has captured the attention of France and the entire world.

'Nonetheless, you may be absolutely certain that starting today, my personality vanishes from the scene so that the facts which I have examined in relation to one another can be seen in action. Was I mistaken when I said, some time ago, "The truth is on the march and nothing shall stop it"? No, I was not; for, notwithstanding all protests to the contrary, and even though no one realizes it, the trial that begins tomorrow will be the first serious step towards the revelation of that truth.

'I have the immense pleasure of having made a slight contribution to this result. Henceforth my role is ended and that of the events themselves begins. I am confident that the light will emerge, by itself, from the atrocious shadows.

'Today I feel even fewer regrets than ever before at having launched this campaign. I am happy to have had the opportunity to use my pen – on which unremitting labours have conferred some fame – in the service of justice and humanity, of a cause on which common sense alone would suffice to shed light if only people's minds could be wrested from the dissensions of the moment and restored to calm. With a clear conscience I shall appear before the jurors, guided by my one strength: the defence of truth, wherever it may be.'

On words such as these, no comment is needed.

Le XIXe Siècle, 8 February 1898

About the Trial
M. Zola at home, in the rue de Bruxelles

Before leaving for the Palais de Justice, M. Emile Zola received a number of friends who had come to assure him of their support. The parlour and the billiard room of his house had been abundantly and tastefully decorated with flowers and plants by Mme Zola.

The eminent novelist did not appear the least concerned over the outcome of the trial.

'Whatever it may be, I shall be satisfied. My conscience cannot reproach me with anything, for my conduct has been dictated by my conscience alone and I place that verdict above all other verdicts. Whether I am convicted or acquitted is of no importance to the only real trial, the one taking place before mankind's universal conscience. If my conviction could hasten the solution of this controversy, in which I have pledged my rest and my honour, I would certainly prefer it to my acquittal.'

And M. Zola – who for the past three months has interrupted his work in order to devote himself to the fine cause of justice, as we know – added, with a smile,

'If I am convicted, prison will make me a free man again. It will be the solitary retreat where I will be able to meditate and resume my work.

'I have no ties to the Dreyfus family. I have never seen M. Mathieu Dreyfus and I do not know Mme Dreyfus. I have consistently and firmly refused to consent to any meeting with them so as to preserve my freedom of action. I am entitled to proclaim my independence before the jury and I shall assure it, in no uncertain terms, that the only motive guiding me has been my conviction that a miscarriage of justice had been committed and that the obstinate refusal to make it good constituted a very serious danger both for individual liberty and for public liberties.

'In my opinion, Dreyfus's innocence is as clear as the light of day.

'I am fully confident in our ultimate success.'

*

Throughout the morning small groups moved back and forth in front of M. Zola's house. A dozen policemen were on duty in the rue de Bruxelles but they did not need to take any action.

At 10:45, M. Zola stepped into the hired coupé that was waiting for him. . . .

R. Racot
L'Aurore, 8 February 1898

Statement to the Jury

Gentlemen of the Jury,
In the Chamber of Deputies, at its session of 22 January, M. Méline, the Prime Minister, declared – to frantic applause from his indulgent majority – that he had faith in the twelve citizens in whose hands he was placing the defence of the French army. Gentlemen, it was you he was talking about. And just as General Billot had dictated his order to the court martial – which has been instructed to acquit Major Esterhazy – by directing his military subordinates, from on high, to observe the most absolute respect for the previous verdict, so M. Méline tried to order you to convict me in the name of respect for the army, which he accuses me of having offended. I declare before the consciences of all decent people that I denounce this attempt by the government to put pressure on the system of justice in this country. Such conduct in politics is abominable. It is a dishonour to a free nation.

Gentlemen, will you obey him? We shall see. But it is not true that it was

M. Méline's wish that I stand here before you. Only with the utmost reluctance did he bow to the necessity of taking legal action against me, for it meant the truth would be on the march, taking a new stride, and he was terrified. Everyone knows this. I stand here before you because I wanted it that way. I and I alone decided that the obscure Affair, the monstrous Affair would be laid before you, and it is I and I alone who, of my own free will, have chosen you as the loftiest and most direct embodiment of French justice so that all of France would know the facts in full and come to its decision. My action has no other goal but this. I personally am of no importance. I have sacrificed all personal considerations. It is enough for me to know that I have placed in your hands not only the honour of the French army but the endangered honour of the entire nation.

You must forgive me, then, if things are not already entirely clear in your minds; that is not my fault. It seems I must have been dreaming: I hoped to lay all the evidence before you because I believed you were the only people worthy to have it and competent to deal with it. The first thing they did was to take away from you, with their left hand, what they had seemed to give you with their right. They pretended to accept your jurisdiction, but whereas they trusted you to avenge the members of a court martial, some of the other officers remained beyond your reach, above any justice you might dispense. Understand who may. It is as absurd as it is hypocritical, and what is dazzlingly clear is this: they were afraid of your common sense; they did not dare run the risk of allowing us to say everything and allowing you to judge everything. They claim that they wanted to keep the scandal from spreading. Well, what do you think of *my* scandal? of the action I took because I wanted to lay this Affair before you? because I wanted the people, as embodied in you, to judge it? They also claim that they could not accept a revision disguised as something else, thus admitting that at bottom there is only one thing that terrifies them: the idea of your being in complete control. The law – the law of the sovereign people – is fully represented by you, and it is this law that I, as a good citizen, have insisted on and profoundly respect, and not the tainted procedure by which they hoped to flout your very selves.

That, gentlemen, is my excuse for having taken you away from your usual occupations without having the power to flood you with all-revealing light, as I had hoped. I have desired but one thing – the all-revealing light, and I have desired it passionately. Now, the debate you have heard here proves to you that every step of the way, we have had to combat the most extraordinarily tenacious determination to keep things dark. We have had to struggle to reveal every scrap of truth. They have argued over everything, refused us everything and terrified our witnesses, hoping to prevent us from establishing the evidence. It was for you and you alone that we have been fighting, so that the evidence would be submitted to you in full and you could then reach your decision with no remorse, as your consciences dictate. I am confident that you will take account of our efforts, and moreover, I am confident that matters have been clarified sufficiently. You have heard the witnesses, you will be hearing my lawyer, who will tell you the true story – the story that is driving everyone mad but which nobody knows. I feel serene. The truth now lies within you, and it will have its effect.

M. Méline thought he could dictate your verdict by entrusting the honour of the army to you. But I appeal to your sense of justice in the name of that very same honour. I categorically deny what M. Méline asserts: I have never offended the army; quite the contrary. I have expressed my affection and respect for a nation in arms, for France's beloved soldiers who would rise up at the very first hint of a threat and defend French soil. And it is also false that I have attacked their leaders, the generals who would lead those soldiers to victory. If a few individuals at the War Office have compromised the army itself by their skullduggery, the mere fact of saying so does not insult the entire army, does it? Indeed, saying so is the duty of a good citizen; saying so spares the army from being compromised and sounds the alarm, so that the mistakes which were the sole cause of our defeat will not happen again and will not drag us into further defeats. I do not defend myself, for that matter; I leave it to History to judge my action; it was necessary. But what does dishonour our army, and I do not hesitate to say so, is that the gendarmes are allowed to embrace Major Esterhazy despite the abominable letters he has written! I maintain that our valiant army is insulted every single day by scoundrels who claim to defend it, yet actually besmirch it with their sneaking plots and drag in the mud every good and noble attribute France still has. I maintain that it is they who dishonour our nation's great army when they mingle cries of 'Long live the army!' with shouts of 'Down with the Jews!' And they have even shouted 'Long live Esterhazy!' Great God! The descendants of saintly King Louis IX, of Bayard and Condé and Hoche, the nation that can count a hundred giant victories, the nation that fought the great wars of the Republic and the Empire, the nation whose strength and grace and generosity have dazzled the universe, shouting 'Long live Esterhazy!' Shame upon us! Only our efforts to establish truth and justice can cleanse us of this stain.

A legend has been built up; no doubt it is familiar to you. Dreyfus was sentenced fairly and legally by seven infallible officers, and if we so much as suspect them of having made a mistake we offend the entire army. Amid vengeful torments he is expiating his appalling deed. And since he is Jewish, a Jewish syndicate has been formed, has it not, an international syndicate of individuals who are not loyal to any state, who are manipulating vast sums, hundreds of millions, for the purpose of saving this traitor through the most shameless manoeuvres. Indeed, this syndicate has piled crime upon crime, buying people's silence, stirring up France into a state of murderous agitation; it is determined to sell France to the enemy and plunge all of Europe into the inferno of war rather than renounce its terrifying purpose. There it is – terribly simple; childish, in fact, and idiotic, as you can see. Yet that is the poisonous diet that the foul press has been feeding to this poor nation for months. And if a disastrous crisis ensues, we mustn't be surprised, for when one sows stupidity and lies on such a scale, what else can one harvest but madness?

Certainly, gentlemen, I would not insult you by supposing that until now you have been content to believe such an old wives' tale. I know you, I know who you are. You are the heart and mind of Paris, my great Paris, the Paris I was born in, the Paris I love with infinite tenderness, the Paris I have been exploring and whose praises I have been singing for nearly forty years. And I also know what you are thinking this very minute, because before I came here as a defendant I sat where you are sitting now. You are there to represent the opinion of the average citizen; together you are striving to embody wisdom and justice. In a little while, when you withdraw into another room in order to deliberate, my thoughts will be with you and I have no doubt that you will strive to safeguard your interests as citizens, which you naturally identify with the interests of the entire nation. You may make a mistake; but if you do, it will be with the intention of protecting the welfare of all while protecting your own.

I can picture you, at home with your families, in the evening, in the lamplight; I can hear you talking with your friends, I go with you as you enter your workshops and your places of business. All of you work; some of you are tradesmen, others are in industry, and still others are in the professions. And your very legitimate concern is with the deplorable condition that business has fallen into. Everywhere, the current depression threatens to turn into a disaster: receipts are declining, transactions becoming more and more difficult. And as a result the idea you have brought with you here (I can see it in your faces) is, Enough is enough! It's time to put an end to all this! You have not reached the point of saying, along with so many others, 'What do we care whether an innocent man is out there on Devil's Island! Is the fate of one individual worth upsetting an entire country?' But you do say to yourselves, even so, with regard to those of us who hunger after truth and justice, that the harm we are accused of doing to the country is greater than any good we could achieve. And if you convict me, gentlemen, at bottom your verdict will be based on just that one consideration: the wish to reassure your families, the need to see business improve, and the belief that in striking me down you will put a halt to a campaign whose demands are undermining the interests of France.

Well, gentlemen, you would be totally, totally wrong. Do me the honour of believing that I have not come here to defend my own freedom. If you strike me down, you will only be raising me up. He who suffers for the sake of truth and justice becomes august and sacred. Gentlemen, look at me. Do I look like a man who has sold out? Am I a liar? Am I a traitor? Then why on earth would I be going to such trouble? I have no political ambitions, no sectarian axe to grind. I am a writer and a free man; I have devoted my life to work; tomorrow I will melt back into the crowd and resume my task where I left off. Some people call me the Italian. How silly they are! I whose mother was French, I who was raised by my grandparents from the Beauce, peasants of the good French soil, I who lost my father at the age of seven and never set foot in Italy until the age of 54, and then only to gather information for a book. Which does not stop me from being very proud that my father was from Venice, the resplendent city whose former glory still glows in all our memories. And even if I were not French, what of the forty volumes that I have written in French and given to the entire world, by the millions of copies? Wouldn't they be enough to make of me a Frenchman, serving the great name of France?

No, I am not defending myself. But what a mistake you would be making if you were convinced that by striking me down, you would restore peace and quiet to this poor country! Don't you realize, now, that the nation is dying because certain parties stubbornly insist on leaving it in the dark, where it languishes in doubt and ignorance? Those who govern us heap error upon error, each lie makes another lie necessary and the accumulation is appalling. A miscarriage of justice occurred; and every single day since then, the attempt to cover it up has engendered a new insult to common sense and fairness. Because an innocent man was convicted, a guilty man had to be acquitted; and now they are telling you it is my turn to be convicted because I have voiced my terrible anguish at seeing the country so lost in this dreadful maze. Go ahead and convict me – but you will just be making one more mistake and piling it on top of all the others, and History will judge you harshly for it. If you find me guilty, your verdict will not restore the peace and quiet that you yearn for – that we all yearn for; it will merely sow the seeds of passion and disorder once again. The cup is full, I warn you. Do not make it overflow.

This country is racked by such a grave crisis – is it possible that you do not realize the full extent of its gravity? They say we are responsible for the scandal, we who love truth and justice; they say it is we who are making this country sick, we who are to blame for the riots. Preposterous! They must take people for a bunch of fools. Hasn't General Billot (to mention just one of them) known the truth for the past eighteen months? Hasn't Colonel Picquart warned him that the stormclouds were building up and urged him to bring about a retrial while there was still time? Hasn't M. Scheurer-Kestner begged him, with tears in his eyes, to think of the good of France and spare the country such a catastrophe? Our only wish, let me assure you, has been to make everything easier, to cushion the shock. No, no, if the country is suffering now, it is the government's fault. Anxious to cover up for the guilty parties and impelled by political interests, the government has refused to make a move, hoping against hope that it would be strong enough to prevent the truth from coming to light. Ever since it decided to take that line, the government has been groping in the dark and aiding the forces of darkness. No one but the government is to blame for the desperate bewilderment people are now in.

By now, gentlemen, the Dreyfus Affair is a very minor matter, very remote and very blurred, compared to the terrifying questions it has raised. There is no Dreyfus Affair any longer. There is only one issue: is France still the France of the Revolution and the Declaration of the Rights of Man? the France which gave the world liberty, and was supposed to give it justice? Are we still the noblest, most fraternal, most generous of peoples? Are we going to keep our reputation in Europe as a humane and fair-minded nation? Every single conquest we have made is in danger of being compromised. Open your eyes! Realize that if the soul of France is in such disarray, it must have been stirred to its inmost depths because the danger is truly awful. No nation can be wrought-up to this extent without the very core of its moral sense being endangered. The hour is one of exceptional gravity; the salvation of this country is at stake.

Once you have realized that, gentlemen, you will understand that speaking the truth and acting with justice are the only possible remedies. Anything which delays the revelation and makes the darkness more murky still will only aggravate and prolong the crisis. Good citizens feel how crucial it is to end all this; their duty is to demand a complete revelation. Already, a good many of us hold that conviction. Men of letters, philosophers and scientists are rising up on all sides, pleading on behalf of intelligence and reason. Not to mention how other countries are reacting, how all of Europe is shuddering. Not all foreign countries are necessarily our enemies. I am not talking about the peoples who may be against us some other day. I am talking about great Russia, our ally; about small but generous Holland, about all of the sympathetic peoples of the north, about our fellow French-speaking nations, Switzerland and Belgium. Why are they all so filled with sorrow? Why do they suffer so, along with us? Do you wish France to be isolated from the rest of the world? Is that your dream? When you go outside our borders, do you wish to find that your legendary fair-mindedness and humanity no longer ensure you of a welcoming smile?

*

Alas, gentlemen, like so many other people you may be waiting for a thunderbolt, for proof of Dreyfus's innocence to flash out of the sky like lightning. But as a general rule that is not how the truth proceeds; it calls for a certain amount of diligence and intelligence. Proof? We know very well where we could find it, but only in the depths of our souls do we think of that. As patriots, we tremble, for we have made the honour of our army hang on a lie, and one day the proof may hit us like a slap in the face. I also wish to make it clear that although we have cited people from certain embassies as witnesses, we firmly decided in advance that we would not summon them here. Our boldness caused smiles in certain quarters. But I don't think they smiled at the Ministry of Foreign Affairs, for over there they must have understood. We simply wished to inform those who know the whole truth that we too know the truth. The truth is making the rounds of all the embassies; it will soon be known to everyone, but at this time we cannot drag out the truth ourselves from where it is concealed, shielded by relentless formalities. The government is not unaware of anything; the government is convinced, as we are, that Dreyfus is innocent; and the day the government is ready, it will be able, at no risk whatsoever, to find the witnesses who will reveal the truth at last.

Dreyfus is innocent, I swear he is. I stake my life on that. I stake my honour on it. The hour is a solemn one. Before this court, which represents human justice, before you, gentlemen of the jury, who are the very embodiment of the entire nation, before all of France, before all the world, I swear that Dreyfus is innocent. With all the authority that my forty years of labour confer on me, I swear that Dreyfus is innocent. By everything that I have achieved, by the name I have carved out for myself, by my works which have expanded the influence of French literature, I swear that Dreyfus is innocent. May all of this turn to dust, may my works perish if Dreyfus is not innocent! He *is* innocent.

Everything seems to be arrayed against me – the two Chambers, the civilian authorities and the military authorities, the major newspapers and public opinion, which they have perverted. All I have on my side is an idea, the ideal of truth and justice. I am confident. I shall carry the day.

I did not wish my country to remain mired in lies and injustice. My opponents may strike me down now; but one day, France will thank me for having helped to salvage its honour.

L'Aurore, 22 February 1898

M. Emile Zola at Home

Flowers and bouquets – Tributes and expressions of support –
M. Zola takes some rest – Hope and courage.

As soon as the news got out that M. Zola had been convicted, two evenings ago, expressions of support began to flood in to his home in the rue de Bruxelles. More and more continue to arrive. The vestibule overflows with flowers and bouquets, and each new mail delivery brings heaps of affec-tionate letters.

Upstairs, in the billiard room, where the servant showed me in, there are sheaves of flowers on every piece of furniture. On the billiard table itself lay a large laurel wreath.

'First of all,' M. Zola began, 'let me ask you a favour. I cannot thank all of the friends – those whom I know and those I do not know – who send me cards and telegrams. There are too many of them. Will you please thank them for me.'

We discussed the trial. The courageous writer was perfectly calm, and without the slightest trace of bitterness he talked to me about the negative verdict.

'I was expecting it,' said he. 'It became inevitable the minute General de Pellieux and General de Boisdeffre took the stand to put pressure on the jury in the name of the honour of the army, even though I had in no way criticized the army. The grounds for the action against me were distorted to such an extent that the jury's verdict was made to seem a matter of patriotism. In such circumstances, neither Labori's magnificent eloquence nor Clemenceau's solid reasoning could prevent them from convicting me.'

'Do you intend to appeal?'

'Of course. I already have. Today, I am taking some rest. I am simply receiving a few friends. Those fifteen hearings were exhausting, and I am entitled to a few hours of rest.'

The detestable demonstrations which had occurred the day before yesterday in front of the Palais de Justice came up in the course of the conversation. The Maître told me,

'I do not hold Paris responsible for what happened. It is not Paris – the Paris I love so much! – that was shouting and yelling death threats in the hope of drowning out our voices. I would never confuse the great and generous people of Paris with a gang of fanatics and braying bullies, hired for the occasion.'

As he showed me to the door, the Maître added,

'I have not lost one iota of my faith. The truth will be brought to light. In fact it began to emerge during our trial. I am not disheartened, far from it; I am filled with courage and hope because I am convinced that I am serving a just cause.'

Ph. Dubois
L'Aurore, 25 February 1898

On 2 April, the Criminal Chamber of the Supreme Court of Appeal declared the verdict against Zola and L'Aurore *null and void because of an irregularity. The arguments used by Zola's lawyer, Henri Mornard, had proved remarkably effective. This new development in the legal situation provided an opportunity for Paul Desachy (a journalist who was later to draw up a monumental chronology of the*

Dreyfus Affair) to publish the following interview, written for both Le Rappel *and* Le XIXe Siècle.

At the Home of Emile Zola

Since the Supreme Court of Appeal overturned the verdict against him by the lower court, Emile Zola has flatly refused to grant any interviews. Many journalists have rung his doorbell in the rue de Bruxelles, but in vain. Although he has received a few of them – friends who assured him of their devotion and support during those dark days when doing so was all to their honour, for it entailed some danger – he has been discreet and reserved even with them. He has not wanted perfidious interpretations to denature the satisfaction he must naturally be feeling.

This attitude does honour to the famous writer, and we shall respect it. There is no need to consult him in order to guess what he must be feeling, and how profoundly relieved this ardent supporter of law and justice must have been when he saw a ray of light penetrate the darkest of nights at last.

We cannot publish even a single sentence from the novelist expressing his judgement on the decision by the Supreme Court of Appeal, for that is his express wish. But he will allow us to describe his state of mind while the lower court's verdict still applied to him and to mention a conversation we were fortunate enough to have with him barely a few hours before the final ruling.

Already, at that time, there was some basis for hope of a happy outcome. The conclusions drawn up by the rapporteur, M. Chambaraud – whose unchallenged authority at the Palais de Justice the magistrates unanimously acknowledged – had restored a climate in which the facts could be assessed more equitably. And M. Manau, the public prosecutor, had judged the writer's generous action – the way he had thrown himself into the fray heedless of the dangers that made others shrink back, the way he had revived faltering spirits and communicated his exalted conviction to them – in terms which offset the insults that had poured from the venomous lips of Van Cassel and Paillot, the state prosecutors.

*

Yet, despite those very promising signs, Emile Zola had refused to believe that his trial would be declared null and void.

'No,' he said to me, 'that cannot happen. It won't happen. I don't dare to believe it.'

I could guess what his overwhelming impression was, even though he did not indicate it any other way than with those words: an impression of dreadful chaos, an accumulation of injustices heaped on top of one another, beginning with the first iniquity, the sentencing of Captain Dreyfus, down to this latest one, his own sentencing by a terrorized jury, the links of a fatal chain attached to one another by a sullen determination to continue moving in the wrong direction.

Notwithstanding our legitimate hopes, he was haunted by a single idea: *injustice at every level.* He could not believe that even among the judges of the higher courts, there were still any free men, men sufficiently conscious of the dignity of their function to rise above the blind hatred of mobs unaware of the evil they perpetuate and the brazen threats of a desperate government.

Nonetheless, I told him what a profound change had come about in public opinion, even in the deepest recesses of the people's hearts, ever since he had uttered the words that explain, that enlighten and convince. They had been like seeds about to bring forth new life.

I related to him my conversation of the day before with Anatole France, that other great writer who, like himself, is fiercely committed to the unremitting struggle for truth. Anatole France has sensed how those words were penetrating into the Parisian society all around him. Thanks to his acquaintances in judicial circles, he had predicted what was going to happen in the Supreme Court of Appeal; and on the morning of the very day on which the rapporteur concluded that the trial was null and void, he voiced that idea, which was confirmed a few moments later.

'Yes, no doubt, the process is under way,' Emile Zola said to me, 'and I sense that the nation's soul is being enlightened little by little. But we still have much to fear. The same individuals who dared to threaten France – the mother country, whose safeguard is entrusted to them! – in order to intimidate an impressionable jury are certain to bring pressure to bear. My lawyer, Maître Mornard, should have rejoiced, should he not, at the rapporteur's conclusions. Yet the letter he wrote me after the hearing was actually pessimistic. It is true, however, that since then he too has sensed the process of incubation that you have described, and that in his latest letter to me he is a little more confident that we will succeed.

'As for myself, the result will be a matter of indifference to me, I assure you. I have done the inescapable duty which conscience dictated to me; I had considered all of the responsibilities, all of the consequences. I moved straight ahead on the path I had to follow. What I did yesterday, I would do over again today.

'The ultimate sacrifice does not matter. If, as I expect in spite of my hopes, the court rejects the appeals submitted by my lawyer, I shall give myself up between 15 April and 20 April, once I have settled a few small matters in Médan. Ferocious though my adversaries are, I believe they will not go so far as to deprive me of those necessary few days of freedom; they will permit

me, before I begin the long months of captivity, to see the first rays of the
spring sun rise over the countryside I love so dearly.'

*

Yes, dear Maître, the sun will rise. Already the sky is blue, and the light is
purer, and joy – an immense, profound joy – floods our soul. For in this
dawn hour, as the clouds are swept away, the sun's rays and the radiant
glow of Justice appear on the horizon.

Paul Desachy
Le Rappel, 4 April 1898

*Friday, 8 April. The court martial which acquitted Esterhazy met in Paris, in
the rue du Cherche-Midi, to decide how to respond to the situation which had
just been created. Since the decision by the Supreme Court of Appeal designated
the court martial as the only body empowered to continue legal action (this
had been one of the arguments that Mornard used to obtain the nullification),
the court martial decided to sue, bringing a civil action. As soon as this news got
out, a reporter from* Le Matin *rushed to Médan to hear Zola's first reaction. The
interview appeared the next day, by which time the novelist was writing
to his lawyer concerning the conditions in which the new trial would take place.*

At the Home of M. Emile Zola

A bicycle ride – Informed by telegram.

As soon as the court martial's official decision was announced, we hastened to the Saint Lazare railway station and left for Médan,[1] where M.
Emile Zola installed himself four or five days ago.

It was nine in the evening when we reached M. Zola's home, where not
one light was to be seen. We rang the doorbell, thus disturbing the echoes
of the sleepy little village. In the garden in front of M. Zola's house a poodle
began to bark furiously (this was the dog with which the novelist has
planned to share his period of captivity at Sainte-Pélagie prison). At last a
loud voice asked, 'Who is there?'

It was the servant. From him we learned that M. Zola, who had spent his
afternoon bicycling and was very tired, was preparing to go to bed. We

---

1   The village is some twenty-five miles west of Paris, between Triel and Poissy, in what was then
the Seine-et-Oise (today the département of Yvelines). Zola had purchased his country house there
in 1878.

insisted that our card be sent in to him nonetheless and were soon informed that despite the late hour, M. Zola was willing to receive us.

A lively, cordial welcome. M. Zola, who had guessed the reason for our visit, told us straight away that he knew about the court martial's decision; a telegram from a friend had informed him of it that evening. He knew that further legal action was going to be taken against him. But he had not been informed that the court martial had expressed the wish that he be struck from the list of members of the Légion d'honneur. We were the first to bring him the news.

'Thank you for your visit. Now I am fully informed.'

'What do you intend to do?' we asked.

'Ah, you mustn't ask me that! I cannot tell you a thing. I must confer with my lawyer.'

'Can you at least tell us whether you were expecting the decision the court martial has just taken?'

'Yes, certainly. Deep down inside, I always knew that the ruling by the Supreme Court of Appeal would not put an end to the matter.

'I was expecting more legal action. It was my deep-seated conviction. And yet for the past several days, the fact that a large part of the press and a number of my friends were of the opposite view had shaken my conviction somewhat. Even this morning, I had doubts, up to a certain point. I was beginning to believe that because the trial had stirred up such strong feeling throughout the country, they would think twice before making a second try. As you can see, my first instinct was the right one. So I am not terribly surprised. The government must be more surprised than I am.

'They begged us "to have pity on France". Well, France will realize, after today's decision by the court martial, that it is not we who have tried to create new disturbances throughout the country.'

M. Emile Zola made no further statements and refused to answer any other questions. He made a point, however, of assuring us that he had as much confidence in the cause of which he has made himself the champion as at the very beginning.

'Yes, unshakeable confidence,' he insisted. 'Sooner or later, the truth will burst forth, triumphantly.'

With those words, we shook hands and took leave of M. Zola.

Le Matin, 9 April 1898

Letter to Prime Minister Brisson

Monsieur Brisson,
You once embodied republican virtue; you were once the lofty symbol of

civic honesty. Then suddenly, you stumbled and fell into the monstrous Affair. Now you have been stripped of your moral sovereignty. Now you are nothing but a fallible and compromised man.

What an appalling crisis! And how dismally sad it is, for the silent and solitary thinkers, like myself, who confine themselves to looking on and listening! Ever since I have been obliged to be at the disposal of my country's courts of justice, I have made it an absolute rule to stay away from all controversy. Why, then, am I giving way today to the overriding urge to write you this letter? Because there are times when an anguished soul cannot help but cry out. But in the depths of my silence these last six months, and the silence of so many other consciences – I can feel them quivering – what agony! what patriotic distress has been felt at seeing our poor country's best and brightest sucked down into compromises of all sorts! So many decent, intelligent people have relinquished their honour as citizens and let it blow away on the prevailing winds of folly. It is enough to make you weep, enough to make you wonder how many more victims must be sacrificed to lies before truth will shine once more upon this decimated country, littered with the remains of those we thought embodied its integrity and its strength.

Every morning for the past six months I have felt more and more surprised and pained. Although I do not wish to name anyone, I cannot help thinking of all those I loved and admired, those in whom I had placed my hopes for the greatness of France. Some of them are in your Cabinet, M. Brisson; some are in the Chambers of our legislature; some are writers and artists. They are to be found in every walk of life. And again and again I cry out: how is it that this man and that man are not with us, defending humanity, truth and justice? They seemed to be of sound mind, and I had thought their hearts were in the right place. It defies reason. Indeed, when someone tries to explain their behaviour to me in terms of political expediency, I understand even less. For anyone with any common sense and impartial thinking, it is obvious that these clever people are rushing lightheartedly to their imminent, inevitable, irrevocable doom.

I thought you were too wise, M. Brisson, not to be convinced, as I am, that no government will be able to survive as long as the Dreyfus Affair has not been legally settled. There is something rotten in France, and normal life will not resume until health has been restored. And I might add that the government which does bring about the revision will be a great government, the one that will save France, the one that will win the support of all of us and will survive.

Yet, on the very first day, you committed suicide, although you may have believed that you were creating a sturdy and long-lasting basis for your power. And the worst of it is that soon, when your government falls, you will have lost your political honour in the process. Note that I am thinking only of you; I am not thinking about your subordinates, the Minister of War and the Minister of Justice, for whom you are responsible.

We are witnessing a lamentable sight – the end of virtue, the moral bankruptcy of a man in whom the Republic had placed its faith, deluded into believing that this man would never betray the cause of justice. Yet as soon as he becomes the master he allows justice to be slain before his very eyes! You have just killed idealism. That is a crime. And you will not get away with it. You will be punished.

Look here, M. Brisson, what is this sham investigation, this absurdity you have just allowed to take place? We had assumed that the famous file was going to be brought to a Cabinet meeting and that there you would all set about examining it, putting all of your minds to the task, helping one another to understand, discussing each document methodically, as it deserves to be. But no, nothing of the sort; the results make it clear that nothing has been verified, that no serious debate can possibly have taken place; that the examination was confined to a frantic search through the file, not for the truth, but only for the documents that could most effectively combat the truth by making an impression on simple minds. That way of examining a file is nothing new: the sole aim is to extract from it everything which seems, no matter what or how, to shore up a conviction that has been stubbornly arrived at in advance. There is no well-aired and proven certainty involved in that; there is only the obstinacy of a man whose own state of mind and that of his acquaintances and colleagues have been shaped under such circumstances that, historically speaking, his testimony is worthless.

And what pitiful results all this has produced! Really – is that all you managed to find, in your frenzied efforts to defeat us? And if so, does this mean that that's all there is to be pulled out of that bag of yours? We're already familiar with those three documents you're waving at us, especially the one that has been so noisily produced before the Assize Court – it is the most shameless, most blatant forgery that ever a naive person was taken in by. When I think that a general actually came to read such a monumental piece of mystification aloud, with the utmost seriousness, to a jury, then that a Minister of War actually read it again to the Deputies and finally, that the Deputies have actually had it displayed in every town and village in France, I am stunned. I don't believe that History will ever record anything more stupid than that. Honestly, I wonder how passion can reduce certain men – who are no sillier than others, I imagine – to such a state of mental aberration that they can give the slightest credence to a document that would seem to be a challenge launched by some forger, who is having a good laugh at everybody.

Needless to say I am not going to discuss the other two documents you have produced. We are tired of doing that, tired of proving that they have nothing to do with Dreyfus. Besides, a revision remains absolutely necessary as long as a document that was introduced has not been communicated either to the defendant or to his lawyers. The illegality has taken official form: the Supreme Court of Appeal must nullify the court martial's decision. But M. Brisson, you know all this as well as I do, and that's why I am so incredulous. Since you do know it, how could you listen to the impassioned declarations of your War Minister without shuddering? At that very minute, did a struggle take place within your conscience? Have you fallen so low as to believe that politics takes precedence over all else? that you are entitled to lie in order to bring this country the salvation that you claim your government is bringing it? It is painful for me to think you could be unintelligent enough to feel the slightest doubt as to Dreyfus's innocence; but it would be even more insulting to suppose, for a single second, that you are sacrificing the truth because you believe that falsehood is indispensable to the salvation of France. How I wish I could read your mind! What is going on inside it would be of the utmost interest to a psychologist.

I can assure you of one thing: you are making our government look utterly ridiculous. I hear that on Thursday there was no one sitting in the diplomatic gallery. Of course not. Not one diplomat could have kept a straight face while those three documents were read out loud. And don't you go thinking that Germany, our enemy, is the only country to be amused by all this. Russia, our great ally, is very up-to-date on the Affair, very well informed and absolutely convinced that Dreyfus is innocent; and I wish Russia would do us the favour of telling you what Europe thinks of us. Perhaps you would listen to Russia, our sovereign friend. Have a word with your Foreign Minister about that.

And let him also tell you how the extraordinary action being taken against Lt-Col Picquart is adding glory to France's reputation abroad. A just man respectfully requests you to shed light on a matter, and in response, what do you do? You haul him into court on a trumped-up old charge. The recent hearings before the Assize Court have shown how hollow it is. 'Getting in my way, are you? Very well, I'll get rid of you!' The whole business is comical, in an appalling sort of way. History cannot offer a more brazen example of hypocritical iniquity.

Now, those three documents are merely laughable; but what have you got to say, M. Brisson, about Dreyfus's so-called confession, reported to the French Assembly by one of your ministers as the unshakeable basis for his conviction? At this point, doesn't your sense of decency utter a cry of outraged protest? Such methods will arouse universal indignation. Didn't you realize how abominable they are?

Dreyfus's confession, for God's sake! Don't you know anything about this whole tragic business? Don't you know the true story – how he was imprisoned and publicly humiliated? And his letters – haven't you read them? They are admirable. I have never read anything loftier or more eloquent. From the depths of pain, they reach sublime heights, and later on, when the works of writers such as myself may have sunk into oblivion, his letters will live on as an imperishable monument. All of human suffering can be heard sobbing in those letters. The man who wrote them cannot be guilty. Read those letters, M. Brisson. Read them one evening at home with your family. You will be in tears.

And yet people come and talk to us seriously about Dreyfus's confession, when the poor man has never ceased to proclaim his innocence! They dig about among the shaky recollections of men who have contradicted themselves a dozen times; they produce pages from a notebook that has nothing authentic about it; they display letters that other letters cancel out! From all sides comes testimony to the contrary, but they do not want to hear it. And there again, nothing is legal; there are no minutes signed by the guilty party; it's mere gossip, at most. That so-called confession is emptiness itself. It is non-existent. It would not hold up in any court.

Well then, since it is clear that reasonable people with any degree of culture will not be taken in by that alleged confession, why bother to wave it about? Why make such a fuss about it? Ah, this is where your dreadful cleverness comes in, this is where you have been so crudely calculating: you toss that glib, so-called proof to the common people, the simple minds. You're hoping, aren't you, that once the ordinary people in both town and country have read your posters, they will all be on your side. And talking about those of us who thirst for truth and justice, they will say, 'What a nuisance they are! Why do they go on and on about Dreyfus? He's a traitor! He has admitted he is!' And the way you see it, that will be the end of it; the monstrous act of iniquity will have been accomplished once and for all.

Are you aware, M. Brisson, how appalling such a manoeuvre is? I defy any decent man not to be horrified by it; his hands cannot fail to tremble with rage and indignation. Far, far away a poor soul who has never ceased to proclaim his innocence is enduring the worst sort of torture, torture of the most exceptional kind and as illegal as the sentence that inflicted it on him. And yet you quite simply go ahead and claim that he has confessed to the crime he never committed; and you use his so-called confession to confine him ever more harshly in his cell. But he is alive and he can still answer you – fortunately for you; for the day he dies, your crime will become irreversible, whereas while he is still alive you can question him and hear him cry out his innocence, once again. But no, while the unceasing cry of this unfortunate man, his unceasing plea for truth and justice, is carried away on the wind and out to sea, you find it so simple to maintain that he has confessed, simple to convince the people it is true. I know of nothing more despicable or cowardly than that.

And you are in collusion with the foul press. You follow its lead. You do what the foul press is doing: feeding the nation a poisonous diet of lies. You cover the walls of our towns with forgeries and idiotic falsehoods, as if you deliberately wanted to worsen the disastrous moral crisis we are going through. Poor humble people of France! What a splendid lesson in civic-mindedness you are being given! When what you really need today, for the sake of your salvation tomorrow, is a harsh lesson in truth.

*

One last thing, M. Brisson, while we sit here having our little chat. I feel I ought to warn you that I am extremely curious to see how you are going to deal with individual liberties and respect for our judicial system next Monday, at the trial in Versailles.

You are well aware of the incidents that occurred in Paris before and after each of the fifteen hearings during the first trial, and then in Versailles, when the single hearing during the second trial took place. Through those incidents France – our great and generous France – offered the civilized world a dreadful sight. The world saw a handful of thugs insulting a man and threatening to kill him; yet that man was a defendant who of his own free will had chosen to appear in his country's courts of justice. What do you think of that, M. Brisson, you who are a decent man, you who care about republican virtue, you who revere the rights of man and the rights of citizens? Wouldn't you agree with me that only cannibals behave that way? Wouldn't you agree that we have fallen very low, that the whole world despises us and is disgusted by us?

We might have some excuse if the entire nation had lost its wits, if a crowd of well-intentioned people had panicked and run amuck, in the grip of some passion, even some criminal urge. But since you are the Minister of the Interior, have a little talk with your chief of police, M. Charles Blanc, who is a keenly intelligent man and altogether a man of the world. He is very well informed, of course. He will explain to you how and where those gangs were recruited, how much the men were paid, what impartial and impassioned support was provided by the pro-clerical circles, how many thugs were involved and how many bigots, and finally how many idle onlookers might have ended up going along with the troublemakers and making the whole thing a very dangerous game. After that, you will no longer have the slightest doubt, I hope, about how the rowdiness was organized. You will realize that the organizers' aim was to deceive France and indeed the entire world, to make them believe that all of Paris was rising up against me and to poison public opinion and put the most abominable kind of pressure on our judicial system.

And that is not all that M. Charles Blanc could tell you, you who are his superior. He will explain how the police had to step in to protect us every single evening, whereas a few arrests on the very first day, followed immediately by legal action, would have put an end to the trouble. Now, I am not complaining about the police, who were very active and protected me with great devotion. It's just that, higher up than the chief of police himself, there seems to have been some desire that things should happen in a certain way. Every single insult was allowed, every single threat as well, all of them filthy and despicable; no one was arrested. The demonstrators were even allowed to come close enough to constitute a genuine danger. And the police did not step in and save me until the very second when things threatened to get out of hand. It was done with considerable skill. Obviously people in high places wished to achieve one effect: they wanted the world to believe that it took a real battle, every single evening, to rescue me from the justly indignant clutches of the people of Paris.

Well, M. Brisson, I am curious to see what kind of campaign you are going to map out with M. Charles Blanc. You will be the sole master; not one of your subordinate ministers will be able to intervene, because in addition to your authority as Prime Minister, you are the Minister of the Interior as well. It is you who are responsible for maintaining law and order. So we are going to find out what conditions you think should prevail when a defendant is to appear in court; whether you think people should be allowed to insult and threaten him, whether such a barbaric sight does not dishonour France totally. I don't believe that my friends and I were ever in any serious danger. But that is not the point. Since anything is possible, M. Brisson, I hereby declare in advance, that if we are murdered on Monday, the murderer will be you.

*

In conclusion, I must voice my astonishment once again: what petty little creatures all of you are!

I suppose I can accept the fact that not one of you is enamoured of the idea of justice, not one of you is lofty and ardent enough to step forward, devote his fortune and his life to the sole joy of being just and then merge back into the crowd once truth has triumphed. But what about ambition? You do have ambition; the whole crowd of you in fact are nothing but ambitious men. Well then, how is it possible that there is no bold, sharp-witted, forceful man among you, no ambitious man of real scope, who could take in the situation at a glance and act swiftly, a man able to discern what is really at stake and make the right moves with courage and conviction?

Let's see. How many of you would like to be President of the French Republic? Every single one of you harbours that ambition, isn't that the truth? You all keep an anxious eye on one another; you all believe you are steering your course more cunningly than the others, some of you using caution, others using popularity and still others, austerity. You make me laugh, for not one of you seems to realize that three years from now, the politician who moves into the Elysée Palace will be the one who has restored our veneration of truth and justice by bringing about a revision of Dreyfus's trial.

Take it from me. Poets are seers, to some extent. In three years' time France will no longer be France. Either France will be dead or our President will be the political leader, the wise and equitable minister, who will have pacified the nation. And the petty, cowardly, calculating creatures, the unintelligent men who were blinded by passion, all who made a mockery of the law and took sides against mankind's legitimate hopes will be punished as they deserve. They will be flung to the ground, their dreams shattered to pieces, and the public will abhor them.

That is why, every time I see one of you give in to the prevailing folly by doing the dirty work of this Dreyfus Affair and being silly enough to believe, perhaps, that in this way he is hastening his own election, I say to myself, 'There goes another one who will not be President of the Republic!'

M. Brisson, I beg you to accept the assurance of my utmost esteem.

L'Aurore, 16 July 1898

Zola's lawyer had hoped that as a result of the hearings at the trial in Versailles, the previous verdict would be overturned; but on 18 July it was confirmed. That evening, at a meeting with Georges Charpentier, the Clemenceau brothers and Labori, it was abruptly decided that Zola would leave the country that very night. He had just time to warn Jeanne.

To Jeanne Rozerot

Paris, Monday evening [18 July 1898]

Dear wife, matters have taken such a turn that I am obliged to leave for England this evening. Don't worry; just wait quietly for me to send news. As soon as I've been able to make some decisions, I'll be in touch with you. I'm going to try to find a place where you and the children can come and join me. But there are things to be settled and that will take several days. Anyhow, I'll keep you informed. I'll write to you as soon as I am abroad. Don't tell a soul where I'm going.

My tenderest love to the three of you.

Part Two
Beset by Uncertainty

Zola left for London so that the sentence could not be served on him in the form required by the law. His entire effort, during the first several days of exile, was focused on keeping out of sight as much as possible so as to foil any attempt by the French legal system to find him, including the possibility of a registered letter officially informing him of the sentence. As soon as he arrived at the Grosvenor Hotel near Victoria Station, he was able to contact his English translator, Ernest Vizetelly, who saw to it that Zola had the benefit of advice from his own lawyer, F. W. Wareham. (In his letter to Labori of 21 July, Zola refers to Wareham in English as a solicitor.)

In France, meanwhile, on 20 July, L'Aurore published an article signed by Zola and entitled 'Pour la preuve', in defence of the strategy adopted. In fact, the author of it was Georges Clemenceau.

To Fernand Labori

London, 19 July 1898, Grosvenor Hotel

My dear Labori, I am sending you a letter for Vaughan – I ask him to have a talk with you about the damages claimed by the experts, which it is painful to have to pay, truly it is; and a letter for my wife; would you be kind enough to give it to her tomorrow, Wednesday, when she stops in to see you, before coming to join me. It is I who advised her to call upon you in case you had something you wanted her to tell me. If you happen to go out, leave the letter with somebody, with orders to give it to my wife.

I arrived here easily enough but with a very heavy heart, I must confess. From the boat I could see the lights of Calais disappear in the night, and my eyes filled with tears. Ah, what an abominable thing! One day I shall describe how heartbreaking it is. But truth and justice must triumph.

You did not give me the little note, about the legal situation, which I will need if I write a page to explain my departure. Please send it to me, but I am not in favour of our acting in haste, and especially not of my committing myself personally. Clemenceau, in one of his articles, can very well explain my attitude and that of *L'Aurore*. – I dare not ask you to keep me informed, for I know how overwhelmed with work you are. But have Maître Hild[1] drop me a line, if anything really interesting happens.

My respects to Mme Labori, and my most affectionate thoughts to you.

---

1   Labori's secretary, a lawyer named Joseph Hild.

To Fernand Labori

[London, 21 July 1898]

My dear Labori, I cannot stay here, at the hotel, because I run the risk of being recognized here any minute. Therefore tomorrow I am going to rent a small flat in the London suburbs. I'll give you the new address as soon as I can.

The lawyer you recommended to me, Mr Fletcher Moulton, is not in London. But I have just consulted a solicitor who is very devoted to me. He maintains that the sentence cannot be notified to me through diplomatic channels. Never, through any channels whatsoever, will an official of the English judicial system take the responsibility of notifying to me a sentence delivered by a French court. Which means beyond a doubt that in order for it to be notified to me, a French bailiff would have to be able to come here, on English soil, lie in wait for me, seize me as I went by in the street and order proceedings to be taken against me. Is that possible under law and in fact? That is what I would like to be informed about straight away. Send me a decisive answer on this point as soon as possible so that I will be reassured and can make arrangements accordingly. As long as you do not have my new address, write to me at the hotel, where I will send someone to fetch my mail.

What an adventure, my poor friend! I'm still feeling thoroughly shaken up.

My respects to Mme Labori, and my most affectionate thoughts to you.

Zola moved a few miles away from the centre of London, settling in Surrey. He first stayed in the Oatlands Park Hotel in Weybridge but soon left it to rent a house called 'Penn' close by.

When Alexandrine (here referred to as 'Alexandre') said goodbye to Zola in Paris on the evening of 18 July, she promised to join him in England, but several obstacles stood in the way of this project.

To Fernand Desmoulin

[Weybridge, 26 July 1898]

My dear friend, I have received your telegram and at the same time a letter from Alexandre. I do understand that there are real difficulties but in my opinion all these precautions are quite useless. I have just written to the

lawyer for the defence to say as much. The newspapers here report
that I have been seen in London; and besides, if the letters from Jean[1]
have been opened, as I suspect they have, they already have the good
solicitor's address, if not my own. In a few days' time, they will be here
and I warn you, I will not lift a finger to hide any more than I already am
hiding. I have had enough. I am going to settle somewhere and then I
will not budge any more. I do not think the sentence can be notified to
me, and we could always challenge the legality of such a notification
carried out on foreign soil. So that, when I return to Paris, the situation
will be one of the following: either the notification will be considered
valid, in which case I shall go to prison and declare that they are fleeing
the revelations that a new trial would bring; or else the notification will
not be valid, in which case the trial will recommence and our tactics
will have triumphed. What I do not want is to continue running away. I
think I am simply going to stay where you left me, live as quietly as possible
and await developments. If I try some other refuge, that one will be the
last one.

Has Jean received the letter in which I gave him the solicitor's address?
I'm quite worried about that because I imagine the letter has been inter-
cepted. If he hasn't received it, give him the solicitor's address so that he
can at least write to me.

Yesterday was a good day, a day of silence, which did me a lot of
good. But today all the problems are starting up again. I repeat, these
problems will not stop until the day the situation is clear; by that I mean
the day they know where I am. They will play their little game and we
will play ours. It is ridiculous to think that I can live incognito in the
situation I am in: I have no luggage, I do not speak the language, I am
at the mercy of a chance encounter and can be recognized any minute.
Go and tell that to the lawyer for the defence, and let our plan of action be
bold and out in the open. Give me an answer on this point as soon as
possible.

Love to you, my faithful companion.

*

If Alexandre cannot come then he must immediately send a suitcase with
some underwear and clothes, not the manuscripts, to me at the solicitor's
address and he must send the suitcase key to the solicitor in a little box, for
the customs.

I am going to run out of money. Go to the rue de Grenelle[2] and tell them
to hurry.

---

1   Jeanne Rozerot.
2   That is to his publisher, Eugène Fasquelle, who was supposed to send him some money.

To Fernand Desmoulin

[Weybridge, 27 July 1898] Wednesday, 2 o'clock

My dear friend, I beg you not to put any pressure on Alex. Leave him absolutely free to decide what he prefers. I don't count. I can always manage. Your letter talks about very serious complications and there is no denying that if Alex. comes to spend only a few days, that is very tiring and even very imprudent, all for the painful pleasure of being together for an instant and then having to part straight away. Although it would make me happy to be able to give him a hug, I believe it would probably be wiser for him not to come, under those conditions. But enough. I do not wish to express any opinion. Let him decide for himself.

You know that W[areham] is to come and see me this evening, at six. I shall probably rent the house, unless there is some very serious news. I have heard nothing since yesterday but the fact that I am in England is known, and I may have to throw people off the scent once again, depending on the news. – At all events, if you come back, I think it would be best if you did not show yourself at this hotel again. You would do better to go no further than London; you would go to the solicitor's office or inform W., who would bring you to me. But above all, dear old friend, do not go out of your way for me. Take care of your own affairs; do not rush anything. You know that the prospect of being alone does not frighten me, and if my loved ones cannot join me, I shall manage very well by myself. – Your devotion is admirable, and I love you and thank you with all my heart.

If you cannot see J.,[1] try at least to see that he gets the letter that I gave you for him, for he has had no news from me and must be worried.

I am glad the bookseller[2] has taken the necessary steps; I think I will be stronger once I have received what he is sending me. – Try to send me the suitcase tomorrow (Thursday) for that too is one of the things that causes me concern, having no underwear and no clothing, like a beggar roaming the countryside. The suitcase should be sent to the solicitor, as I said before, not forgetting the key in a little box.

That is all, my dear friend. I am not too uncomfortable here. But I always feel as though someone here is about to recognize me, and that is why I am going to arrange it so as to go away as soon as possible.

With love.

1 Jeanne.
2 Eugène Fasquelle (see previous letter, note 2).

*Fernand Desmoulin continued to be an effective confidant and go-between. Ulti-
mately, Alexandrine did not make the voyage to England. For the time being, she
chose to stand aside; and it was Jeanne who came over first, with the children, on
11 August. Penn provided a calm atmosphere in which Zola was able to resume
work at a regular rhythm. He turned his attention once again to* Fécondité, *his
novel in progress, and began to write the first pages of it.*

To Alexandrine Zola

[Weybridge, 3 August 1898]

Dear wife, my poor heart is filled with uncertainty and anguish. For six
long days now I have been discussing with our faithful Desmoulin what the
best course of action would be. And I just don't know. By now I am in a
state of extreme anxiety since I cannot talk to you and find out what you
yourself want to do.

I persuaded Desmoulin to leave so that he could convey my hesitation to
you along with my wish to leave the decision absolutely up to you. He will
explain to you all of the possibilities I have considered; the two of you can
discuss them. But I beseech you, in the name of all we have shared, in the
name of our past thirty years together: decide as if only your own happiness was involved and I didn't exist. I want you to be as happy as possible,
even now and only on that condition will I be happy myself.

I kiss you with all my poor, sore heart. I am heartsick at not knowing
what to do any more.

*

Give Desmoulin my love. He has been marvellous and has been a great
comfort during this dismal time.

To Alexandrine Zola

[Weybridge, Saturday evening, 6 August 1898]

Dear wife, Desmoulin has written to tell me your decision and announced
that a letter from you is on its way. But since I have not received it this
evening, I will not have it until Monday evening, because in England, on
Sundays, everything is dead. I don't want to wait until then to give you
news of myself and tell you how terribly upset I am at the idea that I will not
see you until the end of September, in more than six weeks, no doubt. I am

going to have the children here with me; but they are not everything, and if you only knew how full of you my poor heart remains, how it suffers at what is happening. I have no more peace of mind; my whole life has been turned inside out. I have developed a constant nervous tremble because of uncertainty over the future.

Nonetheless, I believe you have made the right decision. I could not urge you to take it as I would have seemed to be putting off the day when we would be reunited. But I approve your decision. You are wisdom itself. Only, please, do not say yet that you will not go to Italy. Wait until the courts have their recess, which will calm down everything in Paris; then leave for Rome, and come back and wait for me in Genoa at the end of September. That is something I dream of, and it would be very sweet to see the dream come true. I will not consent to stay here beyond the last days of September, unless some very serious developments occur.

I am writing to you in a hurry so that you will have a letter from me straight away. Once I have received yours, on Monday evening, I will write to you again, a long letter to tell you what my life here is like. I have not gone out for four days, and I am working; I've begun to write the first chapter of my novel. But I have trouble keeping my mind on it. Luckily I am well.

I kiss you with all my heart, dear wife. At this time it is you who are the devoted guardian, you who represent and defend me.

You may be sure that I will never forget how courageous and admirable you are amid these dreary circumstances. If I didn't still love you the way I do, your attitude at this time would fill me with remorse.

To Fernand Desmoulin

[Weybridge] Saturday evening, 6 August 1898

My dear old friend, I have just received your letter this very minute. It makes me happy and at the same time so sad. I am going to have my children, but you would never believe how distressed I am when I think of my poor wife. Did you tell her everything? that above all I do not want to hurt her, that I will not be happy unless I know that she is happy?

All of this is so disturbing, and although I keep turning over and over, no matter which side I lie down on, I can feel the thorns.

Ever since you left, four days ago, I have not stepped outside. I have begun to write my novel; but even though this work brings some comfort, I feel the most extreme moral anguish. My habits have undergone too much change, there is no affectionate presence near me and uncertainty over the future leaves me in a continual state of nervous expectation. Well, once the children are here, perhaps I shall calm down a little. But even so my heart will not be full, and I'll miss my poor wife so much!

I enclose a note for Jean; deliver it to him, or have it delivered, immediately. The date when he will have to take the 9 a.m. train will be specified to you in the telegram we agreed on, that you will receive the day before. I have some fairly complicated arrangements to make here and I don't think the departure can take place before Tuesday or Wednesday. As soon as you have received my telegram and you are sure he will be leaving the next day, send Vizetelly a telegram saying, 'I leave at nine tomorrow. Valentin.'

That takes care of everything, doesn't it? Thank you, my dear old friend, for your devotion to a poor banished soul; you are so helpful, just like a brother. My heart swells with gratitude.

A warm and brotherly hug to you.

Note for Jean

If possible, do not go to Paris to fetch anything; when packing, simply make do with what there is in Verneuil.[1] Bring some warm clothing, however. Bring me my complete bicycling suit. Do not bring any women's trousers because a skirt will be necessary.[2]

Do not bring either the cook or the housemaid; dismiss them, saying that they will be taken on again at the end of September, so as to avoid making enemies out of them. Above all, make sure those two women do not know what country you are going to. In fact it might be a good idea to mislead them; hint that you are going to Belgium, or Switzerland.

As for the departure, here is what I would advise. The day before, Desmoulin or some other person would pick up the trunks and come back to Paris with them. He would leave them at the station, in the cloakroom. The next morning, he would come back at eight to pick them up and take them to the Gare du Nord, where he would register them for Victoria Station, after having purchased two full-price tickets and one half-price ticket for the child who is under seven. Buy return tickets provided it is possible, after one month, to extend them by ten-day periods.

Give Jean clear instructions for the trip. Jean and the two children will leave Verneuil in the morning by the 6:40 train, I believe. When they reach Paris they will take a carriage which will bring them to the Gare du Nord, where they can have breakfast in a café. They will

1   Jeanne and the children lived in Verneuil, near Médan.
2   For their future bicycle rides in the English countryside.

meet Desmoulin inside the station, near the London ticket window. Bring along food for the journey. On arrival at Calais, the boat that is right alongside; on arrival at Dover, the train that is alongside. And do not get off the train until the end, at Victoria, where someone will be waiting for the travellers.

Tell the person looking after the house in Verneuil to keep all of the newspapers and all of the letters. Do not give any address to anyone. Disappear.

Jean will give Desmoulin the money for the tickets and the luggage.

To Alexandrine Zola

[Weybridge] Sunday, 7 August 1898

Dear wife, it has been pouring with rain since yesterday; and since I am shut up here with not even the slightest possibility of stepping outside, I'd like to have a little chat with you, while I wait for your letter, which will certainly not arrive until tomorrow evening. I would like to provide you with a few details about the way I am living here even though our good friend D[esmoulin] must have given you some information. I am shut up like a monk in a small house with, as servant, a maid who does not know a word of French and is supervised by one of Vizetelly's daughters, who does not know any more than she does. Most of the time I have to use sign language. For whole days at a time I do not open my mouth, and I have not gone outdoors for five days. The scenery is superb – endless lawns, giant trees. The only problem is the dreadful weather. So far I have had only two bright sunny days. First it was terribly windy, and now this rain. The worst part is that the instant it begins to rain, fog seems to well up from the ground. Actually, none of this disturbs me too much because, as you know, I don't dislike cool weather such as this, and the only thing I suffer from is loneliness, the feeling of being abandoned in a foreign country.

Fortunately, I set to work on Thursday, and I have already written twenty pages of my novel. I get up at eight and have breakfast at nine, which enables me to sit down to work before nine o'clock [*sic*]. That gives me good long mornings, and I have begun my novel with a very clear mind. The hardest part of the day to get through is the afternoon and evening. I do read some of the books that have been lent to me, but it gets on my nerves, really. And anyhow I can't spend all my time reading. I have had not a single newspaper so far, and I have just made arrangements to receive at least *L'Aurore* and *Le Siècle*.

Today, however, V[izetelly] sent me both of those papers, the Friday numbers, and that is how I found out some news: that *Le Petit Journal* has been sentenced,[1] that our appeal has been rejected, and above all, the new revelations about the relations between Esterhazy and du Paty de Clam.[2] I believe those revelations are of the utmost gravity, very disturbing for our opponents. However, I am not optimistic, as you know; and in my view, the decisive victory is still a long way away. And the uncertainty continues to make me acutely anxious on my own account.

Do not worry about my wardrobe and my personal effects. You did not forget anything; what you sent is very complete and will be more than enough until we are reunited. I am convinced that in two or three weeks you will be free and you'll be able to take your trip to Italy. As you can well imagine, lawyers and judges too are very eager for some holiday themselves. So everything will quiet down for a while and you will be free. Let me have Bertolelli's[3] exact address because it would be preferable for me to send you my letters at his address, one envelope inside another so that our name will not appear on the first one. And in the meanwhile I am going to write to you regularly twice a week, using the good doctor[4] as a go-between, except of course in special cases. For instance, you could have someone fetch my letters in Paris every Tuesday and Saturday. That would spare you unnecessary trips. Beware of Sundays: the letters that you put in the mail on Saturday will not reach me until Monday evening.

Thank your cousin for kindly offering to send me her son who, as you so rightly put it, would be of no use to me. Send the three of them my most affectionate wishes. – And tell all our friends that I am fine, since after all physically I am very well and my life is now perfectly peaceful. The only thing is that my poor heart continues to bleed; because of these abominable events, I am afflicted with an internal tremor that will stay with me for a long time.

To Fernand Desmoulin

[Weybridge], Sunday, 7 August 1898

My good friend, I have just discovered that the letter I wrote to you yesterday, Saturday, will not be collected until eight o'clock this evening. What a charming country! So you will receive this one at the same time. – I did a good deal of thinking last night; and finally, for simplicity's sake, I think it's best if you don't wait for a telegram from me before you send me

1   On 3 August; see the Chronology.
2   An allusion to Reinach's articles in *Le Siècle*; see the Chronology.
3   Count Edoardo Bertolelli, a friend of the Zolas, in Rome.
4   Dr Jules Larat, Desmoulin's cousin.

Jean and the children. My mind is made up. Send them to me as soon as you can, Wednesday, or Thursday at the latest. I doubt that Jean will be ready before Wednesday. That would be a good day. Mind you, you won't receive this letter until Monday evening. If everything is ready, then wire Vizetelly on Tuesday just to say, 'Leaving tomorrow.' That will mean that Jean will take the 9 a.m. train for Victoria the next day, Wednesday. Vizetelly will then wire me, and we will both be at Victoria the next day.

It's agreed, then. I'll be expecting them Wednesday, or Thursday if an extra day is needed to prepare everything. Naturally, in that case you will not wire Vizetelly until Wednesday.

It has been pouring with rain since yesterday. I am leading a solitary existence, deep in my work. But I admit that six weeks of such a life would terrify me.

Thanks again, my good friend and brother, and all my love.

Note for Jean

Don't bring the camera. I have mine.

There is a piano, so bring a little music.

Be very wary of the maids, when you dismiss them. They might warn the neighbours that you are leaving, or might even go to Paris, where they may have left some clothing. Do whatever is necessary to make absolutely sure they do not know a thing and cannot alert anyone.

Don't forget to take along some food for the voyage. Beyond Dover, they do not accept French money. On the boat, if the sea is calm, it is best to stay on deck and sit there. If the sea is rough, go down into steerage, and if the children are sick, take refuge in a cabin.

I don't think the customs officers inspect the trunks until London. So we will be there. Have the keys ready. At Dover, the train is close to the boat. To be sure you don't make a mistake, show the tickets to an employee, repeat to him 'Victoria', and let him seat you. Then do not get off the train until it stops at the end of the line, in London.

To Alexandrine Zola

[Weybridge] Monday evening [8 August 1898]

Just as I thought, dear wife, the letter you sent on Friday did not come until just now, at seven o'clock, as I was about to have dinner. I was waiting for it anxiously and it breaks my heart because you tell me that when you feel overcome with sadness and begin to fret, you think of my happiness, in order to feel a little less miserable. That is what I want to avoid. The idea that I can cause you the slightest unhappiness, or make these abominable days still worse for you, is more than I can bear. You must promise me to go out and enjoy yourself as soon as you can. My poor heart is so pulled in two directions these days that it can find no rest. When evening comes and it is almost time for the mail to arrive, I begin to tremble as if expecting a disaster. Well, the days will pass and perhaps we shall be happy again. – The fact that you are in Paris is useful; I do realize that. That is why I have accepted your decision. And I can only thank you for your devotion – it is so immense, so fine. Everything you write to me in that connection moves me to tears. – And I am so touched by what you write about the flowers that you put in my study and the orderly way you arrange the papers and documents that are sent to me, as if I were coming back that evening. Do you know that these past few days, when I've felt so dreadfully lonely, I have had thoughts of taking the train and coming back to our house at night? I would have hidden there and we would have lived a quiet life. But then I decided that it would be folly. Thank you for the flowers, and for wanting to create the illusion that I am still at home.

You mustn't send me the papers or the little comb, and above all don't send me the [photographic] plates. I have no need of those things at this time. When you go to Rome, take the papers and the comb with you, and you will give them to me when I join you in Genoa.

I don't understand which papers you are looking for. The letter I mentioned to L[abori] and that I thought I had left in the drawer of the contador [*sic*] may have been torn up by me. You mustn't let it worry you so. As for the other paper, is that Lorenzo's letter? I have found it here, in a file that you sent to me, mixed in with the files for my novel, and I am sending it to you. There are other papers in this file, notes that you gave me. Tell me more clearly what L. asked you for and I'll see whether by any chance I have it here.

Don't let yourself be overly alarmed or pushed about by the people who are looking after our affairs. They are very devoted but they do not fully realize what problems we face. I don't want to tell you in writing how the abruptness of my departure and the two dazed weeks that followed still rankle. With a little more forethought, the full horror of it all could have been avoided. It makes me desperate to know that you are in their hands. Do only what you feel it is reasonable to do and break free as soon as you can.

I plan to finish the first chapter of my novel tomorrow. The weather was awful again today and it is as cold as in winter. There was nothing I could do but work all day.

The poor dog-wolf-cat has been badly battered by the storm. When will he go back to his little daily routine in his poor little home? Until then, he will be frantic.

My dear wife, you who are so valiant and tender, I kiss you a thousand times over, with all my heart.

Jeanne and the children reached Penn on the evening of 11 August. But despite that long-awaited reunion, the tone of the letters is chiefly one of keen anxiety. In addition to the bitterness of exile there were Zola's financial worries, for the verdict reached in the experts' trial sentenced him to pay thirty-two thousand francs in damages.

To Alexandrine Zola

[Weybridge] Thursday, 11 August 1898

Dear wife, today I shall begin to send you two letters regularly every week, so that you will have one on Tuesday and one on Saturday. That way you can be sure of sending someone to fetch them at the right times, and it will be less inconvenient for the doctor[1] as well.

Your letter of 7 August has saddened me, since I seem to have offended you; I gather I didn't explain things clearly enough. Dear God! the last thing I want to do is to hurt you in any way! Therefore I will not come back to the subject all over again, even if I could be clearer this time, because never have we gone through a period when we had a greater need to love one another and get along well together. That is why I beseech you to let me know what your wishes are, always, so that I can try to do as you wish. Let us be in agreement on everything; that way we will suffer less.

I have not gone out for nine days. It appears that I was recognized at the hotel where I was staying with Valentin.[2] There was a note in one of the newspapers so, to be on the safe side, I lie low.

Yesterday I finished the first chapter of my novel and this morning I began the second. I am pleased with my work. It is what has saved me from being bored stiff in this lonely house where I don't even utter three words a day. If only I could go out and go for a walk! My life is so dull, so totally uneventful that I have absolutely nothing to tell you about. I am expecting the children this evening and they will put an end to the loneliness. But

---

1   Jules Larat, Desmoulin's cousin. See the letter of 7 August to Alexandrine Zola, note 4.
2   i.e. Desmoulin.

those poor children – I almost feel remorseful at having them come because they will not have the big garden they are used to in V[erneuil] or their playthings. And the sky is so grey! It is very selfish of me, no doubt.

You are right to be extremely cautious when you write me and not mention anyone by name. But I would be very grateful to you if could give me a little information on our affairs. I have not yet received any newspapers. And anyhow, it is not the public facts that I want to know but what Lab.[3] thinks, what he predicts, where he thinks we are headed. – You say the future frightens you. Alas, I am more pessimistic than you are; ask our faithful Valentin how little hope I have. Personally, I think a happy ending is far in the future and I expect to remain outside France for a long time, unless I come back to be immolated. That is why I am so eager to see you in Genoa in late September or the early part of October, for we simply must have a serious talk so as to come to some decision.

I have sent you Lorenzo's letter. The little volume you went to such trouble to look for was given by me to Lab. And finally, the letter he had you look for on the basis of my recollections may not exist any longer; I may have torn it up. If it is not in any of the three places I mentioned to you it could only be among the bundles of letters you made, dating from 20 May up to the day we left for the country. Otherwise, I repeat, it has been destroyed.

I am fine. But all of these recent events have had such an effect on my nerves that tears come to my eyes at the slightest pretext. I do not recognize myself any more; I would have thought I'd be more stalwart. When this is all over, if ever it is, how much peace and quiet I shall need in order to recover completely! What annoys me the most is that I have been deprived of my freedom so completely that I can't go out any more, even in a foreign country, and I am compelled to live in seclusion, in hiding, as if I were a criminal.

And you, my poor wife, I see all the vexations and problems you have because of having to go to Paris so often and all the complicated precautions you must take. You need so much tenderness and devotion to overcome all that. And that's what makes me even more furious about the way they insisted I leave, so hastily. My departure was so stupid, and will it even serve any purpose? I doubt it. However, we must drain this bitter cup to the dregs. – I am pleased to hear what you say about the servants. How lucky it is that the people around you are loyal; otherwise, the complications would have become worse still. Tell them I am thinking

3   Labori.

of them and I thank them for their devotion to you. – Don't neglect Monsieur Pin,[4] whose company in times of loneliness is not to be despised. He's quite bad-tempered with other people; but he is fond of us, and you're never altogether alone when he is there to trot along by your side. Give him a nice little kiss from me; tell him I think of him every time I see a dog go by on the road.

So be brave, dear wife; say to yourself that such an abominable situation cannot last. And if it does last, we shall have to accept it, wind up our affairs and settle down somewhere, in the most modest conditions possible. We are too old now to start life all over again, and all I ask is to live my last days in peace, even if it has to be in some backwater.

I believe Lab. himself will be leaving on vacation. Try to confess him before he leaves; then you can tell me how the future looks to him.

My heart is so heavy that perhaps I ought not to have written to you today. But say to yourself that I am in good health and that the rest is simply because my poor nerves are on edge.

I thank you again, dear wife, for all you are doing and I kiss you long and tenderly, with all my heart.

To Fernand Desmoulin

[Weybridge] Friday, 12 August 1898

My faithful friend, Jean and the children arrived last night in fairly good condition. But it seems the poor children were very sick on the boat even though the sea was admirable. They were put to bed and slept well, and this morning they are as happy as a couple of larks. They are going to be a great consolation to me in my lonely existence, for I must admit that my poor heart is still distraught.

My very affectionate thanks to you for all you have done, for your devotion and the trouble you went to to send the little darlings to me. I wanted to write to you immediately to let you know how they are and tell you how grateful I am to you.

The newspapers that Jean brought me from France have incensed me all over again. So once again Esterhazy and du Paty are out of danger. Oh yes, the truth is on the march – but at a snail's pace! We will all be dead by the time it triumphs. My pessimism continues. You know that I am receiving neither *L'Aurore* nor *Le Siècle*. Would you please do *whatever is necessary* so

---

4   Pinpin, Zola's favourite dog.

that they do not overlook me, because in the end this total lack of French newspapers is putting more strain on my nerves.

We have now settled down and I am working very well. That is what will keep me going unless I get clubbed over the head again by something else. It seems someone recognized me at the hotel, but one newspaper reported that I had gone back to London. So I hope that here I will be left in peace. Besides, our plans are all ready if we have to disappear quickly and take refuge somewhere farther away. But is that any way to live?

One little incident has brought me some pleasure: I found my cane, which had got hidden in a corner.

See Alexandre as often as you can. He is very fond of you; you will make things a little less harsh for him. Please tell your cousin again how touched I am by his friendship and the trouble he has gone to. From time to time I shall write to you.

Love to you, my faithful friend.

To Fernand Desmoulin

[Weybridge] Saturday, 13 August 1898

My faithful friend, I did not receive your letter of Thursday evening until this morning. Thank you for expressing your fears about having Jean and the children stay here with me. But everything you have said to yourself I had already said to myself long ago. And do you know why I went ahead anyhow? Because I don't give a damn! I am fed up, thoroughly, totally fed up! I've done my duty and I want to be left in peace. And if they don't want to let me have peace and quiet, I'll go out and get it myself. The only thing I've ever believed in is work; I have gone back to work and the rest doesn't matter any more. They can say what they like, do what they like; it doesn't bother me. Once I have done whatever needs to be done so that my family and I are as happy as possible, the world can collapse all around us and I won't even turn my head to look. I assure you I will not come back home until there is some justice in France, and the latest developments prove that that is not going to happen overnight.

I have given enough thought to other people, my faithful friend. I repeat: I consider that my public role is finished and I am determined to think only of my family and myself. – There! Nonetheless I shall take all the precautions I can but I refuse to worry unduly about them. I cannot take any more struggles and sorrows.

I would have written to you today anyhow to tell you that the two newspapers finally arrived last night. So don't do a thing. And thanks again, with all my heart.

In haste. Love to you, my friend and brother.

To Alexandrine Zola

[Weybridge] Sunday, 14 August 1898

Dear wife, your good letter dated Wednesday has given me great pleasure, because I can sense that you are a little more reassured. Since then, however, I have had the feeling that things in Paris are going from bad to worse. And in that connection, when I learnt that the Court of Appeal had doubled the sentence, in the experts' trial, and that the amount to be paid added up to nearly forty thousand francs,[1] I immediately thought that, just as with the trial in Versailles, the full amount was going to have to be paid immediately. So I wrote a letter to Lab. to ask him to approach Vaughan and our other friends, because I really do think it is altogether unfair to abandon me in these circumstances and let me bear the entire burden of the costs. If you see Lab., talk to him along those lines too. They promised me they would come to my assistance. Surely that famous syndicate (where is it, in Heaven's name?) will step in, sooner or later.[2]

I am incensed at all this! My heart swells with indignation! I am doing a good deal of thinking here, but I cannot and will not tell you everything I decide as I wait for events to take their course. But my mind is made up: I shall not come back until there is justice in France, and what is going on proves that that will not happen overnight. I have done my duty; let other people do theirs. The one thing that matters now is taking care of you and the two little ones, getting back to work so that we will at least have bread to eat until the very end. As for developments that do not concern us directly, I want nothing more to do with them. I've had enough! And that is why I want you to meet me in Genoa. You tell me it would not be wise. Well, for heaven's sake, suppose they do find out where I am! Let them! Then it will be all over. No later than early October, we absolutely must make our plans for the winter; we will certainly not be able to spend it in France. Nor do I want to spend the winter here, for all sorts of reasons. So the best thing to do will be to go somewhere sunny. That way you will be comfortable and I will be able to put in good long days of work. Do not

1 See the Chronology. In fact, the amount was thirty-two thousand francs.
2 An allusion to the 'syndicate' which, the nationalist press claimed, was financing the pro-Dreyfus campaign. See above, the article of that name which Zola published in December 1897.

worry; I am thinking of everything, I am arranging it all in my head; and once you are in Italy, when the time comes, I shall explain to you how I picture things. We will stay at the seaside, between San Remo and Genoa. You will make all the preparations; then I will simply come and join you.

Desmoulin is absolutely right when he tells you over and over again that you must go and rest in Rome. I think you will be free once the matter of the experts is settled. All the rest is unimportant. And really, since everyone else will be taking a holiday, it would be a monstrous thing if you didn't take one as well. It would really make me feel badly if you were stuck in the country with no one to keep you company.

As I was telling you, the children arrived here on Thursday evening. The poor little things were horribly seasick even though the sea was as smooth as glass. They must have been very tired because, the day before, they had to leave V[erneuil] at six in the evening so as not to be seen by the neighbours who were on the look-out, go through the woods, with almost no luggage, and take the train at the station where the man with the flageolet used to play. Then they spent the night at the home of a reliable friend who was originally supposed to fetch them in a motor car but was forced to abandon that idea when other difficulties arose. So they were worn out by the time they reached here. But today they are fine and naturally they are brightening my solitary existence. I hope they will not be too bored even though they have no playthings. Since they arrived, the weather has turned fine, but fine in a way that is typical of this region: the sun beating down during the daytime, and thick fog both morning and evening. I find this crushing heat a bit hard to take. Nonetheless, I get through my five pages regularly every morning and I plan to finish my second chapter tomorrow.

Yes, I have received a letter from Belle-Isle.[3] Our faithful Valentin finally gave our address to Ch., whose letter is very affectionate. It has given me some pleasure, because he speaks the harsh truth, as he sees it, about this unfortunate country of ours. He feels that we are up against such unscrupulous scoundrels that I must not come back to France for any reason. At all events, I repeat: I will not come back until I can come triumphantly. Otherwise it would be silly of me to come looking for insults and a martyrdom that would not be of use to anyone. The scoundrels who have just released a man like Esterhazy yet keep Picquart in prison will stop at nothing.

If you do go to Italy, as I hope, I imagine you will write to me far enough ahead of time for me to tell you which things of mine you should take with you, so that you can give them to me there. I've already told you:

---

3   From Georges Charpentier, who was on holiday at Belle-Ile-en-Mer, in Brittany.

Emile Zola as photographed by Paul Nadar, March 1898.

Alfred Dreyfus.

(*Facing page, top*) Esterhazy, Lucie Dreyfus, Mathieu Dreyfus and Lt-Col Picquart. (*Below*) Dance Step. Cartoon showing General Mercier, Major du Paty de Clam and General de Boisdeffre with Esterhazy, the 'traitor'.

C. ESTERHAZY   Mme DREYFUS

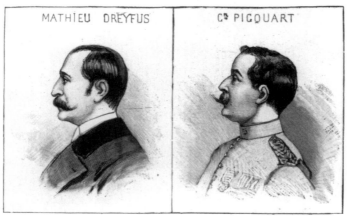

MATHIEU DREYFUS   Ct PICQUART

MERCIER   PATY   BOISDEFFRE   ESTERHAZY

PAS-A-QUATRE

'A Ball at the Elysée Palace', *Musée des Horreurs* (freak show), no. 26, 1900. Lithograph by V. Lenepveu which shows (*left to right*) Grand Rabbi Zadoc Kahn, Lt-Col Picquart, Joseph Reinach, Alfred Dreyfus and Emile Zola being invited to the Elysée Palace by President Emile Loubet (*centre*).

L'AFFAIRE ZOLA

Zola au Palais de Justice

The Zola Affair. 'Zola at the Palais de Justice', *Le Petit Journal*, 20 February 1898.

Zola at one of the hearings during his trial, *L'Illustration*, 26 February 1898.

Lt-Col Henry testifying at Zola's trial, *L'Illustration*, 19 February 1898.

Monsieur Jaurès. 'The truth is on the march. Spectacular drama. Down with the army! Long live Dreyfus! Long live Zola!' Cartoon by Gyp, *Le Rire*, 21 May 1898. (Truth is traditionally depicted as a naked woman emerging from a well.)

Waiting for the Mail. Zola says, 'Not a word from Schwartzkoppen. And the Emperor of Germany doesn't write to me. It's inconceivable!' Cartoon by Forain, *Psst...!*, 9 July 1898.

Obsèques de Bismarck

DISCOURS DE M. ZOLA : — « Messieurs !... Hier encore, le Monde comptait deux Géants... Aujourd'hui, je reste le seul !... » (*Et il continue.*)

Bismarck's Funeral. 'Speech by Monsieur Zola: "Gentlemen, just yesterday there were still two giants in the world. Today I am the only one left!" (And he continues.)' Caricature by Caran d'Ache, *Psst...!*, 6 August 1898.

La Revision

La Revision ?... soit... Mais avec le poteau et les douze balles, cette fois

Revision. 'A revision? All right, but with a firing squad and twelve bullets, this time.' Cartoon by Caran d'Ache, *Psst...!*, 3 September 1898.

Anti-Dreyfus demonstration in Paris in October 1898, when the case for revision
was being examined.

Photographs by Emile Zola: near the Crystal Palace (*top*), outside London; cemetery in Addlestone (*below*).

Photograph by Emile Zola: Jeanne and the children at the window of the house in Weybridge.

Photograph by Emile Zola: Alexandrine Zola taking a walk in the English countryside.

The Sponge. Indian ink drawing (inscribed to Joseph Reinach) by H.G. Ibels, a pro-Dreyfus cartoonist: General Mercier thrusts a sponge soaked in vinegar at a crucified Alfred Dreyfus.

my little comb, my file entitled 'Impressions during the hearing'.[4] Maybe you could also take along a little underwear for me, and some winter clothes.

You would leave all the servants in the country, and we would see later.

All I want is for the days to go by quickly, so that we will know where we stand and can organize our new life. Try not to worry too much. Be well. Get some rest. We will always find some way to make the best of things.

If Monsieur Pin behaves himself, give him a fond stroke or two for me. – I kiss you with all my heart, my dear wife, and send you my immense gratitude again for all the trouble you are going to, and I beg you to think of yourself a little and get some rest, for the sake of your health.

To Alexandrine Zola

[Weybridge] Thursday, 18 August 1898

Dear wife, I have received your letters and Mirbeau's letter, and I see that you both feel that at a given moment I should come back and turn myself over to the authorities, without going back to Versailles. I don't think that is logical. Lab.[ori] would certainly stand in the way of such a plan, and he would be right. We mustn't forget the purpose of my leaving France. The sole reason was so that we could remain in command of the situation and begin the trial again at what we considered the most auspicious moment. So I would be a traitor to the cause if, upon coming back to France, I didn't try to shed a little more light on the affair. – The truth is that, in logical terms, I am going to be forced to choose between two alternatives: either go back so that the trial begins again, or else remain outside France as long as we believe that there cannot be any point in starting the trial again. Obviously the second alternative is the one we must choose; and as I do not see when it might be useful for the trial to begin again, since there is no justice any more, I conclude that I am going to be in exile for a long time to come. – So it is with that thought in mind, and confirmed in my mind more forcefully every day as I mull it over, that I plan to join you in Genoa. It is not just a vague notion but a plan which I am mapping out in detail. It is certainly not my intention that you and I should stay in a hotel in Genoa. I will explain to you as time goes by just how you should make things ready for my arrival. It is my formal wish that the children should be in Paris on 1 October. Personally, had it not been for them, I would have stayed here only one or two weeks if the plan had been for me to go back on the 15th;

4   Containing the notes that Zola had taken during his trial in February.

but since that will be impossible, and since I have absolutely no desire to spend the winter here alone, the simplest thing is for me to come and join you in some country where we can conveniently settle down. And do not bother yourself with the idea that all is lost if they find me: that is not true. On the contrary, the day they find out where I am, we will be relieved of a great worry. Italy will be a fine place for us to wait for events to take their course, and if anyone objects, I don't care. I have had enough. In the end I will tell France what I think of it. I am perfectly calm, I promise you; I am thinking through our situation very clearly here in my refuge, and it is my intention to act very cautiously.

There is only one thing I regret, if we are forced to settle somewhere in the region of Genoa, and that is this: I do not know how I will manage to have the poor chevalier[1] come. You will not be able to bring him with you. I'll find a way.

If *L'Aurore* pays half of the forty thousand francs, that is something, at least. But Vaughan did not seem very eager to do it. If it became necessary, you could go to see him at the newspaper; you will find him there between 5 and 7 p.m.

This business with the experts is the least of my worries, because we are going to run out of money. I would like to have time to finish my novel in peace, so as to put us back onto an even keel.

I don't need to tell you to try everything you can to persuade people to help us. You are as familiar with our situation as I am and your devotion throughout this whole affair moves me to tears. As soon as you have got rid of this last chore, you will be able to leave.

Have no fear, I am being careful here and other people are being careful for me. Nothing of a disturbing nature is happening. A week from Saturday I shall change my retreat again, and once I am in a new house, it will be impossible, once and for all, for anyone to find me. Not a day goes by without people looking after my safety. I am telling you this so that you will not be haunted by fears, which I find perfectly understandable.

No news that could be of any interest to you. My life goes on, to as strict a schedule as if I were in a monastery. Every morning, very regularly, I do my five pages. I have begun my third chapter. There was a very violent storm the other night. Luckily the children did not wake up. They are relatively good; they play in the little garden and go out very little, which is the way I prefer it. The weather is fine again. I am sitting in the room where I work. My greatest wish is to get as far ahead on my novel as I can until the end of September, and to go and continue it this winter on the shores of the Mediterranean.

---

1   Nickname of Pinpin, the dog.

I am going to answer Mirbeau. Thank him anyhow, for I am very touched by his devotion. Shake hands with all our friends for me.

What I can promise you is that I will put a letter in the mail to you on Thursday evening and another on Sunday evening, so the first one should reach you on Saturday and the other on Tuesday. But with the postal service here, I can't guarantee a thing. – Thank you for all the comforting things you write to me; they are like balm on my soul. Actually what I suffer from the most is having had to leave my poor home so abruptly and not even knowing when I will be able to go back to it. Which is why I feel so moved when you write that it seems to you I am still there. Ah, my poor dear wife, when will we be there together again? You were quite right to make the clock work. It looked as though as it was dead. I am happy to know it is alive again and is striking the hours, as it did when I was there. – When you go away, leave everything as if we were going to come back. But if we do not come back we will have to take a decision, because we will not be able to keep up the expense of such a household.

I think of you when I kiss the children. How lucky they are, not to understand anything and to live so gaily, with not a care in the world!

I kiss you with all my heart, dear wife, and in spite of everything I dream fine dreams of peace and affection!

The day they leave us alone, we will be able to live more happily, and we will only need very little to live on.

The dismissal of the case against Esterhazy, on 12 August, increased Zola's pessimism. He felt as if there was no way out. Would it not be better for him to come back to France and face the term in prison? He tried to convince Labori that it would.

More than ever, he was touched by the support expressed by faithful friends: Octave Mirbeau and his wife Alice, whose sympathy was warmer than he had expected, and Alfred Bruneau, a loyal companion during the dark days, with whom he discussed a projected opera, L'Ouragan *(The Hurricane), which was being written at this time.*

To Fernand Labori

[Weybridge] 19 August 1898

My dear friend, your very affectionate letter gave me great pleasure. I too embrace you with all my heart for all the dreadful trouble you are taking, for the superhuman courage with which you are defending truth and justice. Do not bother to write to me often, for I know how exhausted you must be. Try to get some rest; get back your strength for the struggles to come. I hope they will at last let you take some vacation; it is in the interests of all of us. We want you to be strong and awe-inspiring, always.

You ask me how I am. The first two weeks were awful. I did not even have any clothing or underclothes, and there I was in a country where I do not speak the language and I was forced to hide. Then I managed to arrange my existence fairly well; staying here has become bearable, especially as I have been able to get back to work. That is what has always saved me. Only, deep in my heart, I still feel an anguish that will not diminish. My poor nerves continue to quiver with indignation and anger. Although I live an utterly calm and solitary life, I am filled with fury. You cannot imagine how horrified I am by the news that reaches me from France.

You ask me what I think of the latest developments, with the hindsight I now have. Well, I've nothing good to say about them! Esterhazy has now been cleared by the civil courts just as he was by a military court. That is enough to disgrace a nation forever. So we can no longer count on the judicial system. I am like you: my only hope lies in some sort of surprise, some unforeseeable development. We need either a bolt from the blue, or else the patient efforts of infinitely small creatures who keep gnawing away until they carry off the prize. Victory is sure to come, but in how many months – or years?

Thank you for the victory you won in the *Petit Journal* affair.[1] It has brought me some brief consolation, and I owe it to you. Naturally, I leave it up to you to have us bring a civil action in the forgery case, if you feel that it is in our interest to do so; and I am sending you the letter you requested for Maître Collet. – Thank you also for your efforts to avoid letting the entire pecuniary burden fall on me, in the experts' case. I have written to my wife. And I also know that Mirbeau is approaching people. In short, I hope that I will be spared serious difficulties.

Lastly, I enclose a note which I beg you to read closely and to have our friends read. Ask them all for their opinions and tell me yours, after having thought it over carefully. In fact, I do not want a reply until early September; then I can organize my life in accordance with the decision we will have reached.

Ah, what a hero Picquart is! I am so moved when I think of him. Give him a very affectionate hug for me when you see him and tell him that not a day goes by without my thinking of him.

And you, my brave friend, my heroic friend, I embrace you too with all my heart and beg you to tell your wife how happy her affectionate support makes me, and how touched I am.

---

1   An allusion to the verdict against Judet on 3 August; see the Chronology.

Note

After the verdict was reached, in absentia, at the hearing in Versailles on 18 July, all of our friends took the view that I must leave France immediately so that the sentence could not be served on me and we could thus remain in complete control of the situation. In particular, we wished to be free to choose the date on which we might feel that it would be useful for the trial to resume, so as to bring the facts to light and ensure that we would win our case. In fact, everything hinged on a matter of dates; we wanted essentially to be able to choose that date ourselves.

I must add that at that time Esterhazy and his mistress were behind bars, that du Paty de Clam was going to be compromised as an accomplice, and that we felt it necessary to await the findings of the investigation; because if legal action was taken against all of them and they were convicted, then it became possible for us to be acquitted. There is no longer any such reason to wait, since the case against them was dismissed for lack of evidence. I would simply like to point out that this attitude – this injustice – on the part of the judicial system proves that now it will stop at nothing and it is just waiting for us in Versailles so as to throttle us.

Therefore, in these circumstances, I wish to know what our friends think about the probable date of my return to France, in other words the date when it will clearly be in our interest and in the interest of the cause to resume the trial in Versailles. I emphasize that it has been proven that it is impossible for the public prosecutor's office to serve the sentence on me abroad and that we are in command of the situation: we can postpone the date of my return as long as we want to.

There are only two alternatives, in my opinion.

As we said when we were counting on action being taken against Esterhazy and his mistress, I could come back in October even if nothing new has happened between now and then, and we could be throttled in Versailles, for the beauty of yet another judicial crime. We will be booed and hissed, threatened and convicted; we will certainly not be able to bring anything new to light; and then I will serve my year in prison. If it is felt that that is useful, that I will be serving the cause by doing so, I am prepared to accept that.

Or else I stay abroad as long as is necessary and wait until such time as we can speak up loud and clear; be on the alert for the circumstances that will enable me to return solely in order to triumph; let the trial hang over their heads like a threat that is about to become reality; remain in command of the agitation, so that we can open the wound again at any time and make it bleed; refrain from taking our trial off their hands, see to it that this ultimatum is always staring them in the face, deprive them of all hope of ever seeing it end since we will be free at all times to start up the whole process all over again.

I want our friends to read this note, discuss it and then let me know which course of action they feel I ought to take.

Distance sometimes made it difficult to have a dialogue with Alexandrine (who now wondered whether she was going to travel to Genoa, as originally planned). The amount to be paid to the experts as damages still constituted a major source of worry.

To Alexandrine Zola

[Weybridge] Sunday, 21 August 1898

Dear wife, I see that you simply do not understand my letters. You re-read them, and you do not understand them any more than you did the first time. That must be because I speak to you as if you were aware of my thoughts, day by day, whereas you, on the contrary, live amidst very different thoughts, those of the people you see. I fear that the people who could give you precise information on the situation we are in are not doing so. Besides, only Lab.[ori] could do so because only he knows and understands. But he has other fish to fry and in addition he looks at the affair from his own particular angle. So that while I may seem so obscure and even a little crazy to you, that is because I am thinking out loud with you without having told you first what probabilities my thoughts are based upon. When we see each other again, I will explain what seems so obscure to you, and you will see that although I am still very courageous and determined to go through with my role to the end, nonetheless I can take the liberty of thinking that once again I have been made to do useless and dangerous things. – Anyhow, you are perfectly right. What is the good of planning what we will do next month since new developments, between now and then, can change everything several times over? So I shall stop telling you that I will go to join you in Italy. First of all we'll see whether you go to Italy, and then whether there is any point in my going there to join you.

But let me calculate the probabilities. It seems likely that the Chambers will not be in session before 20 October. Now, I think it would be impossible for me to come back before they are in session; and in fact before the interpellations that will occur and that may bring down the government. So that would take me to the middle of November. If the children have left me on 1 October, what will I do then and where will I live for six weeks, until it is time for me to come back? I have written to Lab. at length and I have sent him a note so that he can think about the date of my return to France[1] and discuss it with our friends; and I am waiting to hear his opinion. I have outlined to him the alternatives we have, as I see it. – Don't think I am discouraged; don't go thinking I am losing my mind. I am as willing to make sacrifices as I was on the very first day. But, I repeat, there are several ways to consummate the sacrifice, and so far it has seemed to me my return would involve dangers of all sorts and would not do anyone any good. Which will not prevent me from coming back if it is judged necessary for me to do so. For the time being, let's wait; that's the only wise course of action. And don't let my letters make you sad; take them as the informal talk of a man who is doing a good deal of thinking and judging the events in France from a distance and at their true value.

I despair at the delays which may prevent you from taking some vacation. I still hope that things will go quickly enough for you to have at least the month of September for yourself. And let's say the month of October as well, because I am still convinced that they will not need us in October. Keep me informed. It will make me so happy to know that at last you are disentangled from all this and at last you can get some rest.

The cheque from the firm of Macmillan represents my share of the royalties on the publication of the American translation of *Paris*. I had been expecting it. Keep the cheque until I can talk it over with Viz[etelly]. If it is preferable for me to cash it, you will send it to me when I tell you to. So everything is fine in that respect.

You are right. If you go to Italy, don't take anything for me, no underclothes, no clothing. First of all I don't know whether I will join you there. And besides, on second thoughts, there is absolutely nothing I need. Don't send me anything here, even if you have the opportunity. I live in a nightshirt. For three weeks now I haven't put on a proper shirt and I've been wearing my indoor jacket and trousers.

I'm not surprised to hear that *L'Aurore* is being turned down everywhere when it asks for financial assistance. That's the work of the famous syndicate! Isn't it marvellous how we are supported by Jewish gold and foreign gold! But even so, I still hope that the burden of those forty thousand francs is not going to fall on me. Lab. has written me a fairly reassuring letter on that score. Keep me informed about it; it's the only question that still worries me. I have written to Mirbeau to thank him.

Naturally I have nothing to tell you about life here. The days go by, and they are all the same. I continue to work very regularly, and I am pleased with my work. The heat is heavy and humid and makes me very uncomfortable. All around me is perfect peace and quiet.

Tell the chevalier that once I am in prison I will ask for only one favour,

1   See above, the letter to Labori dated 19 August.

and that is to have him with me. That will console him for my absence. – And you, dear wife, don't worry about my letters; you tell me they upset you and make you feel bad. I will stop thinking out loud since I cannot give explanations along the way; that would take pages and pages.

Tell yourself that I am fine, that I am working well and that in the last analysis I will do whatever it will be noble and useful to do. – What I would like, I repeat, is for things to develop in a way that allows you to take some vacation; you certainly deserve it, after all the worries you have had to deal with alone for the past month. I will not feel reassured until I know that you too are far away from the idiots and the scoundrels, and getting some rest.

The tenderest of kisses from the poor dog-wolf-cat to his poor wolf-cat-dog.

To Alexandrine Zola

[Weybridge] Thursday, 25 August 1898

Dear wife, I am very sorry for your sake that you have to give up the idea of your trip to Italy. I picture you alone, in this appalling heat, obliged to go to Paris frequently, and worried and weary, and I feel heartsick, knowing how upset you are and what strain you are under. You are having a really dismal summer. But I fully understand the reasons that prevent you from leaving. I know the worries you would take away with you if you left the servants in Médan. You would constantly fear that things would go from bad to worse and that would spoil your trip. Stay, then, if that is what you prefer, even though it was my keenest wish to see you get some rest. In that case I obviously won't have you go to Genoa so that I can meet you there. That would be quite illogical. If you had already been in Italy and if I had been free, then, not wanting to remain in England, it would have been perfectly natural for me to go to Genoa to join you. Then we'd have come back to France together, at the necessary time. Now, I would not do that unless I was going to spend the entire winter abroad; because in that case it would be more pleasant to spend it in a sunny climate. But since it is becoming likely that I will go back to France early in November, at the latest, the double trip to Genoa, each of us travelling separately so as to meet there, would be a useless complication. I am waiting to see what will happen in September and I will arrange things differently. I will let you know what seems to me the wisest thing to do. I think your idea of moving the servants to Paris by the first of October is a good one and we'll see about yourself later. It will depend to some extent on the way Lab.[ori] answers the note I sent him, in which I ask him to indicate the date he recommends for my return to France. I will discuss that date if need be. Then, once it has been set, we will make our final arrangements. There is no point in our talking it over today because we would run the risk of changing our minds several times again.

As for my novel, I did not commit myself to Vaug[han]. I simply told him that, assuming other offers were equal, I would give him the preference. So I am as surprised as you are by his way of looking at the matter and I promise you that before signing anything final I will take every possible precaution.

I am not counting on anyone, any more than you are, to come to our assistance in pecuniary terms. I have calculated it; I know roughly how much harm may be done; and if I am left in peace to work, the breach should not be too difficult to repair. But that doesn't mean that we shouldn't make every effort, even useless ones, to try to persuade the newspaper at least to pay its share of the costs.

You ask whom I want you to go and see. Nobody; you of all people! Promises were made to me, but I do not want to send you here and there soliciting. Only Lab. can take action, and once Vaug. has reached a decision, we will just have to accept it. When I come back, I will look into the matter, if there is still time. Don't fret over it any more.

I have talked to Viz[etelly] about the draft from America.[1] He feels that since it was sent here, the best thing would be for me to cash it here. I would endorse it and we would take it to another bank, as if it came from France, so as to avoid the danger of having it expire. Furthermore, it seems to me that the money could be useful in October if new complications should arise. So simply send me the draft in a letter, since I don't believe there is any danger.

You are going to so much trouble over my chain,[2] my poor Loulou. I have thought of that chain several times since I have been here, the way I think of the things in our dear house, and everything I had to leave so abruptly. That is what I cannot forgive, because all of that could have been avoided; and although I am determined to stop thinking aloud in my letters so as not to confuse you still further, you may be sure that I will make up for it in person when I see you again. Then you will understand what seemed incomprehensible to you and you will see that even today we can choose between two alternatives and that the one that would consist of returning to France is perhaps not the best one, from every point of view. – What you decided concerning the chain is fine; we will look at both designs and choose together.

Over here I have had the repercussions of your heatwave in France. For a week the sun was dreadful. You know how uncomfortable it makes me.

1 The royalty cheque from Macmillan; see above, the previous letter to Alexandrine Zola.
2 A watch chain that Alexandrine had had repaired.

But since yesterday it has been almost cold; the wind must have veered to the north. I am pleased that the hot spell did not stop me from working. I have begun the fourth chapter of my novel, and that is putting me on my feet again. Besides, I lead a cloistered life, and it would be fine if only I didn't continue to feel such terrible uncertainty about the future. – The children are well. The boy is slightly disorientated and his general state of health reflects that a little, but nothing serious.[3]

Thank you for the jasmine blossoms. All I can send you in return are two small white pansies that I pick in front of the little room where I work alone for hours on end. They will tell you that you are here with me, very often. – Give the chevalier a kiss and try not to feel too sad as you spend September in our poor old Médan; I cannot think of it without a very heavy heart. Nonetheless, I do not despair about the future; we will manage to organize it in such a way as to be quite happy. – Dear wife, I send you all my love, and hope that our vigilance will triumph over all our woes.

Zola left Penn for 'Summerfield', a house in Addlestone, a few miles away. Did this new retreat plunge him still deeper into exile? At that very moment, in France, it was decided to prosecute Picquart, a fact which did not incline Zola to optimism. One piece of good news did, however, emerge: persuaded by Octave Mirbeau, Joseph Reinach very generously agreed to pay the damages that Zola had been sentenced to pay to the experts.

To Alexandrine Zola

[Addlestone] Sunday, 28 August 1898

Dear wife, I moved to another house yesterday, I have taken refuge farther from the capital, in a more deserted spot. Here the garden is very large and well-shaded, which makes me very happy for the children's sake; they can at least run about as they like. There are all sorts of hiding places in this garden, so they will play in it very happily.

The house is also more convenient, and the rent is the same. Since I had only rented the other house for four weeks and since the owner was coming back from the seaside, I was forced to move. But I was delighted at having to; I would have changed my place of refuge at all events because I didn't feel safe any more. The trouble stemmed from the fact that when I left the hotel, I did something silly: I did not change names. I rented the

3   Jacques, who was frail.

house using the same name[1] as I had used at the hotel and as a result, when a newspaper reported on my stay at the hotel under that name, the owner of the house had read that paper and therefore realized who his tenant was. So I was at his mercy. By the way, I have nothing but good things to say about this country when it comes to discretion; the people who have recognized me have all kept perfectly quiet. Never mind, I am safer here. I have changed my name again and I am in a region where no one will come looking for me. This time I am absolutely certain they will not find me.

For that matter, has anyone looked for me? I doubt it. They are only too glad to be rid of me. Not to mention that they would have absolutely no way of doing anything to me if they did find me. I have consulted [lawyers]; they have no practical means of having the sentence served on me. There is not a doubt about that, and I could make my presence known and come and go freely without any danger whatsoever. The only reason I continue to stay quietly in the background is to avoid the horde of reporters and especially so as to live undisturbed and overlooked, and work in peace. When I wrote to you that the best thing would be to make my presence known and that everything would go more smoothly thereafter, I meant that if the sentence had been served on me and if I had not registered a protest, the verdict would have become final; whereupon the situation would have been just what you want it to be; that is, the trial would not be able to resume in Versailles and all I'd have had to do was to give myself up, at a time of my own choosing. Hiding and preventing the sentence from being served, as Lab. advised me to do, means acting in such a way that everything begins all over again. I might add that if I decided one day to live abroad openly, I would do so without any danger; and if that were to happen, I assure you I would adopt an attitude that all of Europe would applaud.

By the way, I have received a very nice letter from Mme St Blaise,[2] in which she talks about you with so much affection and admiration that I am very touched. Her opinion, very clearly, seems to be that I should stay abroad. She says that if I decided one day to announce publicly that I am here, the entire country and even the entire government would be on my side and would protect me, if necessary. She offers to approach important people whom she knows. I shall answer her in the next few days and thank her, but refuse her offer. I wish to go on living undisturbed and out of the way. Besides, you know that I have not yet come to any decision; I am waiting for the next developments and for Lab. to consult our friends. In fact I am almost certain that I will come back to France at

---

1   Jean Beauchamp.
2   Alice Mirbeau, wife of Octave Mirbeau.

the end of October or the beginning of November. It will even be a heroic act and a useful one, I hope. Anyhow, I will talk it over with you when the time comes, so that we will know what we should do in October.

Mme St Blaise gives me some news that will make me very happy, if it is confirmed. She announces that her husband has found a person[3] who is willing to advance the forty thousand francs. I imagine your next letter will tell me more.

I did not receive my mail last night because of the move. It reached me this morning but there weren't any letters, only the two newspapers. Today being Sunday, there is no mail. So I will not hear from you until tomorrow evening, if you wrote to me on Saturday, as I imagine you did.

The weather has taken a turn for the worse. I moved yesterday in pouring rain, then the sun came out a little this morning but it was very windy. My work was disrupted for only one day; this morning I resumed my fourth chapter. I am in the midst of a difficult passage and I got only four pages done. But it doesn't matter; I feel quite steady and fit. – This morning, what knocked me over a little was the newspapers I received, because I read that it has been decided to prosecute Picquart.[4] What an abominable thing! The guilty man goes free and now Dreyfus's martyrdom is not enough; another innocent man must be thrown into prison. Once I go to prison as well, that will make three of us. I have never heard of such a monstrous thing.

I see in the papers that it is not so hot in Paris. I am very glad to hear it because I was really worried about those frequent trips you were making in such terrible heat; take good care of yourself, rest and try to shield yourself as much as possible from the dreadful things surrounding you. – I have not had a letter from you since the last one I wrote to you; and that's why this one is a bit empty.

Tell Monsieur le chevalier that the dogs over here are a very unlucky lot because they always wear muzzles. I petted one yesterday, a little white one, who seemed very gentle and appealing.

With my tenderest kisses, dear wife, from a heart that is filled with hope in spite of everything and awaits the happier days that are bound to come.

*

We do agree that you will continue writing to me under the same name, care of the solicitor.

---

3   Joseph Reinach.
4   See above, the letter to Labori dated 19 August.

As September began, dramatic events in France gave new impetus to hope:
Colonel Henry was arrested, then committed suicide. The prospect of indefinite
exile faded away. But nothing had been decided yet. The waiting continued.

To Alexandrine Zola

[Addlestone] Thursday, 1 September 1898

Dear wife, last night I received the telegram that the good doctor sent to the
solicitor for me: 'Victory. Tell Beauchamp immediately'. You can imagine
what a happy shock I felt, because I understood straightaway that some
important event had just taken place, in our favour. I confess that all night
long I was unable to sleep. This morning I could not settle down to work. I
will not be receiving the French newspapers until this evening and you can
imagine my impatience at being without any detailed news whatsoever.
Finally I bicycled over to the next village and bought the English newspapers, in which I have such trouble deciphering a few words. And that is
how I have just learnt, roughly, what has happened: Henry was arrested,
he admitted to his forgery, and he committed suicide. But I still have no
details and I am on tenterhooks, as you can imagine. Not one piece of
reliable news from France. But I have the impression that although this
does not yet put an end to our woes, nonetheless the truth has just taken a
giant step forward. I fear they will still try some equivocal manoeuvre or
other and will still persist in refusing a revision. Never mind. This is the
beginning. The enemy is being routed.

From your last two letters I see that you are thinking again of going to
Italy and I am very glad, because although you had good reasons to stay
until now, I do believe that developments will allow you to get some rest
and amusement. Once the matter of the experts has been settled, there will
be nothing serious any more to keep you in Paris. You could go there some
time in the next few days, install the servants, turn over M. le chevalier to
them and go to Rome, where you would stay until the end of October. I
repeat, I don't think I will be able to come back myself before then. And
if these recent developments did allow me to come back sooner than
expected, I'd find the house reopened and ready to receive me, and then it
would be I who would wait for you, as I have in previous years. You would
have nothing to worry about, because it could only be very promising
developments that would hasten my return. So feel free to make your
decision and go and get some rest, yourself; you must need it so badly.

I received the cheque from America.[1] Thank you. I shall cash [it] soon,

---

1   The royalty cheque from Macmillan; see above, the letter of 21 August to Alexandrine Zola.

when an opportunity arises. You were quite right to thank R. for advancing the money.[2] I would rather not write to him at this time. A letter from you should be enough. The note from me which he thought over for two days is the one I sent to Lab. and in which I spell out the two alternatives open to me, either coming back or not coming back.[3] I can well understand that he is giving it careful thought, since the question, in the terms in which I put it to my friends, is a very grave matter. Besides, depending on what is happening today in France but that I am unaware of, all of that would become secondary, particularly if all I had to do was to come back in triumph.

I received a kind letter from Amélie and will reply to it.[4] I answered Mme St B. and thanked her.

I forgot to mention that I also received a letter from our faithful Valentin which I answered immediately, calculating that my reply would barely have time to reach him since he is supposed to be in Paris on the third.

You did exactly the right thing with regard to Roux![5] I cannot feel comfortable at the idea of seeing him come to our house again. Henceforth there are things which it will be difficult for us to tolerate. After having upset our entire lives, this monstrous affair will obviously make some changes as to the people we continue to see.

You talk about the places there might be near here where I could spend the winter. I am familiar with them but not for anything in the world will I spend a winter in this country, if I am not able to come home. I still plan to send the children back at the beginning of October unless it really makes things simpler to keep them here two weeks more. But in that case, I would doubtless spend those two weeks in the house where I am, for you cannot imagine how worrisome it is for me to make the slightest move. And besides, I repeat once again, it is impossible to foresee what I shall do in a month, especially with these latest developments.

This evening, I shall go back to buy the local papers, so as to have fresh news. I'll manage to decipher it after a fashion. – How extraordinary to think that here I am surrounded by fields and total silence, everything is perfectly calm, and I cannot receive any news, and meanwhile in my country events are taking place on which my fate depends!

Here in the garden I have found more of those little white pansies and I am sending you two of them to thank you for your jasmine, which brought me a little whiff of home.

2   An allusion to Reinach's gesture.
3   See above, the letter of 19 August to Labori.
4   Amélie Laborde, Alexandrine's cousin.
5   Marius Roux had been a friend of Zola's in their youth but was now the sub-editor of Ernest Judet's *Petit Journal*. He wanted to have news of Zola and had expressed the desire to pay a call on Alexandrine.

I kiss you with all my heart, dear wife, and I kiss you in the hope that the serious problems we have had are going to end. You have shared my distress with me so closely, and you will share the victory as well.

To Alexandrine Zola

[Addlestone] Sunday, 4 September 1898

Dear wife, I was very happy to receive a letter from you last night, since the days on which you write to me work out badly because of that blasted Sunday which is sacred to these people over here – how idiotic of them! The letter you send on Saturday does not arrive until Monday evening and the one you send on Tuesday reaches me on Wednesday evening, so that every week I have a letter on Monday and another on Wednesday, then nothing, from Wednesday to Monday! That leaves a big gap, as you can see. It's because of the days on which you go to Paris to fetch my letters.

So last night, when I recognized your writing, I was overjoyed. I had suspected there would be a letter from you because I sensed that you must be desperate at the idea of not being able to tell me about the important events that were taking place. They surprised me, just as they must have surprised all of you in Paris. I must admit that for a minute I felt ecstatic. Today, I have calmed down. Certainly a giant step has been taken towards the truth; in fact I quite sincerely believe that now the truth will become obvious and undeniable. But our troubles are not yet over. We shall still need a great deal of patience. From Mirbeau's letter and from yours as well, I see that our friends' opinion is the same as the one I had the instant I was informed. From now on there can be no more question of exile. I shall come back; that is certain. Only, if there is to be a revision, it is absolutely imperative that I wait until it is completed and then come back, fully victorious, when all is over. It is not my triumph that I am concerned about, for it will be my ardent wish, as you know, simply to be left alone. No, I am thinking of the beauty of the campaign we have led and I want it to be complete, one superb stroke all the way to the end, concluding like a work of art. – So I may remain far from France for a long time yet to come. Until 15 October, I can stay in this house. After that, a decision will have to be made. I do not want to plan too far ahead. I am waiting to see what happens.

From your standpoint, I can understand that the latest developments are delaying your trip and even making you hesitate. News like that has such serious consequences for us that, if you were abroad when it reached you, it would have a very profound effect on you. So do as you think best. It is impossible for me to give you any advice. As far as material factors are concerned, it's all right for you to leave, since all immediate necessities have been taken care of and you can go away confident that we will not be bothered any more.

The government has too many problems to think about me; there is absolutely no doubt that it is going to leave me alone. I am no longer in danger. But on the other hand, further dramatic events may happen any day, and it is better not to leave if you think that their effects would fill you with anxiety while you were abroad. From now on it all depends on your personal feeling about it, on what you would prefer to do.

This house is really very comfortable. The garden, which is terribly unkempt, is like an island of greenery in the midst of the fields. The children can roll about in the tall grass from morning till night. I spend the afternoons lying there myself and reading. For the past week the weather has been delightful: sunny but not too hot, and hardly a cloud in the sky. – I lost a day's work because of the excitement caused by the great news. But yesterday I resumed my task and began chapter five. The novel is going very well; it is my sole consolation. I think I will not feel unworthy if I return to Paris with a substantial amount of work done. I have stopped rushing to read the papers because I know it will take many days yet before justice is done. I have fully recovered my equilibrium and am perfectly calm once again. – Yesterday I wrote to Amélie. Aside from your letter, and the two that our devoted Larat[1] wrote to inform me of events, I have not yet had any letters from anyone. Mirbeau's letter arrived last night, at the same time as yours, and moved me to tears; it is so charming and expresses so much solidarity. At last a little reward, a little happiness coming our way. – In fact I am very touched by what you say about the servants, about Eugénie, and how overjoyed they are. Their joy may enable me to forget how dreadful the cooking is over here. Apart from various kinds of roast meat, and fried or grilled fish, I am being poisoned. I will spare you a recital of my heroi-comical difficulties with the two maids I had to hire but who speak not one word of French. At home, we wouldn't want them, not even for doing the washing up. However, those are minor cares.

Tell Monsieur le chevalier that he is a naughty rascal to go up to bed without his mistress and cause her so much worry. But I send him my love all the same. – And as for the two of us, dear wife, I think we are beginning to be fine dogs-wolves-cats once again. The cat-wolf-dog kisses the wolf-cat-dog with all his heart.

---

1   See above, the letter dated 11 August to Alexandrine Zola.

Writing to Labori and Mirbeau, Zola gave free rein to his joy.

Vaughan asked him to speak a few words of support for a public meeting that L'Aurore was to organize at the Tivoli-Vauxhall auditorium. Zola refused, in line with the reserved attitude he had consistently taken.

To Fernand Labori

[Addlestone] Thursday, 8 September 1898

My dear and valiant friend, you don't need to write to me – never fear, I know that you hold me dear and that I am in your thoughts. And besides you are having to make such efforts, to perform such a complicated task, that I would not want to take up a single hour of your time unnecessarily.

Yes, your good letter finds me in a very joyful frame of mind. I think that we are finally marching towards victory. Nonetheless, I still feel some anxiety and I beseech you, as I beseech our friends, to be doubly wary and cautious as we near our goal. Our battle will not be won until D.'s innocence has been recognized and he is free. The day he is put on trial once again, my heart will stand still, for that will be the day of the real danger. You understand perfectly well what I mean and all of you must now have but one thought in mind: make sure that the evidence presented that day is so irrefutable that any criminal attempt to conjure it away becomes impossible.

I agree with you, of course, concerning the date of my return. It is impossible to set a date at this time. The only logical date, in my view, would be after the results of the revision, so that our trial in Versailles would be the victorious conclusion to the entire affair. So I shall wait – not in peace, no, because I am too overwhelmed with anxiety for that – but at least in hope, for the day when I shall be able to resume my ordinary life as a working man, with my task accomplished. And in fact, I am well and working, and I suffer only from being here, out of my element, far from my wife and in a country of which I do not speak the language.

And I think of you, my courageous and glorious friend, who are going to be so instrumental in bringing about victory. I have always told you that it is you who made my trial into an irresistible, all-conquering campaign. Although I felt bitter pangs of remorse, at one point, fearing that I had dragged you into a hopeless case, when the good news came my first thought was that now the future belonged to you, to us – and I cried like a dumb beast, thinking of that tormented innocent man whom we are going to restore to his wife and his children. – Please convey my most cordial regards to your wife. Affectionately yours.

These mid-September letters echo with scenes from daily life in exile: among them English cooking, the weather, and the games that Denise and Jacques played in the big garden at 'Summerfield'. In Paris, Brisson's procrastination and the fact that each successive Minister of War was bent on defending the same positions of refusal made hopes of a revision retreat into the distance.

To Alexandrine Zola

[Addlestone] Sunday, 11 September 1898

Dear wife, I was quite overjoyed to receive your extra letter, which reached me last night. I do not want us to exchange more than two letters a week because it is still a little dangerous to correspond and especially because of the trouble you have to go to, to collect my letters in Paris. I only regret that because of our arrangement, one of your letters reaches me on Monday evening and the other on Wednesday evening, so that when I write to you on Thursday I am answering both of your letters at once and when I write to you on Sunday I have no letter from you to answer. But no matter how hard I think about it, there seems to be no way to arrange things better. So let us continue writing to one another regularly on the agreed days until the end of the month. Then, once you have gone back to Paris, you will send me one letter on Sunday and the other on Wednesday before five o'clock. That way, things will work very well, you'll see, and we will answer one another's letters very regularly.

I continue to keep up with the news very closely. But I must admit that I am doing so more calmly since I realize that the conclusion is less and less likely to take place soon. That does not shatter my confidence. I am still convinced that whatever they do, they will be forced into a revision. They may still delay things with wicked tricks, but they will merely be putting off the inevitable outcome. The trouble is that what with their dithering and their formalities, I don't know by now how much longer they are going to oblige me to stay here. I am trying to figure it out, and I begin to believe that if we set the date for my return on 15 November, we are being too optimistic. I am impatient because my poor heart still feels very heavy at being far away from you for so long, after having been separated in such a dreadfully sudden way; and even though I am not alone, and I am fairly comfortably installed, still, I am in a foreign country, far from everything I am accustomed to and all my friends. Two more long months! It seems a century. There are evenings when I feel altogether hopeless, swamped with despair, and I begin to tell myself all over again that we will never emerge from this situation. Well, we must be courageous and patient. On 15 October, once the children are not here any longer, I shall have to make other arrangements. The idea of a month all alone in London terrifies me. I won't talk about it here because it is still impossible to foresee what events may lead me to do.

Yesterday, to my great joy, I finished my fifth chapter. It is not just the end of a chapter, you realize, but also the end of Book One; and that Book had me quite worried because it was very tricky to do. I am pleased with it; I believe I have managed to get everything in, without offending the prudes overmuch. And also, it makes a coherent whole; it completes a sweeping tableau. It is a hundred and fifty-five pages long, only five more than the number I had decided on in advance. Since the novel consists of six Books, this means that one sixth of it is done, and I have five more Books to write. I shall start the second one tomorrow. I have finished the outline of its first chapter.

Since I began my novel five weeks ago, I have worked on it every morning but two: the one when I moved to this house and the one when I got news of the great events. So as you can see I am in fine shape, since keeping to a regular schedule of work is the very balance wheel that regulates my life.

After the terribly hot weather we had here, I was afraid there would be storms and heavy rain, but no, not at all, the wind has simply shifted and the weather has got cooler but is still very beautiful. For three days now, it has been delightful. I do not set foot outside the garden, where there is a wicker chaise longue. I lie in it for hours at a stretch to read the papers. There is also a hammock, and Denise and Jacques shake it about to their hearts' content. This garden is a real find. Tall grasses grow in it unhindered, while oaks and acacias provide shade. It is truly a little haven of solitude and untamed nature where you might think you were a hundred miles from any other dwelling. The problem is that as soon as the first rains come we will be obliged to flee, for I imagine the dampness will make it impossible.

Don't worry too much about the letter I wrote to Amélie. From the second letter she sent me, I knew that Albert[1] had stayed behind in Chamonix for a few days. So he must have received my letter and sent it to his mother. You are right to warn Amélie, by the way, so that she can go and inquire about it if she has not received it, for it would be dangerous if it went astray.

What you tell me about the gardeners is again beginning to disturb me and make me angry.[2] I suppose it is difficult to get rid of them at this time, but you mustn't let them get out of bounds. Next spring is a long way off; we can't leave enemies in the house until then. Once I have come home,

---

1 Albert Laborde, son of Alexandrine's cousin Amélie.
2 Octave and Léonie Lenôtre, the gardeners, who had been overly talkative on numerous occasions. Alexandrine was wondering if she was going to keep them on until the spring.

we'll have to talk seriously about what to do. We mustn't let them get away with it.

Tell Mirbeau I was delighted that he refused to fight Millevoye,[3] who is an idiot. For a minute I was afraid he would feel obliged to do him the honour of fighting with him. I would have felt shattered. All our friends, who are being insulted and provoked most abominably, should agree not to fight with scoundrels, for whom a duel is now the only way to climb out of the mud in which they are floundering.

If you had come and if we had had Eugénie, we would have eaten very well here, because the meat is exquisite, although the vegetables are dubious and fruit is completely lacking. But the worst part is their astonishing recipes; for a French person, they spoil everything. I'll explain some of them to you. They're horrible. And such dirt! such a profound lack of well-being in the country of cleanliness and comfort!

If Monsieur le chevalier continues to misbehave, I shall cease to have any respect for him. He will not be invited to the party we will have when I come back.

How heavy time hangs, dear wife. There are days when I am patient, and others when I feel totally lost, like a body without a soul. Well, I kiss you with all my heart and long for the moment when I'll be able to tell you how dreary it has been, all these long days, not having you here with me.

To Alexandrine Zola

[Addlestone] Thursday, 15 September 1898

Dear wife, over here I have felt the repercussions of all your impatience and anxiety at the new dithering and new obstacles we are faced with; and the distance has made me twice as feverish. I am prepared for anything but, even so, I feel the pressure of events. And so, since Monday, I have been on tenterhooks once again. You should see me at eight in the morning, when the local newspapers reach me and, from the dispatches, I try to make out what happened in Paris the day before. Nothing else of a decisive nature is going to happen before Saturday. And since Saturday's news would not reach me until Monday, because of Sunday, I am writing to the good doctor to beg him to send me a telegram on Saturday evening. Believe me, it takes a great deal of courage for me to get down to work every morning, when I feel so impatient and distraught. Thus far, I have had the strength

---

3   Lucien Millevoye (1850–1918) was the political editor of *La Patrie*, an anti-Dreyfusard newspaper, and a Deputy from Paris; an ardent nationalist, he had been one of General Boulanger's chief advisers.

to sit down at my desk, my head in a whirl, and force myself to continue my task in spite of everything.

You tell me Lab. is very optimistic. Well, I am certainly not like him; not that I doubt that we will triumph in the end, but it seems to me that our troubles are not yet over. We are up against too many scoundrels and idiots. It is the idiots especially, certain Ministers, for instance, who become very dangerous. No doubt they will decide in favour of a revision, but I wouldn't be surprised if they delayed it again through their cowardice and stupidity. Furthermore, even when the revision has been decided on, we will still have to live through periods of doubt and excruciating suspense. Then, if the full complement of judges has to be present in the Supreme Court of Appeal, we must wait until the end of the recess, that is, November. And finally, calculate the time it will take to bring the prisoner back, and that takes us up to January or February. I am filled with consternation. What am I going to do? Where shall I wait until then? Naturally, I am saying these things to you only so as to talk about them, for I am determined not to make any decisions in advance; and once again, I repeat, I am waiting to see how things develop. I hope that a month from now we will be able to come to a decision.

You tell me you have made up your mind to return to Paris on the 24th and then to leave for Rome on 1 October. And you add that in your next letter you will explain what you have in mind and will ask me if I approve of your plan. What I approve with no hesitation is the idea of your getting some rest and relaxation at last. You certainly have earned the right to go somewhere else and forget the abominations you have been subjected to for the past six months. So I am absolutely in favour of your going away if you wish to. As for the rest, it will work out, no matter where you are. The idea of spending the winter here terrifies me, and I have no intention of doing any such thing. Jersey, which you suggest, is six or seven hours away by boat; moreover, there are a great many French people there. Besides, I do not want to remain separated from you beyond early November. Therefore, I repeat, we shall have to decide, depending on developments. But in the event that my exile should be prolonged, your being in Italy would not make matters worse for me; on the contrary, because then I might decide to revert to my original idea by going there to join you. Well, let's wait and see.

I do understand that you had no choice but to give the go-between's address to R[einach] for Monod.[1] But I am upset about it because, if Monod comes, it will be a real nuisance for me. I do not want to see him here; someone will have to bring him to some place close by; and you can imagine the complications, all for the sake of a matter that is not of the

1   Gabriel Monod the historian, one of the leading Dreyfusard figures.

slightest importance. I am totally convinced of that in advance. I beg of you, refuse, on my behalf, to give anyone the address; tell people I do not wish to receive anyone and tell them they can write to me by giving their letters to our faithful doctor.

I have had a letter from Albert and Lili.[2] Rest assured; Amélie received my letter. But tell the children that, to be on the safe side, I will not answer them. – I will not answer Bruneau either as long as he has not returned to Paris. I know his new address is in the rue La Boétie but I'm no longer sure whether it's number 122. Let me have the information as soon you know for certain. – I am delighted you are making such a large quantity of plum preserves since that is my favourite kind of jam. I eat a good deal of it here; I fall back on it when the cooking in this country is not to my liking. Their jam is very good but they leave all the stones in it, which is not very tidy. I still long for Eugénie. If we settle down somewhere for the winter, we must send for her and her husband. – It is very nice of the little Italian cousins to send us presents. Tell all those dear people how I am and say that I send love and kisses. Now, Italy has produced yet another assassin; really, there is a country pursued by fate.[3]

After a few relatively cool days, we are having bright sunny weather once again. The whole region is amazed; never before has anyone seen such fine weather. It has not rained for over six weeks and the sky continues blue with not a cloud. I dare not wish for rain because of the children, but personally, I'd be delighted to feel a bit cold.

When you leave for Italy, I'll feel sorry for the poor chevalier. Give Léon firm instructions not to walk him in the evening while we are gone; I'm so worried that he might get lost. And if I came to join you and we sent for Eugénie and her husband, they would bring him to us. Meanwhile, tell him it is naughty of him to have an accident in the bathroom, but don't scold him too much.

How slowly the time drags by, dear wife, how very slowly! I am getting older and my poor broken heart is not as strong as it used to be. It could really use a little certainty.

I kiss you tenderly, and hopefully too, in spite of everything.

To Alexandrine Zola

[Addlestone] Thursday, 22 September 1898

Dear wife, the letter I received from you yesterday was so sad, and it found

---

2   Elina Laborde, Amélie's daughter.
3   The Empress Elizabeth of Austria had been assassinated (in Geneva) by an Italian anarchist, Luigi Luccheni.

me in a despondent frame of mind as well. How well I understand the distress you feel at leaving our poor house in the country! Here, in exile, I cannot think of it without tears springing to my eyes. When will I see it again? Never, perhaps. Sombre thoughts have flooded over me these past two days, and I must ask you to forgive me for not being able to conceal them from you, but I couldn't possibly write to you if I didn't tell you everything. The worst part of it is that they are not just vague thoughts. I do truly despair, because my faith in a happy outcome in the near future is crumbling little by little. Now that a new general is Minister of War and Zurlinden is being kept on as Governor of Paris, I fear the worst.[1] At heart, Brisson is nothing but a coward and an idiot. Because he alone could have settled the whole affair, courageously and promptly, if only he had been willing to take on the responsibilities of Minister of War. As long as the generals have the slightest influence in this affair, truth and justice will be impossible. And this morning came the cruellest stroke of all: I learnt of their latest infamy with regard to Picquart. Their plan is obvious. They want to undermine him so as to invalidate his testimony during the revision. I no longer have the slightest doubt on that score. When Dreyfus reappears before a new court martial, it will convict him all over again in spite of all the evidence, in spite of everything. If he is not acquitted, I have made up my mind never to return to France.

Once again, forgive me for not being able to hide my thoughts from you. They will out whether I like it or not, because I am so thoroughly convinced that far from nearing victory, we are heading towards the most tragic complications. Mind you, I continue to have total faith in the future; we are the truth, we are justice, and we are bound to triumph one day. But – in how many years? ten? twenty? when the scoundrels we are confronted with today are no longer in power? Ah, my poor wife, we might as well pack up our belongings and begin thinking now of settling abroad once and for all. [. . .]

I am sorry now that this letter starts out so despondently. I was furious. I had just read the articles about Picquart. Even so, we must not despair! But what an appalling struggle! If ever we emerge victorious, it will have been a close shave.

Alexandrine finally decided against her trip to Italy. She prepared to join Zola in England once Jeanne and the children had left, which they did on 15 October. In Paris, the fall of Brisson's government on 25 October accelerated the revision process, despite the military authorities' determination to continue prosecuting Picquart, who had been transferred to the Cherche-Midi prison in Paris on 22 September.

1   General Chanoine had been appointed Minister of War (see the Chronology). He had agreed to reinstate General Zurlinden as military Governor of Paris.

To Alexandrine Zola

[Addlestone] Tuesday, 4 October 1898

Maybe, in the midst of such upsetting news,[1] I was wrong to keep on working away so stubbornly at my novel. Since I've begun spending time in the garden, to get some fresh air while I read, my head has been a little clearer. The weather continues to be admirable. In the morning there is the lightest of mists, which the sun dispels immediately. Never have I seen a more beautiful autumn, one so mild and golden. It would be a pleasure to be alive if I didn't feel that moral anguish which continues to weigh upon me in spite of everything. [. . .]

For the sake of my peace of mind, I wish I could recover the faith I have lost. You remember how serenely I used to proclaim, even during the darkest days of my trial, that the truth would triumph over everything. Now as we are drawing near our goal I no longer dare believe that the triumph of truth is inevitable, because what is going on is such a sorry sight that it has destroyed all the hope I once had in men's reason and decency. I know of nothing more dreadful. To think that they are keeping Picquart in prison, that all of Paris did not rise up at the idea that Dreyfus was innocent, that France continues to be accomplice to so many crimes! That means we can expect the worst kinds of infamy, to hide so many other infamies that have already been committed. That is why I continue to be so pessimistic. Until the very last day, the authorities will do everything they can to make the innocent pay the debts of the guilty. Never has a country gone through a more dreadful period. And I will go so far as to say that, even when Dreyfus has been acquitted, you'll see, they will continue to call us traitors and say we've sold out.

To Alexandrine Zola

[Upper Norwood] Tuesday, 18 October 1898

Dear wife, since Saturday, when the children left, I have had no news, and as you can imagine I am almost going out of my mind with anxiety about what may have happened when they arrived in Paris. My instructions were very clear: what little luggage they had they were to leave at the station; they were not to go directly home; they were to go first to another

---

1   Allusion to Pinpin's death on 20 September. Both Zola and his wife were profoundly affected by it.

house to find out the news; and finally they were to come home on foot as if they had been out for a walk. But this morning I still do not know how it all went. I may have information this evening, tomorrow for sure. – The poor things had no winter clothing, hardly even any underclothes. I wouldn't even have known where to send it. – And as I explained to you, I had absolutely no choice but to make them leave, because every single day I feared that I would be discovered along with them. [. . .]

I do believe that although matters concerning the revision are moving slowly, they are not going too badly. I devoutly hope that the Supreme Court of Appeal will carry out a thorough investigation, even if that means I'll be forced to stay here two months longer. It would be sure to bring victory, and that is the only way I can come back to Paris: victorious.

On 27 October, the Criminal Chamber of the Supreme Court of Appeal began to examine Lucie Dreyfus's petition for a revision. Two days later it declared her petition was admissible and decided to conduct an investigation.

In one of his letters, Labori commented on this development in these terms: 'So it is that, thanks to you, the hour of justice is beginning to dawn [. . .]. I cannot let this day go by without paying homage to you, expressing my profound admiration and affection.' Here is Zola's reply.

On the same day, Zola wrote to Reinach who, a little earlier, had published, in Le Siècle, *a long article entitled 'Esterhazy's accomplices'.*

To Fernand Labori

[Upper Norwood] Sunday, 30 October 1898

My dear friend, thank you for your good letter. I am deeply touched. The feeling which dictated it to you goes straight to my heart. But as you know, I have never accepted your praise without referring a large share of it back to you. You are responsible for this victory as much as I am; my triumph is simply your triumph, for it is you who have made of my protest what it has become; such a resounding inquiry, such an eloquent cry that since then the clamour for truth has swelled throughout the entire world. And today the truth is being revealed, thanks to you.

Last night, at the same time as your letter, I received a telegram from a friend informing me of the decision by the Supreme Court of Appeal. This means our salvation, since it has been decided to carry out a thorough investigation. Henceforth, Dreyfus stands acquitted. I had been terrified of only one thing: the infamous possibility of a new court martial, if all of the facts were not brought to light.

So I am overjoyed. But it does mean that I shall have to remain here two more long months, and I must confess that exile is beginning to weigh singularly heavy upon me. I was quite ill but now I am back on my feet and have been able to resume my work. And my wife has arrived, which is a very great joy to me, for she will help me to bear my lonely situation, far from everything I am accustomed to and all my friends. We are going to organize ourselves so as to spend the winter here as snugly as possible. And besides, I have no right to complain, since Picquart, the heroic Picquart, is far more unhappy than I. I hope that now they will be forced to release him. Give him my most affectionate good wishes, the very first time you see him.

Please assure Mme Labori that we mourn with her and share fully in her grief. My wife, who was very sorry not to see her, sends her her deepest sympathies. And to you, my dear friend, we send our very warmest thoughts.

Affectionately yours.

The next two letters, both to Jeanne,[1] show Zola's keen interest in photography. He took a good many photographs while in exile. Denise and Jacques were his favourite subjects, but he also did a number of landscapes and scenes from daily life in England.

To Jeanne Rozerot

[Upper Norwood] Thursday, 17 November 1898

My beloved wife, you have given me great pleasure by sending me the children's photographs. I think Denise's is very good, though she has a slightly sad expression. As for Jacques, he is making that little face of his, but the trousers change him so much that I mistook him for a real gentleman.

I'd like to have just Jacques's head, his bust, exactly the same size as the one you have sent me of Denise.

I have my eye on a double frame, made of silver, that I have seen at the jeweller's here, and that I would buy if I could use it, that is, if I had the heads of my two darlings, of a similar size and facing each other. I mean, not turning their backs on each other, or rather, both in profile but not facing the same way. Since you tell me that more prints are on their way, maybe you will be sending me one of Jacques's head, similar to Denise's.

1   They were published, in French, in *Les Cahiers naturalistes*, n° 66, 1992, pp. 233–5.

Otherwise you could have one made by giving back a print of Denise's head to Pierre Petit[2] and telling him to do one of Jacques, making it the same size and in such a way that the two heads face one another. [. . .]

No, don't send me the photographs of you all that Mme Triouleyre took.[3] You know how happy I would be to have them, but what's the point of giving them to me if I can't place them on my desk for all to see [. . .]?[4]

To Jeanne Rozerot

[Upper Norwood] Sunday, 20 November 1898

My adored little wife, I have received all of the portraits of the children. No, you didn't get it wrong; you did send me the two different poses of Denise. This makes me very happy because what I asked you for does exist and now I have two pictures of our darlings, both the same size and looking at each other. And I've gone ahead and bought the little silver frame I mentioned to you. It is in the shape of a double heart, very simple and very pretty. I am going to cut out the two photographs and place them on my desk in the frame. I think Denise's picture is much better than Jacques's. His hair is too smoothly combed and his expression does not look natural. He seems to be making a face; no doubt he was told he had to smile. Never mind; he looks sweet nonetheless.

Will you please send me another print of Jacques's picture in your next letter? That way, in addition to the two pictures that I am going to frame, I shall have another pair, since I already have two of Denise. Here are some more snapshots that we took together here. There are a dozen of them but these are the last I shall be able to send you, since only three prints were made of each one. First of all I set aside two complete series, one for you, one for me. Then, out of the third series, Vizetelly took about thirty, the best and most interesting ones, so that the ones I sent you, in three batches, are only the ones he let me keep.

And I am giving you the rest today except for a few that are repeats or that are not very gay, like the cemeteries. But rest assured that I have kept the complete set that I made for you and will put together a nice album of them. However, the pictures stop at 'our arrival at Summerfield'. I have sent about a hundred more to be developed, all the ones we took 'after our arrival at Summerfield', and I won't have those

2   A professional photographer.
3   A friend of Jeanne and the children.
4   An allusion to Alexandrine, who had been at Upper Norwood since 25 October. (She left on 5 December.)

for a month. [. . .] At any rate, they will be developed and I will make prints of them in Paris. [. . .]

Would the investigation ordered by the Supreme Court of Appeal enable the exile to come home at last? (It was not brought to a close until 9 February 1899.) On 5 December, Alexandrine had had lunch at the home of Octave Mirbeau, along with Clemenceau and Reinach, and had found all of them 'extraordinarily pessimistic' on that score. She conveyed this information to Zola.

To Alexandrine Zola

[Upper Norwood] Thursday, 8 December 1898

Your letter has made me somewhat irritated with our friends, and I want them to know immediately how I feel about it. It is out of the question for me to stay here until the end of February, and if people abandon me too harshly, I will do what I have always done: I will act on my own, strictly on my own, and that will suit me just fine. I know that I am right in wanting to come home, I can feel it, and never has my intuition deceived me. I don't care in the least whether I come home in triumph; all I want to do is resume my role in the battle, if necessary. Tell them this.

Note for Labori

I am surprised to see my friends express such keen anxiety at the idea that I wish to come back to France. I don't know as yet what the Court will decide with regard to Picquart, and anyhow his case is not the same as mine. But already a magistrate's court, ruling on a suit brought against him, has decided that the cases closely related to the Dreyfus Affair cannot be judged fairly until the Court has concluded its investigation. And that is enough, it seems to me, to clarify my own situation.

There can be no doubt that my trial is closely related to the Dreyfus Affair. I am being tried on the strength of a single sentence: 'A court martial, acting on orders, has just dared to acquit such a man as Esterhazy. Truth itself and justice itself have been slapped in the face.' Therefore, even if the accusation of libel remains because of the 'acting on orders', there is also the question of good faith, and it becomes very important to know whether Esterhazy is innocent or guilty because, if he is guilty, then of course that will be an extenuating circumstance in my favour. But it is that very point which the Court is in the process of bringing to light, and in fact we know that it has been brought to light, that Esterhazy now stands convicted of having written the bordereau, which is what M. Mathieu Dreyfus's complaint accused him of. He was summoned before a court martial to answer that charge and that charge only, and his acquittal by the court martial signified quite simply that he had not written the bordereau. Now, if the Court establishes, on the contrary, that he did write it, won't that constitute a decisive argument in favour of my good faith? Can I be judged at the present time before the results of the Court's investigation are known? That would be contrary to every notion of common sense and justice.

The fact that military justice is prosecuting Picquart so relentlessly is understandable; they are taking revenge. But why would civil justice pursue me with equal vengeance? – me, of all people? I am not trying to elude justice; I am asking that the truth be brought to light – the light I have so ardently striven to find – before I am judged. And it seems to me that all decent people will be on our side, that it is unthinkable that I should be summoned to appear at Versailles now, until the truth I have been searching for is known in full.

Besides, can anyone believe for one minute that the Ministry of Justice and the public prosecutor's office *really* want my case to come up just at this time? Imagine it! At the very same time that the Court was conducting its investigation, they would allow us to open ours in Versailles! We could make every one of the witnesses called by the Court parade before the jury of Seine-et-Oise. We would be stirring up all of that terrible agitation all over again; we would force the generals to come and perjure themselves once more, in public. Such scandal all over again! What an opportunity to force the truth out into the open! No, they cannot possibly want that to happen. They will be scared. Especially since, whatever happens, our appeal is still pending before the Supreme Court of Appeal which, once again, may rule against them. Even if they did convict me, the disgrace of it would fall entirely on them. Personally, I am prepared to go to prison. Sometimes I'm sorry I'm not in prison. There are times when I even wonder if it wouldn't be an excellent tactic to return to France straight away, so as to show them we're not afraid any more and force them to retreat. – There is an article ready and waiting to appear in *L'Aurore*; it would explain why I'm coming back, and how.

If my friends consider it impossible for me to come back, then let them at least explain to me the reasons for their anxiety, which I do not understand. I'm sure they are not afraid to fight. But then why are they so cautious on my behalf? I will not remain where I am unless they can prove to me that by coming back to France I would compromise the cause.

On a little English greeting card bearing the printed message, 'Joyful greetings', here are a few lines to Jeanne celebrating the anniversary of their love affair, which had begun a decade earlier.

To Jeanne Rozerot

[Upper Norwood] 11 December 1898

To my beloved Jeanne, a thousand loving kisses from the depths of my exile, in remembrance of 11 December 1888, with gratitude for our ten happy years as a couple, and for the bond between us that was strengthened forever by the arrival of our Denise and our Jacques.

The leaders of the Dreyfusards responded to Zola's note of 8 December just as Alexandrine had predicted: it was impossible for him to return to Paris. Labori explained the reasons for their position to Zola, who accepted them. He bowed to the decision with abnegation.

To Fernand Labori

[Upper Norwood] Thursday, 15 December 1898

My dear, faithful friend, thank you for your long and admirable letter in which you explain, so very clearly, what you believe my present situation to be and the obligations that it places on me. For my part, I am still absolutely convinced, I must confess, that it is now possible for me to return to France, that we'd certainly find a way to prevent the government from resuming the trial in Versailles before the Court had completed its investigation and that this would be a new victory for us. But I bow to the decision you outline since you maintain that my return would be dangerous for the other people involved in our struggle and damaging to our cause. Beyond a doubt this is the greatest sacrifice I have made yet to that cause.

I am in a weary mood. I am weary of peace and safety. You cannot imagine the anguish I feel each morning as I read the papers. I have the feeling I'm not the slightest use any more; I'm a dead man, while the others continue to fight. And this is going to go on for months, far away from those I love, far from everything my mind and my heart are accustomed to.

As for changing my place of refuge, what good would that do?[1] I'd be like a sick man: he may turn over and over in his bed but he still has a fever. I have settled in here. If I went elsewhere I'd have to go through the whole difficult and dangerous process again. So I have decided not to budge; that way it is simpler and more dignified. I have all sorts of reasons for staying where I am.

You ask me what I think of events as I observe them from a distance. Henceforth I am certain we will win the day, but I am also convinced that until the very last moment the scoundrels will do all they can to impede justice. The heroic Picquart appears to have been saved – thanks to you, in fact. Now they will hound Urbain Gohier[2] and Reinach; and you can be sure that on the very eve of Dreyfus's acquittal they will still attempt some idiotic and outrageous manoeuvre. Ah, poor France! The thought of our poor country fills me with anxiety every minute of the day. Once our victory has been won, everything all about us will lie in ruins, and how shall we ever reconstruct a sturdy house with such rotting and shattered materials? That is the terrifying prospect.

Thank you for the affectionate and devoted way you are handling all of the secondary matters.[3] I have lost interest in them to some extent, I must admit, because as I said I consider myself a dead man, since I am barred from my own country, and must remain far away and silent, for so many days to come. Well, at least I can work. That is my sole consolation.

Please express my very warmest regards to Mme Labori. And thank you, thank you, my dear and faithful friend, for all the generous things you have done, and all you will be doing in the future.

Yours affectionately.

---

1 Labori was suggesting Italy.
2 A journalist with *L'Aurore*, who was being sued for his articles criticizing the army.
3 The attacks on Zola and his father by Judet, Zola's complaint against Judet in response and the ensuing legal entanglements.

Part Three
Waiting for Victory

Justice

It is almost eleven months since I left France. For eleven months, I forced myself to live a life of total exile and observe total silence, and kept my whereabouts strictly secret. I deliberately lay in the depths of the tomb as if dead, and awaited truth and justice. Today, the truth has won, justice reigns at last, and I am reborn. I have come back to resume my place on French soil.

It was on 18 July 1898 that I bled every drop of my blood, and it will remain the most dreadful day of my life, for it was on 18 July that I gave in to tactical necessity on the advice of my comrades in arms, who were fighting the same battle as I was, for the honour of France. I had to tear myself away from all that was dear to me, from all the habits of heart and mind. And although threats and insults have been heaped upon me in all the days since then, that abrupt departure was surely the cruellest sacrifice I have been required to make for the cause. It was my supreme act of immolation. The base and silly people who have assumed that my purpose was to avoid going to prison and have spread that story everywhere have been as petty as they are stupid.

Avoid going to prison, for heaven's sake! I have never asked for anything else but prison! And I am still prepared to go to prison, if necessary! Anyone who accuses me of running away from prison must have forgotten the entire story, including the trial that I deliberately provoked solely because I wanted it to be the field in which truth would be sown and harvested, and the way I completely sacrificed my peace and quiet and my freedom, offering myself up as a holocaust and willing, in advance, to be ruined, so long as justice emerged triumphant. Isn't it blindingly obvious today that the long campaign led by my legal advisers, my friends and myself, was nothing other than a disinterested struggle to shed the clearest possible light on the facts? Why did we try to gain time? Why did we meet one procedural ploy with another? Because we were responsible for the truth, the way you are responsible for your family, and while the faint glimmer of truth we held in our hands was growing brighter daily, we did not want it to flicker out. It was like carrying a sacred lamp on a very blustery day; we had to shield it from the crowd, whipped into a frenzy by lies. We had but a single tactic: to remain in control of our Affair, make it last as long as we could so that it would cause other events to occur, and let it produce the decisive evidence we were determined to find. We never gave ourselves a thought; every one of our actions was intended to make right and reason triumph. For this we were ready to pay with our liberty and our lives.

Let the reader recall the situation I was in in July, in Versailles. I was being strangled, wordlessly. And I did not want to be strangled in silence, while the Parliament was in recess and demonstrations were filling the streets. We wanted to last until October in the hope that by then the truth would have marched still further and justice would then become inevitable. In addition, you must not forget all the work that was constantly going on behind the scenes, and everything we were expecting to emerge from the investigations under way against Esterhazy and Colonel Picquart, both of whom were in prison. We were aware that if the investigations were conducted fairly, they would inevitably shed vivid light on the facts; and although we could not foresee Colonel Henry's confession, followed by his suicide, we knew that any day there would inevitably be some startling development which would reveal the monstrous Affair in its true and sinister light. In those circumstances, isn't it understandable that we wished to stall for time? Were we not right to use every legal means available so as to choose the most favourable moment, in the best interests of justice? Stalling for time meant winning, after the most painful and sacred of struggles. We had to wait at all costs, because on the basis of everything we knew and hoped for, we could expect victory to come in the autumn. Once again, we ourselves did not count; our only aim was to save an innocent man and avert the most frightful moral disaster that had ever threatened our country. And those reasons were so compelling that I resigned myself to leaving, announcing that I would return in October. In so doing I felt certain of helping the cause and hastening its triumph.

One day, but not now, I will talk about that sacrifice – how bitter it was to me, what a wrench it was. People forget that I am neither a polemicist nor a politician, deriving benefit from every quarrel. I am a writer with no ties of any sort. I have had but one passion throughout my life – a passionate attachment to truth, and I have fought for truth on every battlefield. For nearly forty years I have used my pen and all my courage, all my capacity for work and all my good faith in the service of my country. And it is frightfully painful, believe me, to slip away all alone on a dark night and watch the lights of France fade away in the distance, when all you have wanted to do is defend the honour of France and the justice and grandeur of its people. I, who have sung hymns of praise to France in over forty works! I, whose whole life has been one long effort to carry the name of France to the four corners of the earth! I, obliged to flee, to steal away like that with a mob of scoundrels and madmen hot on my heels, hurling threats and insults at me! Moments such as that are atrocious, and from them your soul emerges as tough as tempered steel, invulnerable to iniquitous wounds. And then came those long months of exile. Can you imagine what torture it is to be struck from the list of the living, to wait each day for justice to awaken and find the awakening delayed each time? I would not wish even the worst criminal to suffer as I did every morning for eleven months upon reading the dispatches from France in that foreign land, where they took on terrifying echoes of folly and disaster. To know what exile means, in the tragic circumstances in which I have just experienced it, you have to have endured such torment throughout the long solitary hours; you have to have relived, far away and all alone, the crisis in which your country was collapsing. As for the silly people who think I went away to avoid going to prison and to have a good time abroad with Jewish gold to support me – all I can feel for them is a little disgust and a great deal of pity.

*

I was supposed to come back in October. We had resolved to stall until the two Chambers were back in session; we were counting on some unforeseen event which, on the basis of what we knew, was certain to occur. And in fact the unforeseen event did not even wait for the month of October. It burst on the scene at the end of August, with Colonel Henry's confession and suicide.

The very next day, I wanted to return to France. As far as I was concerned, the revision was now inevitable and Dreyfus's innocence was going to be acknowledged immediately. Besides, I had never wished for anything but a revision, my role was bound to come to an end as soon as the case came before the Supreme Court of Appeal, and I was prepared to fade out of the picture. As for my own trial, in my view it was no longer anything but a mere formality, since the document on the strength of which the jury had convicted me – the document produced by Generals de Pellieux, Gonse and de Boisdeffre – was a forgery, and the forger had just taken refuge in death. Accordingly, I was preparing to come back when my friends in Paris, my legal advisers and all those who were still in the thick of the battle wrote me very anxious letters. The situation was still extremely serious. The revision was still far from being a foregone conclusion. M. Brisson, the Prime Minister, was constantly encountering new obstacles and being betrayed by everyone; he did not even have an ordinary police superintendent at his disposal. So that if I were to come back while feelings were still running so high, that might be the pretext for new outbreaks of violence and hence a danger for the cause and an additional problem for the government, which was already facing a difficult task. Since I did not wish to complicate matters, I had to give way and agree to be patient a little longer.

When the case was at last referred to the Criminal Chamber, I wanted to return to France. I repeat: I had never asked for anything but a revision; I considered that my role was ended since the Affair had been brought before the highest court instituted by our laws. But again I received letters begging me to wait, not to act hastily. Whereas the situation seemed simple to me, they told me that on the contrary it was full of dark corners and rife with danger. My name and reputation could not fail to be a torch which would rekindle the flames. And on those grounds my friends and advisers appealed to my civic-mindedness, urging me to wait until calm had been restored and public opinion had swung the other way, as it was bound to, so as to avoid plunging our poor country into further upheaval. The Affair was moving in the right direction but nothing was over yet, and how bitterly I would regret it if an impatient move on my part were to delay the triumphant revelation of the truth! And once again I gave way, and continued to be tormented by my silence and my isolation.

When the Criminal Chamber, accepting the request for revision, decided to conduct a sweeping investigation, I wanted to return to France. This time, I must admit, my courage was exhausted. I realized that this investigation would last for many months and I had a presentiment of the continual state of anxiety that I would be in because of it. And really, hadn't enough of the facts been brought to light? Hadn't the report by Justice Bard, the indictment by Manau, the public prosecutor, and the plea by Maître Mornard, the lawyer, established enough of the truth for me to be able to come home, my head held high? Every one of the accusations I had made in my 'Letter to the President of the Republic' was borne out. I had played my role; now all I had to do was step out of the spotlight. Imagine, then, how profoundly sad it made me feel, how indignant and rebellious, at first, when I found that my friends were once again expressing the same resistance at the idea of my returning to France. They were still in the thick of the fighting; they wrote to me that I could not gauge the situation as they could and that it would be a dangerous mistake to let my trial begin again at the same time as the investigation by the Criminal Chamber. The new government was opposed to the revision and might seize upon my trial as the pretext, the opportunity it was looking for to set up new stumbling blocks. Besides, the Court needed to be able to work without any disturbance; it would have been misguided on my part to come and stir up popular feeling, which would infallibly be seized upon and used against us. I protested; I even considered disregarding all of their advice and returning to Paris one fine evening without notifying anyone. Then at last I saw the wisdom of their words, and once again I resigned myself to many long months of torture.

There you have the reasons why I did not come back to Paris for nearly eleven months. By standing aside I was merely being a soldier in the battle for truth and justice, just as on the day when I stepped forward. I was merely the good citizen, devoted enough to go into exile, to disappear altogether, even willing to cease to exist if that would help restore calm in his country and avoid inflaming the atmosphere surrounding the monstrous Affair. I must add that, being certain of the ultimate victory, I kept my trial in reserve as the final resource, the little sacred lamp which we would re-light if the evil powers succeeded in extinguishing the sun. I took my abnegation so seriously that I observed a total silence. I decided to be not only a dead man but a dead man who did not talk. The minute I crossed the border, I said not a word. One must not speak if one is absent and cannot take responsibility for what one has said. No one heard me. No one saw me. I repeat: I was in the tomb, in an inviolable retreat, of which not a single stranger was able to find the whereabouts. The few journalists who let it be understood that they had found me were lying. I did not receive a single journalist. I dwelt in the desert, unknown to anyone. And I wonder what my country, which is so hard on me, can reproach me with during the eleven months of voluntary banishment I suffered, in dignified and patriotic silence, in order to bring peace to it again.

*

It is all over now and I have come back, since the truth is being brought to light and justice is being done. I wish to come back in silence, serenely confident in victory; I hope that my return to France will not cause any unruliness, any demonstrations. It would be unworthy of me if anyone, even for an instant, was able to confuse me with the vile exploiters of mass movements. Just as I kept silent while I was living outside France, it is my wish now to resume my accustomed labours and my place as a peaceful citizen who has come home again, without disturbing anyone or drawing attention to himself.

Now that the good fight has been fought, I do not want any applause or reward, even if it is felt that I did make a useful contribution. It was such a fine cause, such a righteous one that I do not deserve any praise. The victor is truth; no other outcome was possible. From the very first minute, I was certain of it; I moved straight ahead, and as I never doubted, I did not need a great deal of courage. It was all very simple. If they must pay tribute to me, let them only say that I have never, consciously or unconsciously, done any harm. I have my reward already: the thought of the innocent man whom I have helped to raise from the grave where he had been buried alive for four years. Yes, the idea that he will be coming back, the thought of seeing him a free man and shaking his hand, is extraordinarily moving, I admit it, and my eyes brim with tears of joy. That minute will be ample payment for all the cares I have had. My friends and I will have done a good deed, and the goodhearted people of France will be grateful to us for it. What more could we ask for? A family who will love us, a wife and children who will bless us, a man who will embody the triumph of the law and of human solidarity, thanks to us!

But, although my part in the current struggle is over, although I do not wish to use this victory for purposes of revenge or to obtain a term of office, a prominent position or honours, although my sole ambition is to continue fighting for the truth with my pen as long as my hand can go on holding it, I would like to point out – before I move on to other campaigns, other causes – how prudent and moderate I have been in the course of this one. Does anyone recall the abominable chorus of protests that greeted my 'Letter to the President of the Republic'? I had insulted the army; I was a traitor; I was devoid of patriotism. Literary friends of mine were appalled, overcome with consternation; they shrank from me, abandoned me to the horror of my crime. Articles were written which will now weigh heavy on their authors' consciences. Never had any writer, no matter how coarse, or mad, or blinded by self-importance, sent to any head of state a more unrefined, more fallacious, more criminal letter. And now, let them re-read that poor letter of mine. I must confess that by now I am a little ashamed of it – ashamed to see how discreet it was, how opportunistic, I might almost say, how cowardly. Yes, now that I am making my confession, I can admit that I toned down that letter considerably; I even kept silent concerning many things which today are known and proven but which at that time I was still trying to doubt, so monstrous and irrational did they seem to me. Yes, I suspected Henry already, but since I had no proof I felt it was wiser to avoid even mentioning his name. I guessed many parts of the story; certain secrets had been confided to me but they were so appalling that I did not feel I had the right to risk setting off their dreadful consequences. And now they have been revealed and the truth of them has become an accepted fact! And now my poor letter no longer hits the mark and looks altogether childish, a mere mawkish tale dreamt up by a timid novelist, compared with the fierce and awe-inspiring reality!

I repeat: I have no desire and no need to crow triumphantly. Yet I cannot help noting that the events have borne out all my accusations. The guilt of every single man I accused has been demonstrated in the glaring light of the investigation. Everything I announced, everything I predicted stands before us, unmistakable. And something else from which I derive a sweeter pride is that my letter was dignified, worthy of me, indignant but not violent. It contains not one insult, not one word that is uncalled for, nothing but the pure-minded bewilderment of a citizen asking his head of state to render justice. This has been the everlasting pattern with all of my works: never have I been able to write one book, one page, without having lies and insults heaped upon me – even though, the next day, they have had to concede that I was right.

Thus, I am serene; my soul feels no wrath, no rancour. If I heeded the temptation to be soft-hearted, in accordance with the disdain my intellect feels, I would even be in favour of granting a pardon to all of the wrong-doers; the public's lasting scorn of them would be their sole punishment. But I believe that some legal punishment is necessary. The decisive argument is this: if no awe-inspiring example is set, if justice does not strike those in high places who are guilty, the ordinary people will never know how great the crime has been. The pillory must be erected so that the people will know, at last. Thus, while I will not assist Nemesis, I will leave her to carry out her vengeful task. As a poet, for whom the triumph of an ideal is satisfaction enough, I may be indulgent. Yet one cause for the most intense rebellion remains: the dreadful thought that Colonel Picquart is still behind bars. Not one day went by, during my time in exile, without my thoughts turning to him, in pain and brotherhood, in his prison. To think that they arrested Picquart, that for almost a year they have been keeping him in jail, like some delinquent, that they have prolonged his torments through the most infamous mockery of justice! It is a monstrous fact, and it makes a rational mind seethe. All who have been instrumental in this supreme iniquity will bear the indelible stain of it. And if, tomorrow, Picquart is not free, then all of France will be forever branded by the inexplicable folly of having left the noblest, most heroic and most glorious of its children in the clutches of torturers, liars and forgers.

Not until Picquart is free will the achievement be complete. And it is not a harvest of hate that we have sown but a harvest of goodness, justice and infinite hope. We must let it grow. Today we can only predict how abundant it will be. All of the political parties have collapsed, and the country is split into two camps: in the one, the reactionary forces of the past; in the other, the forces of open-minded inquiry, truth and righteousness marching towards the future. Those advanced outposts are the only logical ones; we must guard them for tomorrow's conquests. Well then, to work! To work by the pen! To work by words, by deeds! Let us work for progress and deliverance. Let us complete the efforts of 1789, and bring the peaceful revolution of minds and hearts, the democracy and solidarity which, freed from evil powers and based at last on the sanctity of labour, will make possible the equitable distribution of wealth. Then France, a free nation, holding aloft the scales of justice, ushering in the just society of the coming century, will once again be sovereign among nations. No empire, no matter how many weapons it brandishes, will be able to resist once France has given justice to the world, as it has already given liberty. I cannot picture any other role in history for France, and its glory will be more resplendent than any it has yet known.

I am at home. Thus, whenever it may please the public prosecutor, he can officially notify to me the verdict from the Assize Court in Versailles, which sentenced me, in absentia, to one year in prison and a fine of three thousand francs. And once again we shall come before the jury.

When I forced the law to take action against me, my only goals were truth and justice. Today, they have been established. My trial is no longer useful, and it no longer interests me. The law must simply state whether it is a crime to strive for truth.

L'Aurore, 5 June 1899

Since 1 July, when Alfred Dreyfus returned to France, he had been held in the military prison in Rennes. On 4 July his lawyers, Edgar Demange and Fernand Labori, were able to hand him the court record of Zola's trial in February 1898 and the text of the investigation conducted by the Criminal Chamber of the Supreme Court of Appeal.

To Alfred Dreyfus

Paris, 6 July 1899

Dear Captain Dreyfus,

I was not among the very first to write you, as soon as you came back to France, to express all of my affection and friendship, because I feared that my letter would be incomprehensible to you. And I wished to wait until your admirable brother[1] had seen you and told you of our lengthy struggle. He has just brought me good news concerning your health, your courage and your faith. Now I can open my heart to you, knowing that now you will understand me.

How heroic your brother has been! He is devotion, courage and wisdom personified. It is thanks to him that we have proclaimed your innocence for the past eighteen months. What joy he brings me now, assuring me that you have emerged alive from the grave, that your abominable martyrdom has made you greater and purer! For our task is not yet over. Your innocence must be recognized at the highest level; it must save France from the moral disaster in which the country has nearly been swallowed up. As long as the innocent man is still behind bars we cease to rank among the just and noble nations. At present, your lofty role is to bring us justice and thereby peace of mind, to lay balm at last upon this great but troubled country of ours, by completing our mission, seeing to it that amends are made, showing the man we have fought for, the man who, through our efforts, embodies the triumph of human solidarity. When the innocent man stands up for all to see, France will once again become the land of fairness and goodness.

At the same time you will save the honour of the army that you have loved so wholeheartedly, the army that has been such an all-encompassing ideal to you. Do not listen to those who seek to aggrandize the army through falsehood and injustice, for they blaspheme. It is we who are the army's true defenders. It is we who will acclaim it the day your comrades acquit you, for their willingness to acknowledge that an error was made will offer the entire world a sublime and saintly spectacle. And on that day, the army will be more than a pillar of strength; it will be justice.

---

1   Mathieu Dreyfus, who had been leading the entire campaign for a revision since 1895.

My heart is full to overflowing, and I can only express my brotherly commiseration for all that you and your valiant wife have suffered. My own wife and I would like to send you, through this letter, whatever is best, noblest and tenderest in ourselves, so that you may feel assured that all decent people are on your side.

With my warmest and most affectionate wishes.

Dreyfus's trial in Rennes was about to open. Zola decided not to attend it. He explained why to Philippe Dubois, who once again had come to Médan to interview him. Zola took this opportunity to outline his literary projects and talk about the exile he had just experienced in England.

At the home of Emile Zola, in Médan

Bicycling and photography – Charpentier's gold medal – Why Zola will not be going to Rennes – Why he will never write a novel or a play about the Affair – These things belong to History – The album of exile.

As I pedalled towards Médan, bathed by the cool morning air and relishing the pungent odour of the woods and fields, I said to myself,

'If I find Zola at home in weather like this, I'll be very lucky!'

For I remembered that the author of *Fécondité* was a keen velocipedist, like myself, and that all summer long, the local countryfolk invariably encounter him on the road, wearing his black velvet jacket and his straw 'colonial' as he rides his steel mount.

But when I reached the famous house that has so often been described, situated behind the little church of the charming village where Zola has had his country home for so many years, I looked through the gate, and there in the garden I could see the servant who was carefully polishing his master's bicycle. This sight reassured me.

'M. Zola is in his darkroom,' the servant told me. 'He is developing his plates. I shall inform him of your visit.'

Cycling and photography are Zola's chief occupations when he is on holiday. A few minutes later Zola, in country garb – a white flannel jacket criss-crossed with black lines, and slippers – came to join me in the little sitting room on the ground floor where the servant had shown me in. Smiling, he held out his hand.

'How am I? Quite well. Or rather, better. When I came back from England, I was not altogether well. I'm still not quite over it. But that's a thing of the past now. Fresh air and bicycling will complete the cure.'

Zola informed me that he had been living in Médan for only three days. He had remained in Paris so as to be at his lawyers' disposal for as long as was necessary, living the life of a recluse, going out but little, receiving only a few very close friends, above all avoiding anything that could furnish a pretext for a demonstration of any kind, favourable or unfavourable. When he felt that his presence was no longer useful, he had finally gone away to the country.

'There is nothing to be triumphant about as yet, since Captain Dreyfus is still in prison,' he said. 'That is why I urged our friends to leave Charpentier's gold medal in the safe at the Crédit Lyonnais, where it was placed last year. Just recently they wanted to present me with it.[1] Later, we shall see.'

'They say you will be going to Rennes. Is that true?'

'Not at all. I was offered several places to stay, including a château close by. I refused. What would I do in Rennes? Satisfy my curiosity? I am not a witness. My presence there could be exploited by our opponents. If I took such a step, it might make certain people think that I still felt some doubt as to the outcome of the trial, whereas I have no doubt whatsoever. I shall stay in Médan and await – not without impatience and excitement, I must confess – the news that will reach me each day. I will not budge from here. As for the outcome, once again, I believe we can be confident. The court martial in Rennes will acquit Dreyfus and reinstate him, for his innocence is obvious to all.'

I took the liberty of questioning the eminent writer about his work in progress.

'Since completing *Fécondité*, which *L'Aurore* is publishing, I have not undertaken anything serious. I have merely jotted down a few scattered ideas. Please tell your readers, by the by, that I do not wish to derive any literary benefit from the Dreyfus Affair. In England, Mr Vizetelly, my translator, received on my behalf heaps of letters which contained proposals of all kinds. I was offered vast sums of money to lecture in America.[2] I was promised one hundred thousand francs outright, plus a percentage of the receipts, if I would consent to write a play. I was also asked to write a novel. I have refused everything.

'It would be base and ugly on my part to exploit the Dreyfus Affair. Besides, the Affair belongs to History, and to History only. The story of it is

1   The idea of a medal to commemorate 'J'accuse' went back to March 1898 (see the Chronology). The project had been carried out by a sculptor named Alexandre Charpentier. Not until January 1900 was the medal officially bestowed on Zola.
2   An allusion to the offers made by Paul Meyer and Edmund Gerson in August 1898 through Eugène Fasquelle, Zola's publisher in Paris. Edmund Gerson ran a famous theatrical agency in New York; he urged Zola to write a play 'in four or five acts' on the Dreyfus Affair. Paul Meyer was one of the representatives of the Société des gens de lettres in the United States, especially with regard to the translation of French books.

so beautiful, so tragic, so complete in itself that I cannot picture it in the theatre. Moreover, it involves people who are alive today. Making a play out of it would call for the addition of a fictional element that would denature it.'

Zola was talking rather heatedly, and it was striking to see how voluble he became.

'I insist,' he repeated, *'never will I write a novel or a play about the Dreyfus Affair.* Now, what I may do one day is to sum up, in just a few pages, my personal impressions during my trials or while I was in exile. Those notes will be my contribution to history. I will write them for use by authors who, in fifty years, for instance, when they have the benefit of hindsight, will want to study the events of our time as they truly were.'

Whereupon, leaving the Dreyfus Affair aside, we discussed photography.

'Would it be too inquisitive, dear Maître, to ask for some information about the plates you were developing a while ago?'

'Not at all. They are plates from England – photographs of town houses, streets and pubs in London, and also pictures of some of the poor, ragged cripples you see so many of over there, alas! Poor devils; they are hideous, pitiful. I took three hundred pictures with a little compact $6^1/_2 \times 9$ camera that I attached to the handlebars of my bicycle whenever I went out for a ride. I obtained marvellously sharp, clear pictures with it. I shall collect all my photographs together into the album of my exile. It will be full of interesting documents and mementoes. Unfortunately, while I was travelling, four of the plates, which had already been developed, got broken. One of them showed the wonderful display at a flower-seller's shop. Every morning for two months while my wife was ill, I went to that shop to buy her flowers and brought them to her.'[3]

And Zola added, in the melancholy tone that all amateur photographers share in such a case,

'Naturally, the plates that broke during the journey were the best of the whole collection.'

When I took my leave, Zola returned to his laboratory.

Ph. Dubois
L'Aurore, 29 July 1899

The Fifth Act

I am terrified. What I feel is no longer anger, no longer indignation and the craving to avenge it, no longer the need to denounce a crime and demand

---

3   In January and February 1899, during her second stay in England.

its punishment, in the name of truth and justice. I am terrified, filled with the sacred awe of a man who witnesses the supernatural: rivers flowing backwards towards their sources and the earth toppling over under the sun. I cry out with consternation, for our noble and generous France has fallen to the bottom of the abyss.

We had assumed that the trial in Rennes was the fifth act of the dreadful tragedy in which we have been ensnared for nearly two years. All of the dangerous obstacles had been overcome, it seemed; we believed we were moving towards a conclusion of concord and pacification. After an excru-ciating battle, the victory of the law appeared inevitable, and the drama would have a happy ending, the classic triumph of the innocent man. But no, we were mistaken! A new obstacle has arisen, the most unexpected and dreadful of them all, making the drama more sombre still, prolonging it, dragging it out towards some unforeseeable end. Our minds shudder and reel at the prospect.

Beyond a doubt, the trial in Rennes was only the fourth act. But great God in Heaven, what will the fifth act be like? What new pain and suffering will it be composed of? Into what supreme expiation will it plunge this nation? One thing is certain: an innocent man cannot be convicted twice without the sun turning dark and the peoples of the world rising up.

*

Ah, that fourth act! that trial in Rennes! Imagine my moral agony as it went on. Out of civic duty, I had left the stage and hidden myself away in utter solitude so as to cease being a pretext for agitation and disturbances. How my heart trembled as I awaited letters, newspapers – news in any form! And how I suffered and rebelled with every page I read! Each succeed-ing day of that admirable month of August grew darker. Never have I felt the chill and the creeping shadows of such atrocious mourning, under more dazzling skies.

And yet, for the past two years, suffering has been no stranger to me. I have heard mobs hound me with their death cries; I have seen a filthy flood of threats and insults flow by my feet; I have known the despairs of exile for eleven months. And there have also been my two trials, two deplorable displays of baseness and iniquity. But compared with the trial in Rennes, my trials have been refreshing and idyllic scenes, with hope in full blossom! We had witnessed many a monstrous episode – the legal action taken against Colonel Picquart, the investigation of the Criminal Chamber, and the law on change of jurisdiction which stemmed from it. But all of that was mere child's play. The inevitable movement from bad to worse fol-lowed its course and the trial in Rennes is the crowning development, the huge and abominable flower that has grown out of the accumulation of all those dung heaps.

It proved to be the most extraordinary set of manoeuvres to undermine truth and justice. A band of witnesses steering the debates, meeting every evening to plot the next day's dubious ambush, using lies to interrogate in place and instead of the public prosecutor, terrifying and insulting anyone who contradicted them, throwing around the weight of their rank, their ribbons and braid. Superior officers invading the courtroom and judges overwhelmed by their presence, clearly suffering at seeing them in a criminal role, obedient to an entire and very special set of mind which would have to be analysed at length in order to judge the judges. A ludicrous public prosecutor, raising idiocy to new heights, bequeathing to future historians a final summing up so vapid, so silly and so lethal that it will forever be a source of wonderment, of such senile and stubborn cruelty that it seems senseless, the brainchild of some human animal that has never yet been classified. As for the lawyers for the defence – first they try to assassinate them, then they force them to be seated every time they get in the way and then, when those lawyers wish to bring in the only witnesses who know the facts, they refuse them that opportunity to introduce crucial evidence.

For an entire month this abomination went on in front of Dreyfus, the poor innocent man, become such a pitiful human specimen that it would make the very stones weep. His former comrades came to give him another kick, and his former superior officers came to crush him with the weight of their rank so as to avoid being banished to a penal colony themselves, and in those ugly souls there was not one cry of pity, not one tremor of generosity. And it is our gentle France that has put on this display for all the world to see.

When the complete and detailed minutes of the trial in Rennes are published, they will constitute the most loathsome monument imaginable to human infamy. It outdoes everything. Never will History have seen a more villainous document. Such blatant ignorance, stupidity, madness, cruelty and lies – in a word, crime – are displayed in it that the generations to come will shudder with shame. All mankind will blush at the revelations of our baseness. That is why I am terrified; because any nation that is capable of holding such a trial, such a consultation on its moral and intellectual condition, in front of the civilized world, must be going through a horrendous crisis. Is that nation's death imminent? We are drowning in poisonous mud – will we ever find a fountain of goodness, purity and justice that can wash us clean?

*

As I wrote in my 'Letter to the President of the Republic', after the scandalous acquittal of Esterhazy, it is impossible for one court martial to undo what another court martial has done. That is against the rules of discipline. And the verdict by the court martial in Rennes, with its Jesuitical hedging, a verdict which did not have the courage to say either yes or no, provides overwhelming proof that military justice is powerless to be just since it is not free and it refuses to acknowledge the obvious. It prefers to convict an innocent man all over again rather than place its own infallibility in doubt. Military justice now appears to be no more than a weapon, an instrument of execution in the commanding officers' hands. Henceforth it can only be an expeditious means of justice, in time of war. In time of peace, it must disappear since it is incapable of fairness, incapable of being guided by simple logic and common sense. It has pronounced sentence on itself.

Does anyone realize what an atrocious position we are in, among the civilized nations? The first court martial, deceived by its ignorance of the laws, clumsy in its judgement, convicts an innocent man. The second court martial, which may also have been deceived, this time by the most conniving tangle of lies and fraud, acquits a guilty man. The third court martial – by this time the truth has been brought to light and the highest civilian court in the land wishes to leave to the court martial the glory of making amends for the miscarriage of justice – dares to deny what is glaringly obvious; it convicts the innocent man all over again. That is irreparable. That is the crime of crimes. Jesus was convicted only once! But never mind; let everything collapse, let France be torn apart by factions, let the nation be ravaged by flames and disintegrate into ruins, let the army itself forfeit its honour in the process, rather than admit that one's fellow soldiers made a mistake and that their commanding officers were liars and forgers! Ideas shall be crucified. The sabre shall continue to reign.

And there we are, in this fine situation, for all Europe and all the world to see. The entire world is convinced that Dreyfus is innocent. Even if some remote nation had still harboured any doubts, the dazzling clarity provided by the trial in Rennes would have dispelled them. All the courts of all the great powers, our neighbours, are informed; they are familiar with the documents and have proof of the unworthiness of three or four of our generals and the shameful paralysis gripping our system of military justice. We have lost our moral battle of Sedan, and this is a hundred times more disastrous than the other Sedan, which involved only bloodshed. I repeat, the defeat of our nation's honour seems irreparable, and that is what terrifies me – for how can we overturn the verdicts of three courts martial? Where will we find the heroism to confess our guilt so that we can hold our heads high once again? Where is there a government of courage and public salvation? Where are the Chambers that will understand and take action, before the inevitable ultimate collapse?

The worst part is that we have a rendez-vous with glory. France has decided to celebrate its century of diligent labour, science and struggles for freedom, truth and justice. Never has there been a century of more admirable effort, as future generations shall realize. And France has invited the nations of the world to come and glorify France's victory – freedom won, truth and justice promised to the whole earth. So it is that in a few months' time the nations of the world will come to France – and what will they find? An innocent man convicted twice, truth slapped in the face, justice slain. We have beomce an object of contempt and they will come to snigger at us, and they will guzzle our wines and kiss our servant girls, as if they were slumming in some low dive. Can we really be on the verge of such a thing? Are we going to let our World Fair become an evil den where the whole world will scornfully condescend to have a good time? No! We must perform the fifth act of our monstrous tragedy now, without delay, no matter how painful the penance we may have to do. We must regain our honour so that we can welcome the peoples of the earth to a healed and regenerated France.

I am haunted by that fifth act; I keep coming back to it, trying to picture it. Has no one noticed that this Dreyfus Affair, this gigantic drama that has aroused the universe, seems to have been staged by some sublime playwright, determined to make it an incomparable masterpiece? I need not recall here the extraordinary sequence of episodes and reversals; they have stirred every soul. With each new act, passions have swelled and the horror has intensified. The genius behind this living drama is fate; it is there behind the scenes, pushing the characters about and unfolding the plot, amid the storm it has unleashed. Surely it wants this masterpiece to be complete; surely it is preparing some superhuman fifth act which will recreate a glorious France, leading the procession of nations. For you may be certain of one thing: it is fate which has willed this supreme crime, the innocent man convicted twice over. The crime had to be committed for the sake of its tragic grandeur and its sovereign beauty – for the sake of the expiation, perhaps, which will make the apotheosis possible. Now that we have reached the ultimate in horror, I await the fifth act. By delivering us, making us young and vigorous once again, it will put an end to the tragedy.

*

What do I dread most? Let me state it clearly. As I have hinted on a number of occasions, I have always feared that the truth – the decisive, irrefutable evidence – would come to us from Germany. This is a mortal danger, and the time to keep silent about it is past. Too much has been brought to light. Courageously, we must face the possibility that Germany could hurl the thunderbolt which would open the fifth act.

Here is my confession. Before my trial, in the course of January 1898, I knew beyond the shadow of a doubt that Esterhazy was the 'traitor', that he had supplied M. von Schwartzkoppen with a considerable number of documents, that many of those documents were in his handwriting and that the complete collection was in Berlin, at the War Ministry. Now, I am not a professional patriot, but I admit that I was shattered by the certainties I acquired, and ever since then my anguish as a good Frenchman has never ceased. I live in dread at the idea that Germany, which may be our enemy tomorrow, could slap us in the face with the evidence it has in its possession.

Just think! The court martial of 1894 convicts Dreyfus, who is innocent; the court martial of 1898 acquits Esterhazy, who is guilty; and our enemy has proof of the twofold error committed by our military tribunals, and France, oblivious, persists in the error of its ways and accepts the appalling danger that lies in wait for it! They say that Germany cannot make use of documents it has acquired through espionage, but how can we be sure of that? If war breaks out tomorrow, what might Germany's first step be? Might it not dishonour our army in the eyes of all Europe by publishing the documents and thus revealing the abominable iniquity in which some of the army's leaders have persisted? Isn't such a thought unbearable? Can France enjoy a minute's rest as long as it knows the proof of its disgrace is in the hands of foreigners? Personally, I have lost sleep over it, and I do not mind saying so.

Therefore, together with Labori, I decided to call the foreign military attachés as witnesses. We knew full well that they would never take the stand but we wanted to let the government know that we knew the truth and hoped that the government would take action. But it turned a deaf ear, treated the matter as a pleasantry, and left the weapon in Germany's hands. And that is how things remained, until the trial in Rennes took place. The instant I returned to France I rushed to see Labori and I insisted, desperately, that approaches be made to the government, pointing out to it this dreadful situation and asking whether it was going to step in so that, thanks to its intervention, those documents would be returned to us. (Obviously, nothing could have been more awkward, and in addition, there was the unfortunate Dreyfus whom we were determined to save, so that we were prepared to make every concession out of fear of irritating public opinion, which was already feverish.) Moreover, if the court martial acquitted Dreyfus, it would, by so doing, strip every harmful virus from those documents and smash the very weapon that Germany might use. Acquitting Dreyfus would mean acknowledging the miscarriage of justice and making amends for it. Our honour would be restored.

But my patriotic torments became more unbearable still when I realized that a court martial was going to aggravate the danger by, once again, convicting the innocent man, the man whose innocence will be proclaimed one day to all the world by the publication of those documents in Berlin. Therefore I tried again and again, pleading with Labori to demand the documents, to summon M. von Schwartzkoppen as a witness, for only he can bring the truth to light. And the day Labori – a hero, who received a bullet wound while in action on the judicial battlefield – took advantage of an opportunity that the accusers offered him by bringing an unworthy foreigner to the witness stand, the day Labori rose to ask that von Schwartzkoppen be heard, since a single word from him would put an end to the Affair, Labori was doing his duty to the utmost. His was the heroic voice that nothing will still. His request still stands, although the trial has ended; and inevitably, when the time comes, his request will launch a new trial and conclude it by the only possible outcome, the acquittal of the innocent man. The documents have been requested; I cannot believe that they will not be produced one day.

The presiding judge of the court martial in Rennes put us in still greater danger than before, intolerable danger, by using his discretionary powers to prevent the production of the documents. He deliberately shut the door on the truth – what could be harsher than that? 'We do not want the evidence to be introduced because we want to convict this man.' And so it was that a third court joined the other two in a wilful miscarriage of justice, so that now there are three iniquitous verdicts, which would all be discredited by a denial from Germany, if it came. Isn't that sheer insanity? Isn't it enough to make you cry out in anxiety and revulsion?

The government whose own agents betrayed it, the government that was feeble enough to let simple-minded overgrown children play with matches and knives, the government that forgot that to govern is to foresee – that government must hasten to take action if it does not wish to leave in Germany's hands the power to stage the fifth act, the final scene that should make every Frenchman tremble. It is the government which has the responsibility of performing that fifth act as soon as possible to prevent its being imposed on us from abroad. The government has it in its power to obtain those documents; diplomacy has been known to solve more difficult problems. The day the government makes up its mind to request the documents listed in the bordereau, they will be given to it, and they will constitute the new element that will necessitate a second revision of the case by the Supreme Court of Appeal. This time, I hope, it will be fully informed and will exercise its full and sovereign jurisdiction by overturning the verdict, with no further appeal possible.

*

But if the government backs down once again, the defenders of truth and justice will do whatever is necessary; not one of us will desert his post. Ultimately, we will obtain the proof, the invincible proof.

On 23 November, we shall be at Versailles. My trial will take place, since the aim is for it to take place, down to the slightest detail. If justice has not been done by then, we will help, once again, to see that it is done. My dear, valiant Labori, whose honour has grown ever greater, will therefore deliver at Versailles the plea he was unable to deliver at Rennes. It is very simple. There will be nothing lost. I shall not prevent him from speaking; you may be sure of that. All he will need to do is to tell the truth, without fearing that he will harm my interests; I am prepared to pay for that truth with my freedom and my blood.

Before the Assize Court of the Seine, I swore that Dreyfus was innocent. I swear it before the entire world and now the entire world joins me, as in a chorus. I repeat: the truth is on the march, and nothing shall stop it. At Rennes, it has just taken a giant step. I have but one fear now: that the truth will arrive in a thunderbolt hurled by the avenging Nemesis and will shatter our country, unless we ourselves hasten to let the truth shine forth, like a sunburst over France.

L'Aurore, 12 September 1899

Letter to Madame Alfred Dreyfus

Dear Madame Dreyfus,

They have restored the innocent man, the martyr, to you. To his wife they have restored the husband, to his son and his daughter they have restored the father, and my first thoughts go to his family, reunited at last, happy, consoled. No matter how much I as a citizen may be in mourning, no matter how much painful indignation, how much rebellion and anxiety just souls may continue to feel, I share with you this exquisite, tearful moment when you hold the resurrected man in your arms. He has been raised from the dead! He has emerged from the tomb, alive and free. Surely this is a great day, a day of victory and celebration.

I can picture the first evening, in the lamplight, in the intimacy of the family circle; the doors have been closed and all the abominations of the outside world vanish on the threshold. The two children are there, their father has returned from that long, long voyage – so distant, so obscure. They kiss him and await the moment when he will tell them his story. What confident peace of mind, what hopes for a future that will make amends! The mother, meanwhile, bustles gently about; for after so much heroism she still has a heroic task to fulfil: through her tenderness, her care and her love, she will soothe and heal the crucified soul, the poor unfortunate man who has been restored to her. The snug house is enveloped in sweet slumber, infinite goodness bathes every corner of the smiling family's home, and all of us who have striven for this moment, who have struggled for so many months for this blissful hour, look on discreetly from the shadows and feel rewarded.

Personally, I confess that at first my role was one of solidarity with my fellow man, a role of pity and love. An innocent man was suffering amidst the most frightful torments; that was all I saw, and the only reason I launched my campaign was to deliver him from the evils that beset him. From the moment I was given proof of his innocence I was haunted by a dreadful fear, at the thought of all this poor man had endured and was still enduring in the isolated cell where he lay in agony, struck down by a monstrous and enigmatic fate which he could not even begin to decipher. What devastating thoughts inside that skull! What excruciating anguish as each new dawn brought another endless day of waiting! I couldn't live with myself. My courage stemmed from pity alone, and my one goal was to put an end to the torture, to raise the heavy slab so the victim could come back to the light of day and be reunited with his family, who would bind up his wounds.

Mere sentimentalism, as the politicians say, shrugging their shoulders. Well, yes, it was sentimental! My heart bled and I rushed to the aid of a man in distress; it did not matter whether he was Jewish, Catholic or Mohammedan. At the time I thought it was only a simple miscarriage of justice. I had no idea of the extent of the crime that was crushing this man, keeping him in chains at the bottom of the ignominious pit where they watched him writhe. My anger was not aroused against the guilty parties, for they were not known as yet. A mere writer, my compassion tearing me away from my customary labours, I was not aiming for any political gain; I was not working for any party. From the very outset of my campaign my only party was mankind, and the need to serve it.

Then I began to understand how terribly difficult our task was going to be. As the battle unfolded and spread, I realized that superhuman efforts would be required to free this innocent man. Every force in society was leagued against us; the only force we had on our side was the force of truth itself. We would have to accomplish a miracle in order to resurrect the buried man. Again and again throughout these two cruel years I despaired of ever bringing him back alive to his family. He was still so far away, in his tomb, and although a hundred of us, then a thousand, then twenty thousand tried to raise that slab, the weight of all those iniquitous acts was so heavy that I feared our arms would be worn out by the supreme effort. One day, perhaps, in some far distant future, we would reveal the truth and see to it that justice was done. But by then the unfortunate man would be dead; never would his wife and children be able to celebrate his triumphant return with their kisses. Never, never again!

Today, we have made the miracle happen. Two years of gigantic struggle have achieved the impossible. Our dream has been accomplished: the victim has come down from the cross, the innocent man is free, your husband is with you once again. He will suffer no longer, nor will our hearts. The unbearable vision no longer keeps us awake at night. And thus, let me say it once more, today is a day of celebration, a great victory. Discreetly, all our hearts beat in unison with yours. The heart of every wife and every mother warms at the thought of your first evening together in the lamplight. The entire world is moved; you are surrounded by its affection and sympathy.

The pardon he has been granted is bitter, no doubt. He has endured so much physical torture – must he now be subjected to such moral torture as well? How galling to think that he has only been granted as an act of pity what was due him as an act of justice!

The worst of it is that everything seems to have been contrived so as to culminate in this final iniquity. That is precisely what the judges wanted: to strike an innocent man once again in order to save the guilty parties, even though it meant hiding behind the appalling hypocrisy of a semblance of mercy: 'Is it honour that you want? We only grant you your freedom, so that your dishonour in the eyes of the law will cover up your tormentors' crime.' In all the long series of ignominious deeds that have been committed, this is the most despicable attempt to strip away human dignity. Think of it! Turning divine pity into a farce, making it the instrument of falsehood, using it to slap innocence in the face so that murder can strut about in broad daylight with its medals and plumes!

And how sad to see the government of a great country so dismally weak that it is only willing to be merciful when in fact it should be just! It trembles before the arrogance of a single faction, thinks it will pacify the nation through iniquitous acts, dreams up heaven knows what perfidious and poisonous kiss – this is the height of deliberate blindness. Once the scandalous verdict had been reached in Rennes, shouldn't the government have referred the case to the Supreme Court of Appeal, the highest court in the land, that the government has been flouting so insolently? Wouldn't our country's salvation have lain in that indispensable act of determination? It would have restored our honour in the eyes of the entire world, and restored the rule of law in France itself. Feelings cannot be calmed once and for all unless justice is allowed to take its course. Any act of cowardice will bring feelings to fever pitch once again. What we need is a courageous government that is prepared to do its duty to the bitter end so that a nation led astray by lies can come back to the straight and narrow path.

But we have fallen so low that we are reduced to congratulating the government on having shown mercy. The government has dared to be good! Ye gods! What dazzling boldness! what unbelievable valour! Now it is in danger of being bitten by the packs of wild beasts that have sprung out of our primeval forests and prowl in our midst! I suppose there is some merit in being good when one is not capable of being strong. No matter, Madame Dreyfus; your husband can hold his head high while he waits to be rehabilitated – as he should have been, immediately, for the glory of the country itself – because in the eyes of the entire world there is no innocent man anywhere who is more innocent than he is.

Let me tell you, Madame Dreyfus, how much we admire your husband, how we venerate and worship him. He has suffered so much and so needlessly from human stupidity and wickedness that we would like to bind up each and every one of his wounds with tenderness. We are well aware that no reparation is possible, that society will never be able to pay back its debt to a martyr tormented with such atrocious tenacity. Therefore we have built an altar to him in our hearts. We cannot give him anything purer or more precious than our brotherly and reverent emotion. He has become a hero, a greater hero than the others because his sufferings have been greater. Anointed by the pain of injustice, august and purified forever more, he has entered the temple of the future where the gods reside, the gods whose images move our hearts and make goodness bloom eternally. His letters to you are imperishable. They will be forever more the most heart-rending cry of protest that ever a tortured and innocent soul uttered. Never has a man been struck down by a more tragic fate, and never has a man risen higher in the esteem and love of his fellow human beings.

Then, as if his tormentors wanted to make him greater still, they forced the supreme torture upon him: the trial in Rennes. Here was a martyr taken down from the cross, exhausted, with only his force of character to sustain him, and what did they do but parade in front of him in the most savage, despicable way, covering him with spittle, stabbing him repeatedly, pouring gall and vinegar on his wounds. And he was admirable, stoical, uttering not one complaint, displaying a lofty courage and an unshakeable confidence in the truth that later generations will marvel at. It was such a sublime and poignant sight that the iniquitous verdict – reached after a month of monstrous debate in which each hearing proved the defendant's innocence more eloquently than the one before – outraged nations the world over. Destiny had its way; the innocent man surpassed god so that an unforgettable example might be set for the entire world.

Now, Madame Dreyfus, we have reached the summit. Nothing could be more exalted, more glorious. We might almost ask, what would be the point of a legal rehabilitation, an official declaration of his innocence, since there is not one decent man anywhere in the world who is not convinced of that innocence? And that innocent man has become the symbol of human solidarity unto the ends of the earth. Four centuries were needed before the religion of Christ found its formulation and won over certain nations, but the religion of the innocent man, sentenced once and then twice, instantly spread around the globe, uniting all the civilized nations in one vast human race. Has there ever been, at any time in History, such a movement of universal brotherhood? I can find none. The twice-sentenced innocent man has done more for brotherhood between peoples, for the concept of solidarity and justice, than a hundred years of philosophical discussions and humanistic theories. For the first time ever, all of mankind uttered a single cry for liberation, a rebellious demand for justice and generosity, as if all mankind were but one sole people, the single and fraternal people of whom the poets dream.

Thus, let us honour him and worship him. Suffering has made him the chosen man, through whose person universal communion has just been accomplished.

*

In the sweet refuge of his family, warmed by your pious hands, Madame Dreyfus, he can sleep peacefully, confidently. You may count on us to glorify him. It is we poets who bestow glory; and upon him we will bestow such a laurel wreath that no other man of our times will leave so poignant a memory. Already, many books have been written in his honour; a whole library has appeared to prove his innocence and praise his martyrdom. On his tormentors' side the documents that have been written, the volumes and pamphlets, are few in number, while those enamoured of truth and justice have not ceased and will not cease to contribute to History, to publish the countless items in the immense investigation which one day will make it possible to determine the facts for all time. Tomorrow's verdict is being prepared now. It will be a triumphant acquittal, an overwhelming reparation; every generation will kneel and, in memory of the glorious and tortured victim, will beg pardon for their fathers' crime.

And it is the poets, once again, who nail the guilty parties to the pillory. Those whom we condemn are scorned and hissed by each succeeding generation. The names of certain criminals, when once we have heaped infamy upon them, are no more than vile wreckage forever more. Immanent justice has reserved this punishment as its own; it has instructed the poets to single out, as objects of loathing down through the ages, those whose social malfeasance and measureless crimes exceed the scope of ordinary tribunals. I am well aware that to despicable souls, to men who care only for their pleasure here and now, such punishment appears remote indeed and leaves them unmoved. Insolence in the present moment is all they seek. Trampling their opponents, they win brutal victories which sate their crude appetites. What does the morrow matter beyond the tomb, what does infamy matter, since one is no longer there to blush over it? This accounts for the shameful sights we have had to gaze upon: the arrogant lies, the flagrant fraud, the inconceivable impudence, everything that is bound to fade away after one brief hour and precipitate the guilty parties into ruin. Have they no descendants? Are they not afraid that their children and their grandchildren will blush with shame?

Poor fools! They don't even seem to realize that it is they themselves who erected the pillory to which we shall nail their names. What thick skulls they must have, deformed no doubt by their particular milieu, the spirit that pervades their profession. Those judges in Rennes, for instance, who sentenced the innocent man a second time in order to save the army's honour. Could one possibly imagine anything more stupid? Surely they did the army no favour by compromising it in this iniquitous adventure. Just another example of their crude, immediate goal, with no thought for the future. The few leaders who were guilty had to be rescued even if that meant discrediting all courts martial and casting suspicion on the chiefs of staff, who are now standing by one another. That indeed is another of their crimes: they have dishonoured the army, brought about greater disorder and aroused greater anger. And ultimately, why did the government pardon the innocent man? Because it bowed, no doubt, to the urgent need to make amends, believing it was reduced to this mockery of justice in order to cool heated spirits.

But you must forget this, Madame Dreyfus; above all, you must scorn it. Scorning villainy and outrage is a source of great consolation in life. I have always found it very comforting. I have worked for forty years, and for those forty years what has kept me on my feet is scorn for the insults that every one of my books has earned me. In the past two years, since we began fighting for truth and justice, the ignoble flood of insults has risen so high on every side that we have emerged from it hardened for life. We are invulnerable; no wound can lay us low. Personally, I have erased the foul newspapers and mudslinging men from my life. They no longer exist. When my eye happens to fall on their names, it glides over them; I even ignore the excerpts from their writings when others quote them. It is simply a matter of hygiene. I have no idea whether they are continuing; my scorn has exiled them from my thoughts and one day the sewers will swallow them whole.

I therefore advise the innocent man to scorn and forget those countless, atrocious insults. He is so high above them, in such a different dimension, that they should no longer affect him. He must live again, arm in arm with you, in the clear light of day, far from the rabble, and hear nothing but the concert of universal sympathy as it rises towards him. Peace to the martyred man so badly in need of rest! In that retreat where you will love and heal him, may the presence of every person and every thing be like a gentle caress!

The rest of us, meanwhile, will continue the struggle. We will fight for justice tomorrow as resolutely as we did yesterday. We must see to it that the innocent man is rehabilitated – not so much for his sake, for he is haloed by glory, as for the sake of rehabilitating France, which was slowly but surely dying from such a surfeit of iniquity.

France's honour will be restored in the eyes of the world the day it annuls the infamous verdict, and our untiring efforts will be directed to that goal. A great country cannot live without justice. Our country will remain in mourning as long as it has not washed out the stain. It has flouted its highest court, and this refusal of the rule of law diminishes every French citizen. Social ties are loosened, the entire structure falls apart when observance of the law is no longer guaranteed. Moreover, this denial of the rule of law was perpetrated with such blatant insolence, such brazen impudence that we do not even have the possibility of shrouding the disaster in silence, burying the body in secret so as not to blush in front of our neighbours. No, the entire world saw and heard, and therefore amends must be made before the entire world, in as resounding a way as the wrongdoing itself.

Striving for a France without honour, a France scorned and isolated, is a criminal enterprise. No doubt foreign visitors will come to our World Fair; I have never doubted that they would flock to Paris next summer, as eagerly as one goes to the fairgrounds amid the bright lights and the blaring music. But should that be enough to satisfy our pride? As those visitors stream in from every corner of the globe, shouldn't we be as eager for their esteem as for their money? We will be boasting about our industry, our sciences, our arts; we will display our feats of engineering and ingenuity. Will we dare to display our justice? I remember the cartoon in a foreign newspaper that showed Devil's Island, reconstituted and displayed at the World Fair, in the Champ de Mars. Personally, my cheeks burn with shame. I fail to understand how the World Fair can open unless France has resumed its rank among the just nations. Let the innocent man be rehabilitated. Then and only then, will France be rehabilitated along with him.

But in conclusion, Madame Dreyfus, I shall say, once again, that you may place your trust in the good citizens who have had your husband freed and will have his honour restored to him. Not one will desert the struggle; they know that in fighting for justice they are fighting for the country itself. The innocent man's admirable brother will once again set an example of courage and wisdom. We had hoped to bring your beloved husband to you both free and cleared of all unfounded accusations; since we have not succeeded, we must beg you to be patient a little longer. We trust that your children will not have to grow much older before all blots on their name have been legally removed.

My thoughts keep turning to those children, and I picture them clinging to his arms. I know what lengths you went to, what prodigious tact you deployed, to shield them from all knowledge of the affair. At first they believed their father was away on a long journey. Then their intelligence made them more and more alert; they began asking questions, demanding an explanation for such a lengthy absence. What could you tell them while the martyr was still in that villainous tomb at the ends of the earth, and only a handful of believers knew that he was innocent? Your heart must

have been shattered. But in the course of the past few weeks, as his innocence at last became obvious to all, as the dawn of revelation at last burst
through the dismal night, I would have liked you to take them both by the
hand and lead them to that prison in Rennes; so that the vision of their
father at his most heroic, and their reunion with him, would be engraved
forever in their memories. And you would have told them what he had
suffered and how unjustly, how great his moral stature was, how tenderly
they must love and cherish him so that he could one day forget men's
iniquity. Like finest steel, their young souls would have been tempered by
his manly virtue.

It is not too late. One evening in the lamplight, in the peaceful, grateful
family circle, the father will take them on his knees and relate the
whole tragic story to them. They must know it so that they will respect
and worship him as he deserves. Once he has spoken, they will be
aware that in all the world no hero is more widely acclaimed, no
martyr's sufferings have stirred hearts more deeply. And how proud of
him they will be, how proudly they will bear his glorious name as that
of a courageous and stoical man whose conduct has been sublime in the
face of the most appalling fate that ever human villainy and cowardice
engendered. One day it is not the son and daughter of this innocent
man who will have to blush; it is his tormentors' children who will be
universally reviled.

Madame Dreyfus, I have the honour to assure you of my profound
respect.

L'Aurore, 22 September 1899

In this long interview, Zola explained the meaning of his latest novel, Fécondité,
*published on 12 October. It dealt with the problem of depopulation and vigor-
ously condemned what he called the Malthusian practices in use in France to
prevent population increase. While retracing the origins of the novel, he also
retraced events leading up to and during his exile in England.*

A Visit to M. Emile Zola at Home

The other day I went to pay a call on the author of that fine book,
Fécondité,[1] for he had given me a copy as a present and I wished to thank
him. In the course of the conversation I asked him if his trials and his exile

---

1   *Fertility*, trans. by Ernest Vizetelly and published by Chatto and Windus, 1900.

had disturbed his work. In replying, he gave me information on the circumstances in which he had written *Fécondité*, on the three volumes to come and on his period of residence in England.

What he told me was so interesting that I asked permission to note down his words and pass them on to our readers. M. Zola very graciously agreed to this. Thus, the words that follow are his very own; I was merely a faithful stenographer.

'The subject of *Fécondité* had been going through my head for a long time,' Zola told me. 'As I first conceived it, it was to be entitled *Le Déchet*,[2] and I had not yet thought of contrasting Malthusian practices – the deliberate sterility of a certain bourgeoisie, a practice which leads to vices, the disorganization of the family and catastrophes of the worst sort – with the example of a social group which did not cheat with nature and where the large number of children became a cause of prosperity. *Le Déchet* would have painted a very dark picture with nothing to alleviate it and might have made too painful an impression on the reader's mind. Once I had completed my *Trois Villes*,[3] my ideas on the subject began to change. I decided to place the evil and the remedy side by side, and the book took the shape in which you have now read it.

'Even so, the critics have said that I was presenting too grim a picture. Philippe Gille, in *Le Figaro*, accused me of inflating the figures, exaggerating the number of women who submitted to ovariotomies. But I can assure you that in fact I toned down the figures. And I didn't even tell the whole story. You know how scrupulously I go about documenting my writings. I consulted the official statistics, I questioned the specialists, I studied the books that deal with the question, and finally visited placement bureaux for wet nurses and midwives' consulting rooms. In short, I worked on the basis of figures that were thoroughly verified and cannot be called in question. From that standpoint, I defy anyone to challenge my work. The scourge that I describe does exist and it is a terrifying thing.

'It was late in December 1897 that I began to put together my file for *Fécondité*. It was no easy job! I drew up a general outline of the book and prepared synoptic tables that enabled me to find my way around among Mathieu Froment's twelve children. At the time of my first trial, I was in the midst of this preparatory work. And thanks to the methodical way I approach everything I do, I managed to make preparations for my book and campaign for Dreyfus all at the same time.

'By the time of the trial in Versailles, my outline was finished. The framework for the book was able to stand on its own and I was about to commence writing the first chapter. But since I was almost expecting to be

---

2 'Waste'.
3 *The Three Cities* (Lourdes, Rome and Paris), trans. by Ernest Vizetelly and published by Chatto and Windus, 1894, 1896, 1898.

arrested upon leaving the courtroom, I had said to my wife, "If by any chance they clap me in jail immediately, you will gather together all the pieces of my file and bring it to me."

'I was not arrested. But several of my friends, convinced that I would be in danger if I remained in Paris, made me decide to leave France. Perhaps they were right. And yet, I must admit that it would not have bothered me too much to go to prison. I would have worked there at my ease and I would have experienced new sensations.

'However that may be, I followed my friends' advice. I left abruptly for London without taking my papers with me, without even taking a change of clothing. At the hotel where I stayed, I was recognized almost straight away. Since I was afraid of the reporters and I wanted to be left in peace at all costs, I went to a suburb of London and, using the name Beauchamp as a pseudonym, I settled into an isolated little cottage, first of all, and then in Norwood, near Sydenham, where I stayed at the Queens Hotel. They gave me the suite which had been occupied by Emperor Frederick III when he came to England incognito to consult the doctors for his cancer. There, I was safe! Only my wife and one of my friends knew where I was. They sent me my file and some personal effects. To correspond with them, I put each letter and its envelope inside another envelope addressed to one of our acquaintances in London, who then sent it on to Paris after writing the final address in his own hand.

'I began my first chapter on 4 August 1898, and soon I had hit my stride. I read not a single newspaper; I saw not a soul. I would work all morning and in the afternoon I would go out on my bicycle. Thus, I was in the best possible circumstances to get work done.

'Early in September, I had finished seven chapters when I received a telegram from my friend. The message was very brief: "Victory. Tell Beauchamp immediately."[4] I was very intrigued. At first I thought it concerned some premature hope. I thought that perhaps Picquart had been released. But I said to myself, "Over there they are in the thick of the battle. They may be exaggerating the importance of some incident or other. Let's wait and see." I might add that at that time, I believed our cause was momentarily lost.

'That night, I slept soundly. But the next morning, I remembered the mysterious telegram. Soon it obsessed me to the point where I could not get back to work. I got on my bicycle and hastened to buy a few English papers. Now, I do not speak English, and I did not want to question the people at the hotel for fear of giving away my identity. So I bought a dictionary and a grammar book, and finally I understood that what had happened was Henry's suicide.

4   See above, the letter to Alexandrine Zola dated 1 September 1898.

'The news took my breath away, I can tell you. From that moment on, I began to read the French papers and I went through the same fits of hope and discouragement that you went through. Despite that, I did not abandon my book. Every single day I worked on it; by sheer willpower I managed to set aside my preoccupations for a few hours and think of nothing but literature, and in that way I moved ahead with *Fécondité* until 27 May 1899, when I was able to write "The End" at the bottom of the last page. On 4 June, I came back to France, and the rest you know.'

'What are your ideas,' I asked M. Zola, 'concerning the three other volumes which, together with *Fécondité*, will form your *Quatre Evangiles?*'[5]

'Oh, there is nothing actually firm in my mind. However, I am beginning to put together some notes for my second volume, *Travail*.[6] But I am in a bit of a quandary. I have already dealt with the mines and the factories. But that is not all that there is to work; there is also the land. Now, I have just sung the praises of the land in *Fécondité*; and earlier, I had dealt with the land in the book that bears that title.[7] Well, I shall see. Jaurès has told me about the glassworks at Carmaux. I may look into that. I may try to talk about the socialists' ideal city. In short, I have not made up my mind.'

'And the other volumes?' I asked.

'Well, there will be *Vérité*,[8] which of course will be based on science. Because, you see, I never cease to *believe* in science,' he added, with a vigorously affirmative gesture. 'It is science which, although evolution occurs slowly and human beings sometimes revert to past behaviour, will provide the morals and the aesthetics of society in the future. Contrary to the Catholic doctrine, which teaches that work is a punishment and a form of suffering, I shall show that work is a good, a sacred function. It is only when we work that we are healthy and happy. That is one of my most heartfelt convictions.

'And finally, in my last book, *Justice*, I shall launch into pure Utopia. It will be a dream vision, a lyrical apotheosis of mankind on the march towards beauty and goodness. In short, an ode.'

'And after that, what will you do?'

'After that, I shall rest. I shall have earned the right to stop working, don't you agree? I dream of going to live in the Balearic Islands. They are an admirable place with a delightful climate. I'll try to forget that I was once somebody. I shall set aside all recollection of my struggles, my defeats and my victories. And I shall spend my last years contemplating nature amid peace and quiet.'

5   *The Four Gospels.*
6   *Work*, trans. by Ernest Vizetelly and published by Chatto and Windus, 1901.
7   *La Terre*, trans. as *The Earth* by Margaret Crosland and published by the New English Library, 1962.
8   *Truth*, trans. by Ernest Vizetelly and published by Chatto and Windus, 1903.

'Do you believe that when your trial comes up again in November, you will have to undergo the same harassments as in the past?'

'Oh no, I don't think so. After all, we are winning the battle. Dreyfus's complete rehabilitation is only a matter of time. As for winding up the part that concerns me, we must see how the Chambers decide. I have no reliable information about that. However that may be, I am pleased with what I did. I fought hard; I used my determination in the service of my country. So, my conscience is at rest.

'Work and determination – they are everything in life.'

'Indeed, my dear Maître, you have proved that to us,' I replied as I took my leave. 'And that is why we admire you both as a man and as a writer.'

Adolphe Retté, *Le XIXe Siècle*,
24 October 1899

Letter to the Senate

Senators,
The day on which you so reluctantly voted the law on change of jurisdiction, you committed your initial misdeed. You who are the guardians of the law allowed the law to be subverted by removing a defendant from the jurisdiction of his natural judges, suspected of being judges with integrity. And in fact it was under pressure from the government that you gave in – for the sake of the general good, to soothe troubled spirits, as they told you you would if only you consented to betray justice.

Soothe indeed! Have you forgotten that the day after the decision by the Supreme Court of Appeal, with all Chambers ruling together, agitation resumed, at a bloodier, more violent level? You had dishonoured your-selves for nothing, since the law you had invented just for the circum-stances and which, it was hoped, would lead to injustice, instead turned into a triumph for the innocent man. Have you also forgotten that a military tribunal did prove willing, nonetheless, to consummate the supreme iniquity? What a slap in the face for our highest court! And until this offence is made good, the conscience of our nation will have to blush.

Today you are being asked to commit a second misdeed – the last one, the most clumsy and most dangerous one. This time we are not talking about a law on change of jurisdiction. We are talking about a law of strangulation. All you did the first time was change the judges. Now you are being asked to say that there are no longer any judges. First you accepted the sordid task of adulterating justice. Now you must declare that justice is bankrupt. And once again they are bludgeoning you with the argument of political necessity. They are wrenching your vote from you in the name of the country's salvation. They swear that only this evil deed on your part can soothe the nation.

Soothe the nation, indeed! Only truth and justice can achieve that. You will not soothe anyone by doing away with the judges any more than you did by changing them. In fact you will be even farther from soothing troubled spirits, for you will cause society to fall apart even more; you will plunge the country into more lies and more hatred. All this will be but a pitiful and hasty expedient; and the day that that becomes clear, the day so much buried and rotting trash completely poisons the nation and makes it panic, it is you who will be responsible, you who will be guilty. You were entrusted with a mission, and History will call your weakness criminal.

*

Over two months ago, Senators, when I asked to be heard by your commission, my chief aim was to protest before it against the amnesty bill with which we were being threatened. And today, my only purpose in writing this letter is to protest again, and still more vigorously, on the eve of the day when you will be called upon to discuss the amnesty law. From my own personal standpoint, I consider this law a denial of justice. From the standpoint of our nation's honour, I consider it an indelible blot.

Do I need to repeat here what I said to your commission? In the long run one becomes rather tired, and rather ashamed, of repeating the same things over and over. The whole world knows that story and has long since judged it. Only the French can continue to fight over it, in a frenzy of political and religious passion. I said that after having shut me up so abruptly at my trial in Paris with that impudent 'The question will not be raised', and after having attempted, at my trial in Versailles, 'to tighten the screws on Labori', it was truly a monstrous ploy to refuse me the trial that I have been seeking; I am already indebted to the judges for so many outrages, so many torments and nearly one full year in exile, solely so that truth might triumph. I further said that never had a more unwarranted or more disturbing amnesty flown in the face of the law, for an amnesty is always applied only to misdemeanours and crimes of the same type and only in favour of persons who have been convicted and are already serving their sentence; whereas this amnesty would be applied to the most peculiar ragbag of deeds, of different types, several of which have not even been brought before the courts as yet. And I also said that the amnesty would be applied against us, the upholders of the law, in order to save the real criminals, by shutting our mouths through an act of hypocritical and injurious clemency and placing decent people in the same category as scoundrels. This is the ultimate in ambiguity. It will destroy whatever is left of the nation's conscience.

Moreover, I was not the only person to say these things that day. Like myself, Colonel Picquart and M. Joseph Reinach had insisted on being heard by your commission. It was then treated to the edifying sight of three men each of whose cases is altogether different from the others and yet who have all been the object of the same expedient – a denial of justice – in an attempt to get rid of them. They did not know each other prior to the Affair. They come from three different spheres. One of them is merely faced with the threat of a court martial; the second is currently on trial in the courts; and the third has been sentenced in absentia to a fine of three thousand francs and a year in prison. But never mind that! Their cases have been lumped together, the same bastard solution has been concocted for all three without any thought for the atrocious situation in which this leaves them – their lives are broken; they are not allowed to clear themselves of the charges brought against them or supply proof of their good faith. Their good names are damaged because they are dismissed along with scoundrels by an infamous parody of justice which tries to disguise an act of universal iniquity and cowardice as a stroke of patriotic magnanimity. Can you really expect these three men not to protest, out of their pain as citizens whose interests have been damaged and out of their love for France, the great country whose worthy sons they believed themselves to be? Of course I still protest and I know that Colonel Picquart and M. Joseph Reinach are protesting along with me, just as they did the day we testified before your commission.

But everyone knows these things, Senators. You know them better, in fact, than anyone else, since you are behind the political scenes, and that is where the whole monstrous undertaking was concocted. Your commission knew these things – and that explains the juridical anguish in which it turned and twisted for so long, and its reluctance to sponsor an unworthy project; only pressure from the government, in the circumstances of which you are aware, succeeded in overcoming that reluctance. You secretly acknowledge, I am certain, that never has there ever been such an accumulation of base acts, falsehoods and crimes, flagrant illegalities and denials of justice. In fact it is that very accumulation of violations and shameful deeds that terrifies you. How can the country be cleansed of it all? How can justice be dispensed to each and every one without ruining the France of the past, without shaking its old foundations and without being forced to rebuild at last the young and glorious France of tomorrow? Even in the firmest minds cowardly thoughts arise: 'There are too many corpses; we'll just dig a hole, bury them quickly and hope that no one will ever talk about them again, and never mind if the stench, as they rot away, seeps through the thin layer of soil that covers them and soon makes the entire country die of the plague.'

That is your line of thought, isn't it? We agree on one point, namely that the disease, rising from the hidden depths of the social body and breaking out in broad daylight, is appalling. We differ only on the way to try to cure the disease. You, as men of government, bury it; you seem to believe that something which is no longer visible no longer exists. Whereas we, as mere citizens, would like to purify the atmosphere immediately, burn what is rotten and do away with the ferments of destruction, so that the body as a whole can recover its health and its strength.

The future will tell who was right.

*

The story is a very simple one, Senators, but it may be useful to summarize it here briefly.

At the beginning, the Dreyfus Affair was only a matter of justice. There had been a miscarriage of justice and certain citizens, whose hearts were more just and tender than others', no doubt, wished it to be set right. Personally that is all I saw in it at first. But soon, as the monstrous enterprise unfolded, as people higher and higher up were shown to be responsible – the military leaders, the government officials, the men in power – the question took over the entire body politic, turning a *cause célèbre* into a terrible general crisis in which the fate of France itself seemed to hang in the balance. And so it was that little by little two parties came to blows; on one side, all the reactionaries, all the enemies of the genuine Republic that we ought to have, all those minds which, although they may not realize it, are attracted by authority of any kind, religious, military or political; on the other side, all those who act of their own free will and with thought for the future, all of the minds emancipated by science, all who are drawn towards truth and justice, those who believe in continual progress, whose conquests will one day bring about the greatest possible amount of happiness. And since then the battle has been merciless.

The Dreyfus Affair began in the judicial sphere, and there it should have remained. But it moved into the political sphere, and that is what makes it so venomous. It provided the occasion which suddenly brought to the surface the hidden enterprise of poison and rot at which the enemies of the Republic had been toiling away for thirty years, undermining the regime. Today it is plain for all to see that France – the last of the great Catholic nations to remain powerful and on its feet – was chosen by Catholicism, or I should say by Papism, to restore the declining power of Rome. So it is that an underground campaign began. The Jesuits, not to mention the other tools of religion, seized upon the younger generation with incomparable skill, until one fine morning France – the France of Voltaire, the France which is not yet back in the thrall of the priesthood – woke up to find that it was nonetheless a clerical country in the hands of an administration and a judiciary and an army whose higher ranks take their orders from Rome. Suddenly, deceptive appearances all fell away. We realized that we had nothing of a Republic except the label, that everywhere we stepped was a minefield, where a hundred years of democratic conquests were on the verge of collapse.

France was about to slip back into the hands of the reactionaries. Hence the fear, hence the warning cry. Hence the state of moral decay into which the cowardice of the Chambers and the government has been letting us sink. Once a chamber or a government is afraid to act, for fear of no longer being on the side of those who will be the masters tomorrow, its downfall is swift and fatal. Imagine men who are in power and who find that they no longer control any of the wheels of state – the obedient civil servants, the military men with their scrupulous discipline, the incorruptible judges. How can action be taken against General Mercier, a liar and a forger, when all the generals show solidarity with him? How can the genuine guilty parties be brought before the courts when everyone knows there are judges who will give them absolution? In a word, how can a government govern honestly when not one civil servant will carry out its orders honestly? Under such circumstances, there would have to be a hero in power, a great statesman determined to save his country, by taking revolutionary action if necessary. And since there are no such men for the moment, we have seen a succession of Ministers take to their heels; powerless and clumsy or, worse still, crooks and accomplices, they have tumbled one after the other as panic-stricken Chambers in the grip of factions have fallen into ignominy, obeying only the narrowest self-interest, heeding only personal concerns.

But that is not all. The worst part and the most painful part is that the foul press was allowed to poison the country, to feed it the most brazen diet of lies, slander, trash and outrageous nonsense and so make the country lose its head. Anti-Semitism was only a crude way to exploit ancestral hatreds and revive religious feeling among a nation of non-believers who had stopped going to church. And nationalism was an equally crude way to exploit the noble love of one's native country, an abominable, politically motivated tactic which will lead the country straight into civil war the day they have managed to convince one half of the French that the other half is betraying them and selling them to the enemy, simply because that half takes a different view of things. We have seen majorities emerge by claiming that truth was falsehood and justice was injustice. These majorities have even been deaf to all argument; they have condemned a man because he is Jewish and have clamoured for the death of so-called traitors whose only wish has been to salvage the honour of France from the disaster in which a nation has lost its reason.

From that minute on, from the instant it appeared that the country itself was going over to the reactionaries, giving way to a morbid folly, that was the end of whatever little courage the Chambers and the government may have had. Daring to withstand possible future majorities – how could anyone think of any such thing! Although universal suffrage seems so fair and logical, it has a frightful drawback: the instant a man is elected by the people he becomes nothing more than tomorrow's candidate and hence the people's slave, so overriding is his need to be re-elected. Thus, when the people suffer an attack of madness such as we are witnessing now, the elected man is at the mercy of that collective madness. He goes along with it if he is not stouthearted enough to think and act as a free man. Hence the painful sight we have been witnessing these past three years: a Parliament that does not know how to use its mandate for fear of losing it, and a government which – having allowed France to fall into the hands of the reactionaries, the people who are poisoning the public – trembles constantly at the thought of being overturned and so makes the worst kinds of concessions to the enemies of the regime it represents, all for the sake of being its master a few days longer.

Aren't those the very reasons, Senators, that will convince you to make a new concession by decreeing an amnesty? Not one government has dared to pursue the guilty parties in high places, and your amnesty will definitively shield them from punishment. You believe you are saving your skins when you say that the government must be saved from the deadly trap in which its continual weaknesses have caught it. If only some energetic statesman, some ordinary decent man had collared General Mercier as soon as he committed his first crime, everything would long since have been straightened out. But instead, every time justice has backed down, the criminals have naturally grown bolder and bolder, and by now it is true that the pile of filth has grown so disproportionately huge that it would take amazing courage to liquidate the Affair through judicial channels, to the best of France's interests. No one has that courage. Everyone shudders at the thought of exposing himself to the taunts and insults of the anti-Semites and the nationalists. Everyone has humoured the madness of certain majorities of voters whose minds have been poisoned, so that now you are being forced into yet another act of cowardice. It will be the supreme misdeed. It will turn the country over to the reactionaries. Already they are swaggering more and more boldly.

But don't you realize what a peculiar tactic it is to bury embarrassing questions? how childish it is to think that that puts an end to them? For three years now I have been hearing the politicians say, whenever they have some interest in believing it, that there is no Dreyfus Affair, or there is no longer any Dreyfus Affair. And yet the Dreyfus Affair continues to follow its logical path; for if there is one thing that is certain, it is this: the Dreyfus Affair will not end until it has been ended. No human power can stop the truth once it is on the march. Today a new wind of panic is blowing and you are terrified, determined to decree once again that there is no more Dreyfus Affair and never again will there be one. You are digging a hole, burying the Affair in it and laying the amnesty on top it; and you hope that if you dig deep enough, the Affair will not be resurrected. Your efforts are in vain. As long as justice has not done its work, the Affair will come back like a ghost, like a suffering soul. No nation can be at rest except through truth and justice.

And the worst part of it is that you may be quite sincere when you assume that by strangling all hope of justice you will be putting balm on our wounds. It is for the sake of that much-desired balm that you are sacrificing the consciences of honest legislators on the altar of the nation. Ah, you poor souls! You may be naive or you may be merely clumsy egoists; but once again you will dishonour yourselves and all to no avail. What a fine thing your balm is if it requires delivering the Republic over, member after member, to its enemies, in exchange for their silence. Every time they obtain satisfaction, they shout still more loudly and hurl still more insults. You are about to pass that amnesty law for their sake, to save their leaders from being shipped out to a penal colony – and yet they claim it is we who are forcing you to pass it! You are traitors; the Ministers are traitors; the President of the Republic is a traitor. And once you have passed that law you will have done the work of traitors in order to save traitors. Will such balm soothe anyone? I can't wait to see you, the day after the amnesty is passed: you will have mud slung at you while the cannibals dance to celebrate the massacre and clap their hands in glee.

Can't you see? Can't you hear? It was agreed that we would keep quiet, that we would observe a truce and stop talking about the Affair for the duration of the World Fair, but who is it who has been talking about it all this time? Who assaulted Paris during the last municipal elections by reviving the smear campaign and spreading more lies? Who has been dragging the army into this shameful business once again? Who continues to sneak about with secret documents in an attempt to overthrow the government? The Dreyfus Affair has become the dread spectre of the nationalists and the anti-Semites. They cannot reign without it. They need it constantly so as to hold sway over this country through terror. Formerly, in the days of the Second Empire, the Ministers got whatever they wanted out of the legislature by brandishing the spectre of revolution; today, they have numbed our poor people's brains and need only brandish the Affair to plunge them into a stupor. And here is your balm once again: this amnesty of yours will be but one more weapon in the hands of the faction that has exploited the Affair so that Republican France would die of it. That faction will now continue to exploit it all the more since your amnesty will endow ambiguity with the force of law, yet make it impossible for the nation ever to find out which side truth and justice were on.

In such a grave and perilous situation, there was only one right course of action. Accept the struggle against the coalition that united all the forces of the past. Reform the administration, reform the judiciary, and reform the supreme command, since it was clear that all of them were rotten through with clericalism. Enlighten the country with deeds, not words. Tell the whole truth. Render the whole of justice. Put to use the fabulous practical lesson that was emerging to enable the people to take, in just three years, the giant step that now it may need a hundred years to take. Accept at least the need to do battle for the future's sake, and win as many victories as possible in the interest of our grandeur in days to come. And even today, even though so much cowardice has made the task virtually impossible, there is still only one right course of action. Come back to truth. Come back to justice. For it is certain that only decline and imminent death await any country that stands aloof from truth and justice.

My very dear, great Labori, who was reduced to silence on one of those cowardly occasions I have mentioned, recently had an opportunity to say this, nonetheless, in his superbly eloquent way. Since the government and the politicians have never ceased to interfere in the Affair and to take it out of the hands of the courts, which should have had the sole power to resolve it, then it is the politicians – it is you, Senators – who have the duty to finish it in order to put this nation at peace and further its well-being. I repeat: if you are counting on your pitiful amnesty law to achieve that result, then you are making the wrongs you have done in the past still worse by adding another, a final wrong that may prove fatal and will weigh heavily on your memories.

*

One source of astonishment to me, Senators, is that we are being accused of wanting to start the Dreyfus Affair all over again. I do not understand. There was a Dreyfus Affair. There was an innocent man tortured by tormentors who knew he was innocent; and thanks to us that Affair is finished as far as the victim himself is concerned. His tormentors have had to restore him to his family. Today the whole world knows the truth; our toughest adversaries are not unaware of it; behind closed doors, they confess to it. The victim's rehabilitation will be nothing more than a legal formality when the time comes. In fact Dreyfus does not even need us any longer, for he is free and his valiant, admirable family have rallied around him, ready to help. They have never doubted his honour, never doubted that his deliverance would come.

Then why would we be trying to start the Dreyfus Affair all over again? That would be pointless and, moreover, would be to no one's advantage. What we want is this: the Dreyfus Affair must finish in the only way that can restore calm and strength to this country. The guilty parties must be punished, not so that we can rejoice in their punishment but so that the people will know the truth at last and justice can provide the only true and lasting balm. We believe that France's salvation lies in the victory of the forces of tomorrow over the forces of yesterday, the victory of men of truth over men of authority. We cannot rest happy until the conclusion of the Affair is justice for all and people have learnt from it the lessons that would help us to found the definitive Republic, provided we carried out every one of the reforms they have shown to be so absolutely necessary.

No, it is not we who are starting the Dreyfus Affair all over again; it is not we who are exploiting it for electoral purposes, not we who are pounding it into the people's heads until they are groggy. We are merely demanding our natural judges. It is our hope that justice for all will quickly bring the truth to light and thus pacify the nation. They say the Affair has done France a great deal of harm; it is a commonplace that the ministers themselves bandy about when they want to secure votes. To which France has the Affair done so much harm? To the France of yesterday? Well then, so much the better! Certainly it is true that all of the old institutions have been shaken up. The Affair has revealed that the old social edifice is rotten, through and through, and the only thing to be done with it now is to tear it down. But why should I moan about the harm the Affair has done to the past if it has done good to the future, if it has made the France of tomorrow a cleaner, healthier place? Never has any fever made the skin break out more visibly with the pustules of disease. That disease must be cured. We are not interested in reviving the Dreyfus Affair. We want to treat the disease whose severity it has revealed and make France well again.

But I am haunted by a graver goal, a pressing need. The amnesty that will bury the Affair, attempting to wind up everything in lies and ambiguity, will have a terrifying result: it will leave us at the mercy of a public revelation by Germany. Several times already I have alluded to this dreadful danger. It should make true patriots shudder and give them sleepless nights. It should make them demand the full and definitive liquidation of the Dreyfus Affair as a measure of public salvation. France's honour depends on it. France's very life depends on it. The time has come, at last, to speak up loud and clear. Very well, speak I shall.

Everyone knows that the many documents which Esterhazy supplied to M. von Schwartzkoppen, the German military attaché, are in Berlin, at the War Ministry. They include all kinds of papers – notes, letters and, among other things, they say, a whole series of letters in which Esterhazy passes judgement on his superior officers and divulges details from their private lives that are not very pretty. The papers include other bordereaus, by which I mean other lists of documents offered and supplied. Even the least little one of these papers proves that Dreyfus is innocent and that the man our courts martial have acquitted twice, despite the glaring evidence of his crime, is guilty. Well, just suppose that a war breaks out tomorrow between France and Germany! See what an appalling threat would be hanging over us! Before a single shot had been fired, before a single battle had been fought, Germany would release the Esterhazy file, would make it public knowledge, and we would lose the battle there and then, in front of the entire world. We would be helpless to defend ourselves. The respect and trust which our army must place in its leaders would be undermined; the iniquity and cruelty of three of our courts martial would be laid bare; the whole monstrous fabrication would be revealed in broad daylight and the country would collapse. We would be nothing more than a nation of liars and forgers.

I have often shuddered at this presentiment. How can a government that knows be willing to live with such a threat for even a minute? How can it talk about keeping silent, about remaining in the perilous situation we are in, on grounds that the country wants to be soothed? It is beyond understanding. I maintain that it is even a betrayal of this country to fail to shed light on this affair immediately and by every possible means, without waiting for that light to come from abroad, in some thunderbolt revelation. The day the innocent man has been rehabilitated and the guilty parties have been condemned – then and only then will we have shattered the weapon that Germany is brandishing over our heads, because then France, of its own accord, will have acknowledged its error and corrected it.

But now this amnesty comes and closes one of the last doors opening onto the truth. I have said it over and over again: they have refused to hear the one witness who, with a single word, could shed light on the affair, M. von Schwartzkoppen. In the courtroom in Versailles, he would be my witness, the one whom I would ask the rogatory commission to hear, the one who could not possibly refuse to tell the whole truth at last and to support it with documents he has seen with his own eyes. There and nowhere else is where the ultimate solution lies. Sooner or later it will come from that source, and it is folly on our part not to elicit that solution. It would be all to our honour if we did so instead of waiting for the truth to be flung in our faces, in tragic circumstances.

I was stunned, the day I appeared before your commission, when its chairman asked me, on behalf of the Prime Minister, whether I was in possession of some new fact that I could produce at Versailles. It was tantamount to saying that if I couldn't pull the truth out of my pocket, like my handkerchief, I had no choice but to let myself be amnestied, without making so much fuss. Such a question astonished me, coming from the Prime Minister; he knows perfectly well that nobody walks around with the truth in their pocket and that the whole purpose of a trial is to let the truth emerge from questioning, testimony and pleas. And above all, the irony of asking *me* such a question! After all they have done to keep my mouth shut, to prevent me from establishing the truth, suddenly they were concerned that the truth might be right there in my pocket! I replied to the chairman of your commission that I was in possession of a new fact; that although I was not carrying the truth around with me I knew exactly where to find it; and that I was simply asking the Prime Minister to urge the Minister of Justice to advise the judge presiding over the court at Versailles not to suspend my rogatory commission when the time came for me to ask it to have M. von Schwartzkoppen questioned. And that would be the end of the Dreyfus Affair, and France would be saved from the most appalling catastrophe.

Now, Senators, go ahead. Pass the amnesty law. Strangle the country. Proclaim, along with Justice Delegorgue, that the question will not be raised. Like Presiding Justice Perivier, tighten the screws on Labori. Then, if France is dishonoured one day in front of the entire world, it will be your doing.

*

Senators, I am not naive enough to suppose that this letter will make you waver even for one second from your determination (so I suspect) to pass the amnesty law. It is easy to foresee how you will vote, for your vote will be the sequel to your long, long record of weakness and impotence. You tell yourselves that you cannot do anything else because you haven't the courage to do anything else.

I am writing this letter simply for the great honour of having written it. I am doing my duty, and I doubt that you will do yours. The law of change of jurisdiction was a judicial crime. The amnesty will be an act of civic treason. It will hand the Republic over to its worst enemies.

Pass the amnesty law. You will soon be punished for it, and one day it will put you to shame.

L'Aurore, 29 May 1900

Letter to M. Emile Loubet, President of the Republic

Monsieur le Président,
Nearly three years ago, on 13 January 1898, I wrote to your predecessor, M. Félix Faure, a letter which he chose to overlook. That was unfortunate for his reputation. Now that he is dead and gone, his memory is still sullied by the monstrous iniquity of which I warned him and of which he made himself an accomplice by using the full extent of the power which his high office conferred on him to cover up the guilty parties.

Now you are in his place, and now the abominable Affair – after having tainted the whole succession of cowardly or collusive governments – is about to end, for the moment, in a supreme denial of justice, namely the amnesty law that the Chambers, under considerable pressure, have just passed. History will know it as the villainous amnesty. Like the ones before it, your government is sinking down into wrongdoing by accepting the gravest kind of responsibility. Have no doubt about it: an entire page in the book of your life will bear this blot. Your term as President runs the risk of being sullied in the same indelible fashion as the term of the previous President.

Allow me, then, M. le Président, to express the full extent of my anxiety. Now that the amnesty has been passed I shall conclude with this letter, since an earlier letter from me was one of the causes of the amnesty. Yet no one can reproach me with being over-talkative. On 18 July 1898 I left for England. Not until 5 June 1899 did I come back from England, and throughout those eleven months I kept silent. I did not speak again until September 1899, after the trial in Rennes. Then once again I fell into a complete silence which I broke but once, last May, to protest against the amnesty bill then before the Senate. For over eighteen months I have been waiting for justice to take its course; every three months I am subpoenaed, and every three months my case is postponed until the next session. It has been deplorable and comical. And today, instead of justice, we have this villainous and offensive amnesty. I believe I have a right and a duty to speak up; I have been a good citizen, after all, keeping silent, not wanting to be in the way or make any trouble, waiting so patiently, counting on the system of justice that has proved to be so slow.

I repeat: I must conclude. The first phase of the Affair – what I will call the full crime of it – is now coming to an end. I am duty-bound to take stock of the situation, to state what we have achieved and what we are confident the future will bring, before I fall silent once again.

*

I need not go back to the very first abominations in this Affair. I need only resume with the events that have followed that appalling decision in Rennes, that act of provocation and insolent iniquity which made the entire world shudder. This, M. le Président, is where your government – and consequently you yourself – began to commit misdeeds.

I am sure that one day – with documents to back them up – people will tell what happened in Rennes. By that I mean the way your government allowed itself to be deceived and then felt obliged to betray us. The Ministers were convinced that Dreyfus would be acquitted. How could they have had any doubts on that score, since the Supreme Court of Appeal believed it had boxed in the court martial with the terms of a ruling so clear that his innocence was obvious, without any need for discussion? Why would they have worried in the slightest, when their subordinates and intermediaries and witnesses and even the persons involved in the drama were promising that there would be at least a majority, if not unanimity? They laughed at our fears; they sat back and let the court fall prey to collusion and false testimony and flagrant manoeuvres designed to intimidate and bring pressure. Their blind confidence even led them to compromise you, M. le Président, by not warning you; for I am certain that had you had the slightest doubt you would not have committed yourself, in your speech at Rambouillet, to accepting the court's decision, whatever it might be. Does to govern mean to lack foresight? Here you have a Ministry whose officials are appointed to ensure that the system of justice functions properly and that a decision by the Supreme Court of Appeal is carried out as it should be. The Ministry is aware what danger that decision is in if it is left in the feverish hands of people whose scruples have been gnawed away. And yet it does nothing! Optimism makes it complacent. It allows the crime to be committed in broad daylight! I am willing to believe that those ministers did, at the time, want justice to be done – but then, how would they have behaved, I wonder, if they had not wanted justice to be done?

Then the news of Dreyfus's condemnation burst upon us, a monstrosity such as the world had never seen before: an innocent man found guilty not once but twice. In Rennes, once the Supreme Court of Appeal had carried out its inquiry, his innocence was obvious; no one could doubt it. And then that thunderbolt. France shuddered with horror, as did all nations everywhere. What is the government going to do? – a government betrayed, fooled, provoked, a government whose incomprehensible laxity led to such a disaster? Once again, I am willing to believe that this blow, so profoundly painful to all just men, was also upsetting to your ministers who had taken responsibility for ensuring that the law would triumph. But what will they do now? What action will they take, now that their certainties have collapsed and they have seen that far from having been the architects of truth and justice, their clumsiness or heedlessness has caused a moral debacle which it will take France a long, weary time to overcome? Here, M. le Président, is where your government's misdeeds and your own misdeeds begin; here is where our views and feelings differ from yours, and the gap continues to widen.

In our view, hesitation was out of the question; there was only one way to operate on France and remove the evil that was eating away at it, only one way to cure France and restore genuine peace. Troubled spirits cannot be soothed until our conscience is clear; we will not regain our health as long as the poison of injustice still circulates in our veins. Some way had to be found to lay the matter before the Supreme Court of Appeal again, immediately. Let no one try to say that that was impossible; the government had the necessary facts in its possession, even leaving aside the question of an abuse of power. It should have liquidated all the trials then under way and let justice do its job, without letting a single one of the guilty parties get away. The ulcer should have been thoroughly cleansed; our people should have been given a lofty lesson in truth and justice; honour should have been restored to France in the eyes of the world. Only then would it have been possible to say that France was healed, that balm had been applied to its wounds.

But that is when your government chose the opposite direction. It resolved to stifle the truth once more and bury it; if only some earth was shovelled over it, it would cease to exist. Your government was so aghast at seeing the innocent man condemned a second time that all it could think of was to pardon him, first of all, and then silence the country by using an amnesty law as a gag. These two measures complement one another; they are the devices used by a desperate government, which failed to live up to its mission and wants to paper over the cracks by taking refuge in *raison d'Etat*. The government tried to cover you, M. le Président, since it had committed the error of letting you commit yourself. It also tried to save itself, believing perhaps that it was taking the only practical step possible to save the Republic in danger.

Thus, the great misdeed was committed that day, when the last opportunity was within reach to take action, to restore the country's dignity and strength. Thereafter, as the months went by, it became more and more difficult, I grant you, to achieve salvation. The government let itself be backed into a corner, and when it came before the Chambers to state that it could not go on governing if the amnesty was refused, it was no doubt stating the truth. Yet wasn't it the government which had made the amnesty necessary in the first place, by disarming the system of justice at a time when justice would still have been possible? In short the government that had been chosen to salvage everything let everything fall apart. And when the time came to seek the supreme means of redeeming a catastrophic situation, the best it could manage was to come full circle, to end up doing what the governments of M. Méline and M. Dupuy had begun by doing – strangling the truth, strangling justice.

What a shameful thing it is for France that not one of its politicians has felt strong enough, intelligent enough, courageous enough to live up to the situation, to cry out the truth, to be the man France would have followed! For three years we have watched a succession of men hold power, totter and then fall, pulled down by the same error. I am not talking about M. Méline, the ill-fated man who was behind the whole criminal undertaking; nor M. Dupuy, the equivocal man, determined from the outset to throw in his lot with whoever was the strongest. But what about M. Brisson, who dared to be in favour of a revision? Yet he allowed Colonel Picquart to be arrested, when the Henry forgery was discovered. How painful to see him make that irreparable mistake! And what about M. Waldeck-Rousseau, who spoke out courageously against the law of change of jurisdiction? His speech echoed nobly in all our consciences. Yet he felt obliged to attach his name to this amnesty, which strips justice of its powers more brutally still. Isn't that disastrous? We cannot help wondering whether it wouldn't have been preferable to have some enemy as head of our government, for as soon as the friends of truth and justice are in power, they too can think of no better way to save the country than through lies and iniquity.

*

After all, M. le Président, this amnesty law that the Chambers have so reluctantly voted – it is understood, is it not, that they did so in order to save the country. Having backed itself into a corner, your government had to choose the argument it felt was strongest: the defence of the Republic. The Dreyfus Affair has at least revealed what dangers the Republic was in, the target of a double-barrelled plot by clerical and militaristic forces, acting on behalf of all the reactionary forces of the past. And in response, the government's political plan has been simple: get rid of the Dreyfus Affair by stifling it, make the majority realize that if it is not docile, if it does not obey, it will not get the promised reforms. That would be all well and good if it didn't involve replacing one poison by another, saving the country from clericalism and militarism by letting it continue to agonize in the throes of lies and iniquity as it has for the past three years.

Now, the arena in which the Dreyfus Affair is taking place is certainly the most detestable kind of political arena. Or so it became, at any rate, because the people were abandoned, turned over to the worst sorts of felons amid the stench of the foul press. And I grant you, once again, that at the present time action has become difficult, virtually impossible. But how short-sighted it is to think you can save a people from the disease which is eating it away by decreeing that the disease no longer exists! The amnesty has been voted; the trials will not take place; legal action can no longer be taken against the guilty parties. But that does not alter the fact that Dreyfus, though innocent, was twice found guilty. And as long as reparation has not been made for that frightful iniquity, France will continue to rave, in the grip of ghastly nightmares. No matter how deep you bury the truth, it burrows ahead underground and one day it will surface again everywhere and spread like some vengeful vegetation. Worse still, you are helping to demoralize ordinary people by confusing their feelings of what is just. If no one is punished, that must mean that no one is guilty. How can you expect ordinary people to know any better, when they have been fed a diet of corruption and falsehood? The people should have been given a clear lesson but instead you darken their minds, undermining their moral sense once and for all.

There you have the crux of the whole business. The government maintains that it is putting balm on the country's wounds with its amnesty law, while we claim that it is running the risk, instead, of paving the way for new calamities. Once again, where there is iniquity there can be no peace.

Politics lives from one day to the next and thinks it has achieved eternity when it has gained six months of silence. Perhaps the government will enjoy some respite, and I even grant you that it may put that time to good use. But truth will awaken, and clamour, and unleash storms. Where they will come from, I do not know, but come they will. And then the men who have been incapable of taking action will be so powerless! and the villainous amnesty that they have applied indiscriminately to decent people and rogues alike will crush them with such a weight! Once the country knows the facts, once the country has risen up and yearns to render justice, won't its anger fall, first of all, on the people who did not enlighten it while it was in their power to do so?

My great, good friend Labori has expressed it in his superbly eloquent way: the amnesty law is a law of weakness, a law of impotence. It seems to accumulate the cowardice of one government after another, the inadequacies of all the men who, when they were brought face to face with an atrocious injustice, did not feel strong enough to prevent it or even to make up for it. Faced with the need to strike hard and strike high, every one of them quailed and backed down. And now, at this late date, it is not oblivion that they are bringing us, not pardon, but fear, stupidity, the inability of successive governments to do so much as simply apply the existing laws. They claim they want to soothe our troubled spirits through mutual concessions. That is not true. The truth is that they did not have the courage to take an axe to a rotting, antiquated society; and to hide their inaction they talk about clemency and they dismiss, on equal terms, a man like Esterhazy, the traitor, and a man like Picquart, the hero to whom the future will erect statues. This is an evil deed and it will surely be punished, for it not only wounds the nation's conscience, it corrupts the nation's morals.

Is that a fitting education for a Republic? What kind of lessons are you giving our democracy when you teach it that there are times when truth and justice exist no longer, if the interest of the State requires them to vanish? The doctrine of *raison d'Etat* has been restored to the place of honour by free men who condemned it in the Monarchy and in the Church. Politics must truly have the power to pervert souls. To think that several of our friends, several of those who fought so valiantly from the very first day, have given in to sophistry by supporting the amnesty law, as a necessary political measure! It breaks my heart to see an upright, courageous man like Ranc take Picquart's defence against Picquart himself by proclaiming his joy that the amnesty, which will prevent Picquart from defending his honour, will save him from the hatred that a court martial would undoubtedly unleash against him. And Jaurès! Noble, generous Jaurès, who has expended his energy so magnificently and sacrificed his seat as a Deputy – a wonderful thing, in these days of electoral greed! And now he too goes along with seeing all of us amnestied together – Picquart and Esterhazy, Reinach and du Paty de Clam, General Mercier and myself – at one fell swoop! Does this mean that absolute justice ends where the interest of one party begins? Ah, how sweet to be a solitary man, to belong to no sect, to owe allegiance only to one's conscience! How agreeable to follow one's own path without wavering, to love only truth and strive for truth, even if it shake the earth and bring the skies down upon us!

Back in the days when there was hope during the Dreyfus Affair, M. le Président, we had a fine dream. Were we not confronted with a case that was unique? a crime involving all the reactionary forces, all the forces that impede the free progress of mankind? Never had a more decisive experiment been possible; never would a more lofty practical lesson be given to the people. In but a few months we would enlighten the people; we would do more for their education and maturity than a century of political struggles had done. We would need only to show the people all the forces of evil at work, accomplices in the most appalling crime, the crushing of an innocent man whose unspeakable torture wrenched a cry of rebellion from all mankind.

Confident in the power of truth, we awaited its triumph. It would be the apotheosis of justice – the enlightened people arising as one, acclaiming Dreyfus upon his return to France, the country recovering its conscience, building an altar to justice, celebrating the reconquest of glorious, sovereign law. And to crown the whole, a kiss of universal brotherhood, the troubled spirits of every citizen soothed, all men united in the communion of universal solidarity. Alas, M. le Président, you know what became of that vision: a dubious victory; for every scrap of truth revealed, utter confusion elsewhere; the notion of justice clouded over still more in the minds of the unfortunate people. It appears that our conception of victory was too crude, too eager. The course of human affairs does not bestow dazzling triumphs which raise up a nation, hallowing it in a single day, making it strong and all-powerful. Such heights are not scaled with but one leap; pain and effort are required. Never is the struggle finished; each step forward is achieved at the cost of suffering; only the sons can observe the achievements of their fathers. Now, in my ardent love for our people, the people of France, I shall never console myself for having been unable to complete their civic education through the admirable practical lesson provided by the Dreyfus Affair. But I have long been resigned to seeing truth penetrate the people only little by little, until the day they are mature enough to meet their destiny of liberty and fraternity.

We never had any other thought but that. From the beginning the Dreyfus Affair expanded to become a social affair, a human affair. The innocent man suffering on Devil's Island, crushed by evil forces, by the callous disdain of truth and justice, was but a symptom; the entire nation suffered with him. By saving him, we would be saving all who had been oppressed and sacrificed. But now Dreyfus is free, restored to his loved ones

– and who are the scoundrels, or the fools, who accused us of trying to revive the Dreyfus Affair? They are the same people whose shifty political scheming has forced the government to demand an amnesty while continuing to infect the country with their lies. As for the verdict reached in Rennes, certainly Dreyfus should seek by every legal means to have it revised and we will help him with every means in our power the day the occasion arises. In fact I imagine that the Supreme Court of Appeal will be happy to have the last word, for the sake of its honour as the pinnacle of our judicial system. Only, that will merely be a judicial matter. None of us has had the foolish idea of reviving the Dreyfus Affair as it was before. The only desirable and feasible task today is to draw the political and social lessons of the Affair, the harvest of reforms for which it revealed the urgent need. That will be our defence, in answer to the abominable accusations being brought against us. Better still, that will be our final victory.

There is a phrase that irritates me, M. le Président, every time I hear it. It has become a commonplace that the Dreyfus Affair has done France a great deal of harm. I have heard it said in every quarter, I have seen it written by every pen; friends of mine say it all the time; I may have said it myself. And yet there could be no untruer statement. I won't even mention the admirable example France has set for the entire world through its titanic struggle for a matter of justice, the conflict that has mobilized all of its active forces for the sake of an ideal. Nor will I mention the results already achieved – the offices of the War Ministry cleaned out, all the equivocal actors in this drama swept away, the system of justice having carried out a small part of its mission, in spite of everything. But the Dreyfus Affair has done France the greatest amount of good simply by having been the putrid symptom, the pustule that breaks out and reveals the infection within. Remember the days when people merely shrugged at the danger of clericalism and it was thought elegant to make fun of Monsieur Homais, that backward and laughable Voltairian. All of the reactionary forces had made inroads underground, beneath the paving stones of our great city of Paris, undermining the Republic, fully intending to take over the city and all of France the day the current institutions collapsed. And then the Dreyfus Affair unmasked those forces before they were ready to strangle the country completely. And the republicans finally realized that their Republic was about to be confiscated unless they did something about it. The whole movement in defence of the Republic sprang from that, and if France has been saved from the reactionaries' patient plot, it is to the Dreyfus Affair that France will owe its rescue.

I hope the government will fulfil the task it has just invoked – the defence of the Republic – in order to persuade the Chambers to pass the amnesty law. Only by doing so can the government be courageous and useful at last. But let it not deny the Dreyfus Affair; let it acknowledge that the Affair was the best thing that could have happened to France; and let it proclaim, as we do, that without the Dreyfus Affair, France today would be, no doubt, in the hands of the reactionaries.

As for my personal affairs, M. le Président, I am not recriminating. For nearly forty years I have pursued my task as a writer, unmoved each time a book of mine has been condemned or acquitted. I have left it up to the future to reach a final judgement on my work. That is why a trial that has not been brought to a conclusion does not upset me very much. It is simply one more affair that the future will judge. And although I regret there is no new trial, because it might have brought a stunning revelation of truth, I know the truth will surely find some other way of revealing itself, and that consoles me.

Yet I would have been curious, I must admit, to see what a new jury would have thought of the first conviction pronounced against me, achieved under threats from the generals, who were armed with that terrifying Henry forgery as with a bludgeon. Not that in a trial of a purely political nature I would have much faith in a jury – so easy to lead astray, so easy to browbeat. But even so, the fact of resuming the discussion could have provided an interesting lesson, when the investigation by the Supreme Court of Appeal had proven every one of the charges I originally brought. Can you picture it? A man who had been convicted on the strength of a forgery and who reappears before his judges once the forgery has been acknowledged, admitted to! A man who had accused other men on the strength of facts whose absolute veracity has since been proven by an inquiry by the highest Court! I would have spent a few enjoyable hours, for it would have been a pleasure to be acquitted; and if I had been condemned a second time, well, cowardly stupidity and blind passion have a special beauty of their own that has always fascinated me.

But I must be a bit more specific, M. le Président. I am writing to you only in order to conclude this affair, and it is appropriate that I should repeat before you the accusations which I expressed to M. Félix Faure, so as to establish now and for all time that they were fair and moderate, understatements in fact, and that in granting me amnesty your government's law is granting amnesty to an innocent man.

I accused Lt-Col du Paty de Clam 'of having been the diabolical agent of a miscarriage of justice (though unwittingly, I am willing to believe), and then of having defended his evil deed for the past three years through the most preposterous and blameworthy machinations'. Now that is discreet and courteous, is it not? compared with the report by the formidable Captain Cuignet, who accuses him outright of committing forgery.

I accused General Mercier 'of having been an accomplice, at least by weak-mindedness, to one of the most iniquitous acts of this century'. – Now, here, I apologize; I withdraw the 'weak-mindedness'. But then, if General Mercier does not have the excuse of being feeble-minded, that means he is entirely responsible for the actions which he committed, as the inquiry by the Supreme Court of Appeal established, and which the legal Code classifies as criminal.

I accused General Billot 'of having had in his hands undeniable proof that Dreyfus was innocent and of having suppressed it, of having committed this crime against justice and against humanity for political purposes, so that the General Staff, which had been compromised, would not lose face'. – Every single document that has been brought to light today proves that General Billot cannot have been unaware of his subordinates' criminal manoeuvrings; and I add that it was on his orders that the secret file concerning my father was turned over to a foul newspaper.

I accused Generals de Boisdeffre and Gonse 'of having been accomplices to this same crime, one out of intense clerical conviction, no doubt, and the other perhaps because of the esprit de corps which makes the War Office the Holy of Holies and hence unattackable'. – Once the Henry forgery had been discovered, General de Boisdeffre passed sentence on himself by resigning, removing himself from the world stage: the tragic downfall of a man who had been raised to the highest ranks, the loftiest functions, and who fell into nothingness. As for General Gonse, he is among those whose terrible burden of responsibility has been clearly established but whom the amnesty nonetheless absolves.

I accused General de Pellieux and Major Ravary 'of having led a villainous inquiry, by which I mean a most monstrously one-sided inquiry, the report on which, by Ravary, constitutes an imperishable monument of naive audacity'. – One need only re-read the report on the inquiry by the Supreme Court of Appeal to see that, in it, collusion was established, proven by the most overwhelming documents and testimony. The 'investigation' carried out in the Esterhazy affair was a blatant judicial farce.

I accused the three handwriting experts, Messrs Belhomme, Varinard and Couard, 'of having submitted fraudulent and deceitful reports – unless a medical examination concludes that their eyesight and their judgement were impaired'. – I wrote that in response to the extraordinary statement by these three experts in which they claimed that the bordereau was not in Esterhazy's handwriting, a mistake which, in my opinion, a ten-year-old would not have made. We know that Esterhazy himself now admits to having written the bordereau. And the presiding judge, M. Ballot-Beaupré, solemnly stated in his report that in his opinion there could be no doubt about it.

I accused the War Office 'of having conducted an abominable campaign in the press (especially in *L'Eclair* and *L'Echo de Paris*) in order to cover up its misdeeds and lead public opinion astray'. I will not labour the point. I believe that proof has been provided through everything that has come to light since then and everything that the guilty parties themselves have had to confess.

Finally, I accused the first court martial 'of having violated the law by sentencing a defendant on the basis of a document which remained secret', and I accused the second court martial 'of having covered up that illegal action, on orders, by having, in its own turn, committed the judicial crime of knowingly acquitting a guilty man.' – As for the first court martial, the fact that a secret document was produced has been clearly established by the inquiry conducted by the Supreme Court of Appeal, and even at the trial in Rennes. As for the second court martial, once again an inquiry proved that collusion occurred, that General de Pellieux intervened again and again, and that the acquittal was obtained, as the chiefs of staff at military headquarters wished it to be, under obvious pressure.

As you can see, M. le Président, every single one of my accusations was borne out by the crimes and misdeeds that have been discovered; and I repeat that those accusations seem very pale and modest today, compared with the dismal accumulation of abominations that were committed. Never, I admit, would I myself have dared to suspect there was such an accumulation. Therefore, I ask you, is there a court anywhere, an honest or even simply a reasonable court, which would cover itself with shame by sentencing me once again, now that everything I originally said has been proven in broad daylight? And don't you agree that your government's law which grants me amnesty – I, an innocent man among the heap of guilty persons I denounced – is truly a villainous law?

*

Thus, M. le Président, the initial phase of the Affair – which the amnesty, of course, has ended – is all over, at least for the time being.

By way of reparation, they have promised us that History will do us justice. That is a little like the Catholics' paradise, used to convince the poor – the miserable, starving dupes – to hang on a little longer: suffer, my friends, eat your dry bread, sleep on the bare ground while the fortunate of this world sleep in feather beds and feast on delicacies. Likewise, let the scoundrels lord it over you while you, the just, are shoved into the gutter. And then they add that once we are all dead, it is to us that statues will be put up. That is fine with me, and indeed I hope that History's revenge will be more reliable than the delights of paradise. But a little justice here on earth would not have been an unpleasant thing.

Not that I pity us. No, I am convinced that the end is in sight, as they say. Falsehood has an inherent weakness: it cannot last forever, whereas truth, which is one and indivisible, has eternity on its side. Thus, M. le Président, your government maintains that its amnesty law will bring about peace and we believe instead that it will pave the way for new disasters. Be patient; we shall see who is right. I believe, and I say it over and over again, that the Affair cannot end as long as France does not acknowledge the injustice and make amends for it. I have said that the fourth act was performed in Rennes and that there will inevitably be a fifth act. My heart still shudders at the thought that the German Emperor has the truth in his possession, that he can throw it in our faces if the time comes – and he may choose to have the time come. That would be the frightful fifth act, the one I have always dreaded. No French government should give in to the idea of that terrible possibility, even for one minute.

They have promised us History. Let me refer you as well to History, M. le Président. History will record what you have done. You will have your page in that great book. Think of poor Félix Faure, the tanner who became a god, so popular early in his career, whose democratic good-naturedness even I found appealing. Now and forever more he is nothing but a weak and unjust figure who allowed an innocent man to become a martyr. Wouldn't you rather be remembered, on that marble slab, as the man of truth and justice? There may still be time.

I am merely a poet, a solitary teller of tales who works away in his corner but who works with a will. I have realized that a good citizen must be content to offer his country the work he does the least clumsily, and that is why I shut myself away in my books. Now I am simply going back to them, since the mission I assigned myself has been accomplished. I have done my part to the best of my ability and now I am fading back into silence for all time.

But I shall keep my eyes and my ears wide open. Like sister Anne,[1] I am alert, day and night, to what may appear on the horizon. Indeed I stubbornly hope to see a great deal of truth and justice reach us soon from those distant fields where the future grows.

And I am still waiting.

M. le Président, I beg you to accept the assurance of my profound respect.

L'Aurore, 22 December 1900

---

1   In the story of Bluebeard, sister Anne anxiously waits for her brothers to come to the rescue.

Leading Figures Involved in the Dreyfus Affair and Other Figures Close to Zola

These texts have been taken or adapted from volume IX of Zola's *Correspondance* (Presses de l'Université de Montréal and CNRS Editions, 1993).

ALEXIS, Paul (1847–1901)

Son of a notary public, he studied law but abandoned it after getting his degree. In September 1869, he left Aix en Provence and went to Paris, where he became a frequent visitor at the Zolas' home. Devoting himself to literature, Alexis contributed to several newspapers as well as writing novels, short stories and plays. He was also among the contributors to the *Soirées de Médan*. His friendship with Zola went very deep, and in 1882 Alexis published *Emile Zola, notes d'un ami*, a book of outstanding importance for anyone wishing to know and understand Zola. Zola and his wife were the godparents of Alexis's first son, while Alexis was the godfather of Zola's son Jacques and Mm. Alexis the godmother of Zola's daughter Denise. Alexis and his wife were among the few people to be received in Jeanne Rozerot's home. 'Zola's shadow', Alexis was a socialist and an ardent Dreyfusard.

BERNARD-LAZARE [Lazare, Bernard, known as] (1865–1903)

His father was a tailor. He studied in Nîmes, then came to Paris in October 1886. He frequented the symbolist and decadent poets, registered in the new religious sciences section of the Ecole pratique des hautes études and became literary critic for the journal *La Nation* in January 1891, then director of the review called *Entretiens politiques et littéraires*. Later he wrote for several of the important dailies and for the anarchist press. In 1892 he published a collection of symbolist short stories, *Le Miroir des légendes*. At this stage he was in favour of revolutionary internationalism and the total assimilation of the Jews; in 1894 he published *L'Antisémitisme, son histoire et ses causes*. That same year, for the literary supplement of *Le Figaro*, he wrote a series of acerbic portraits of literary figures, including Zola. In February 1895, he met Mathieu Dreyfus, who soon won him over to his cause and suggested that he write a pamphlet on the Dreyfus Affair. Bernard-Lazare published this work in 1896; in the weeks that followed, he had talks with several political and literary figures, including Zola, and campaigned in favour of Alfred Dreyfus in the columns of *L'Aurore*. Also in 1896, he came into contact with Theodor Herzl and, in 1898, he was a delegate to the second Zionist congress, in Basel. Although he broke with Herzl a few months later, he continued to militate in favour of the creation, in Palestine, of a Jewish nation based on democratic principles and freed of 'ritualistic and Talmudic superstitions'. On his death he left an unfinished work, *Le Fumier de Job*, intended for Péguy's review, *Cahiers de la quinzaine*.

BERTILLON, Alphonse (1853–1914)

He invented a method of identifying criminals called anthropometry. As director of the criminal records office at the Paris prefecture of police, he was appointed by General

Mercier, in October 1894, to make an expert appraisal of the bordereau. Bertillon concluded that the handwriting was that of Alfred Dreyfus.

BILLOT, Jean-Baptiste (1828–1907)
Minister of War from April 1896 to June 1898, he obstinately refused the idea of any revision of Dreyfus's trial, even though he was a friend of Scheurer-Kestner.

BOISDEFFRE *see* LE MOUTON DE BOISDEFFRE

BRISSON, Henri (1835–1912)
He was a Freemason, and an anti-clerical radical. Elected President of the Chamber of Deputies in 1881, he was appointed Président du Conseil (Prime Minister) in 1885. In 1894 and then in 1898 he again became President of the Chamber. His second Cabinet, formed on 28 June 1898, fell a few months later, after his three Ministers of War – Cavaignac, Zurlinden and Chanoine – resigned one after the other, just at the time he himself had been won over to the principle of a revision. He was President of the Chamber again in 1904 and 1906.

BRUNEAU, Alfred (1857–1934)
The son of a violinist and music publisher, he won first prize in cello in a competition at the Conservatoire in 1876, then second prize in the Rome competition in 1881. In March 1888, he asked Zola for permission to set *La faute de l'abbé Mouret* to music; but since Zola had sold the rights to Massenet, he offered Bruneau his new book, *Le Rêve*. The librettist Louis Gallet versified it, and the work was performed at the Opéra-Comique in June 1891. This success encouraged the two authors to adapt Zola's short story, *L'attaque du moulin*, which was performed in November 1893. For a year Bruneau had also been a music columnist first for *Gil Blas*, then *Le Figaro* and *Le Matin*. Zola and Bruneau, now close friends, worked together on several other operatic works: *Messidor* (at the Opéra, February 1897), *L'Ouragan* (at the Opéra-Comique, April 1901) and *L'Enfant roi* (Opéra-Comique, April 1905; the score had been completed a few weeks before Zola's death). In 1925 Bruneau was elected to the Institut, to succeed Paul Dukas. In 1931 he published a book of recollections of Zola, *A l'ombre d'un grand coeur*.

CAVAIGNAC, Godefroy (1853–1905)
Son of Eugène Cavaignac (who put down the insurrection of 1848 and was named head of the executive branch of government) and a graduate of the Ecole polytechnique, he was elected Deputy in 1882 and became Under-Secretary of State for War in Brisson's first Cabinet in 1885, then was Minister of the Navy and the Colonies in the Léon Bourgeois Cabinet in 1895–6. After Méline's government fell, Cavaignac was made Minister of War in Brisson's second Cabinet. An energetic man, he proclaimed, in his celebrated speech to the Chamber on 7 July 1898, that he was prepared to put an end to the Affair; he believed he could provide incontrovertible proof that Dreyfus was guilty. On 13 August, Captain Cuignet, his military attaché, discovered the 'Henry forgery'. While Cavaignac did not deny this discovery, he continued to oppose revision and on 3 September he resigned. He then joined the Ligue de la Patrie française and until the end of his life continued to oppose all attempts at revision.

CHARPENTIER, Georges (1846–1905)
Son of Gervais Charpentier, the publisher, he started out as editor of the news-in-brief department for *Le Journal des débats*. With Maurice Dreyfous as his partner for five years, he succeeded his father, publishing Zola (beginning in 1872), Goncourt, Flaubert, Daudet, etc. In his own words, he became the 'publisher of naturalism'. In the spring of

1872 he married Marguerite Lemonnier, daughter of Gabriel Lemonnier, who had been jeweller to the Crown. Her salon, at 11, rue de Grenelle in Paris, was one of those that were most in vogue in her day. Every Friday, beginning in 1875, it attracted men of letters, society figures, politicians (Léon Gambetta, Jules Grévy, Charles Floquet, Henri Rochefort, Jules Ferry, Georges Clemenceau, etc.), musicians and painters. She supported the Impressionists, particularly Renoir. After both of their sons died, Charpentier sold his publishing house to Eugène Fasquelle, his friend and partner, in 1896. Until their death, he and his wife devoted themselves to various good works, in particular a day nursery which Marguerite Charpentier started in 1901 and in which Alexandrine Zola was active. The Charpentiers were very close friends of the Zolas; they saw each other frequently and went on holiday together several times. Zola was godfather to their son Paul.

CLEMENCEAU, Georges (1841–1929)

After completing his studies at medical school in Paris in 1865, he mingled with the young republicans and wrote in opposition papers such as *Travail* (for which Zola wrote between 1860 and 1862) and *Le Matin*. He spent some time in England, then four years in the United States. He then practised medicine in France. Elected to the National Assembly on 8 February 1871, he was one of the 107 Deputies who rejected the preliminaries to peace. After the repression of the Commune, he resigned from the National Assembly. On 20 February 1876, he was re-elected from the 18th arrondissement in Paris and on 16 May 1877, he was among the Deputies who opposed de Broglie's government. Continually re-elected until 1893, he was in favour of the revision of the Constitution, the adoption of a sweeping national plan for education, and economic and social reforms, and led vigorous attacks on the expansionist colonial policy. He was first in favour of, then opposed to, General Boulanger. The Panama Affair caused his political downfall, whereupon he reverted to a career in letters and journalism. From 1897 to 1899, he campaigned in *L'Aurore* for the revision of Dreyfus's trial. He supported Zola and went to see him in England in January 1899 and again in May. As Senator from the département of the Var in 1902, Minister of the Interior (March 1906), and Prime Minister from October 1906 to July 1909, he was instrumental in bringing about the separation of Church and State and repressed trades union agitation, which made the socialists openly hostile to him. On 19 November 1917, at Poincaré's request, he formed a new Cabinet and led France to victory. He presided over the Paris peace conference in 1919. After the Versailles treaty was signed, he withdrew from public life and wrote two volumes of personal meditations, *Demosthène* (1926) and *Au soir de la pensée* (1927).

DEMANGE, Edgar (1841–1925)

A lawyer, he defended Alfred Dreyfus before the first court martial in Paris (December 1894) and before the second in Rennes (7 August–9 September 1899).

DEROULEDE, Paul (1846–1914)

He became a member of the Paris Bar in June 1870, then volunteered for service in the war of 1870–1. He wrote plays and published volumes of verse. In 1882, with Henri Martin, he founded the Ligue des patriotes; five years later, he placed it at the service of General Boulanger. He was Deputy from Angoulême from 1889 to 1893 and was elected again in May 1898. In September, he reorganized the Ligue des patriotes, which had been dissolved in 1889, and in the months that followed appeared at the head of the anti-Dreyfusard movements. During the funeral of Félix Faure, in February 1899, he attempted a coup d'état; he then plotted another attempt and in January 1900 was finally sentenced to ten years' banishment. He returned to France after the amnesty law was passed in 1905.

DESMOULIN, Fernand (1853–1914)

He intended to become a doctor but for financial reasons had to abandon his studies and make a living from his talent for pencil sketches and engraving. He made his debut as painter at the Salon in 1892, where he exhibited landscapes and other subjects derived from his travels to Bruges, Prague, Monaco, Venice, etc. A contributor to *La vie moderne*, he became friendly with Georges Charpentier, founder of the review, and then, beginning in 1887, with Zola. He actively supported Zola during the Dreyfus Affair and did Zola's portrait in 1890 (for the illustrated edition of the *Soirées de Médan*), in 1893 and 1898. He also did portraits of Colonel Picquart, Scheurer-Kestner and Waldeck-Rousseau. Towards the end of his life, Desmoulin devoted himself to preaching to the inmates of Saint-Lazare prison.

DREYFUS, Alfred (1859–1935)

He came from an old family of Alsatian Jews (in 1871, when Alsace and Lorraine were annexed by Germany, his father, a wealthy industrialist, had chosen French nationality for himself and for his children who were under legal age). In 1878 he entered the Ecole polytechnique and in 1880 the Ecole d'application in Fontainebleau. In 1882 he was made a lieutenant in the 31st artillery regiment and in 1889, with the rank of captain, was assigned to the Ecole de pyrotechnie in Bourges. In 1890 he entered the Ecole de guerre and married Lucie Hadamard. Two years later he became a probationary officer on the army's General Staff. On 15 October 1894, he was arrested by Major du Paty de Clam, who accused him of having written the 'bordereau' announcing the delivery to the Germans of documents concerning French national defence. Sentenced on 22 December 1894 to deportation for life in a fortified place and to military degradation, he was put aboard ship on 21 February 1895 for Devil's Island. After the verdict of 1894 was nullified, he was again found guilty and sentenced in Rennes on 9 September 1899, but was pardoned by Emile Loubet, President of the French Republic, on 19 September. He went to live in Carpentras, with one of his sisters, then to Cologny, near Geneva. On 5 March 1904, the Supreme Court of Appeal declared that his petition for a revision of the Rennes verdict was admissible, and on 12 July 1906, the verdict was definitively quashed. The next day, the Chamber of Deputies passed a law reintegrating him into the army, with the rank of squadron chief. Decorated with the Legion of Honour, he was placed in charge of the artillery of Vincennes, then commanded the artillery of the arrondissement of Saint-Denis. He retired in October 1907 but was mobilized during World War I, assigned to an artillery park near Paris and then to a combat post in the Aisne and near Verdun, where he helped direct munitions depots.

DREYFUS, Lucie (1869–1945)

The daughter of David Hadamard, a diamond dealer, she married Alfred Dreyfus in April 1890. They had two children, Pierre (born in April 1891) and Jeanne (born in February 1893).

DREYFUS, Mathieu (1857–1930)

Alfred's older brother. At the beginning of 1895 he left the responsibility of managing the family firm to his two other brothers, Jacques and Léon, in order to campaign for the revision of Alfred's conviction. He led the Dreyfusards discreetly but vigilantly. His memories of the Affair, *L'Affaire telle que je l'ai vécue*, were published in 1978.

DRUMONT, Edouard (1844–1917)

An employee at the Seine prefecture, he soon left the civil service and entered journalism. In 1886 he became director of a newspaper called *Le Monde*, and in April that year published *La France juive*, a veritable manifesto of anti-Semitism which soon ran into one hundred and fifty editions and earned its author fame, as well as a conviction requiring him to pay a heavy fine, and two duels. In the same vein, Drumont went on to publish *La France juive devant l'opinion* (1886), *La Fin d'un monde* (1889), *La dernière bataille* (1890), *Le Testament d'un antisémite* (1891), and *Le Secret de Fourmies* (1892). On 20 April 1892, in order to give his campaign broader scope, he launched his newspaper, *La Libre parole*, subtitled '*La France aux français*' (France for the French). In May 1898, thanks to the anti-Semitic riots in Algiers, Drumont was elected Deputy from that city. In the Chamber of Deputies, he proclaimed himself leader of the anti-Jewish party. He strongly opposed a revision of Dreyfus's trial and demanded that legal action be taken against Zola.

ESTERHAZY, Ferdinand (1847–1923)

Son of General Walsin-Esterhazy, an illegitimate descendant of the French branch of one of the must illustrious families in Hungary, he was nine years old when his father died. In 1865 he became a student at the Paris law school. In 1866 he tried, and failed, the competitive entry examination for Saint-Cyr, the French officers' training school, and in 1868 he joined the pontifical Zouaves. He was promoted to second lieutenant in 1869 and joined the Foreign Legion the following year. He took part in the Franco-Prussian War (1870–1) and in 1874 became General Grenier's aide-de-camp, in Paris. This was when he discovered the Parisian 'dolce vita', becoming a member of several clubs, dabbling in speculation on the stock market and engaging in a number of love affairs, in particular with Léonide Leblanc, the renowned 'horizontale'. Thanks to that affair, he was detached to the Intelligence Bureau in 1877 and there made the acquaintance of Captain Joseph Henry. In 1886 he married Anne de Nettancourt, aged 22, but his marriage did not improve his financial situation, which was already irrevocably compromised. In July 1894 – by which time he had become a Major – he offered his services to Maximilian von Schwartzkoppen, the German military attaché in Paris. In November 1897, Mathieu Dreyfus denounced Esterhazy as the person having written the bordereau, but a court martial acquitted Esterhazy on 11 January 1898. Discharged on 31 August when the 'Henry forgery' was discovered, Esterhazy went into exile in England, where he became the London correspondent of Drumont's *Libre Parole*. From 1908 on, he lived in Harpenden, in Hertfordshire, calling himself Count Jean de Voilemont. From 1911 to 1917, he contributed articles to *L'Eclair*.

FASQUELLE, Eugène (1863–1952)

He began as a clerk in a stockbroker's office in the rue Drouot (and was later able to supply Zola with abundant information on the Stock Exchange for use in *L'Argent*). In 1886 Fasquelle became a secretary in Charpentier's publishing house, and in 1887 he married Jeanne Marpon, daughter of Charles Marpon, the publisher. By 1891 he was Georges Charpentier's partner and in July 1896, when Charpentier retired from business, Fasquelle became full owner of the publishing house, situated in the rue de Grenelle. Fasquelle published the works of Alfred Jarry, Pierre Louÿs, Maurice Maeterlinck, Marcel Pagnol and Edmond Rostand, but in 1912 he rejected the first version of *A la recherche du temps perdu* when Proust submitted it to him. The professional relationship between Fasquelle and Zola became a close friendship, and the Dreyfus Affair brought them still closer together. In February 1898, when Zola appeared before the Assize Court, Fasquelle, Bruneau, Charpentier and Desmoulin constituted his faithful bodyguards at the Palais de Jusice. Fasquelle went to see Zola in

England and accompanied him back to France in 1899, when his exile came to an end. Fasquelle was also the executor of Zola's will.

FAURE, Félix (1841–99)

Born in Paris, he settled in Le Havre, where he a founded a business in skins and hides which made him a wealthy man. He was a member of the Le Havre chamber of commerce and in 1881 was elected Deputy for the Seine-Inférieure, representing the Union républicaine movement. He was Minister of the Navy in the Dupuy government in 1894 and stood for President, against Waldeck-Rousseau and Brisson, when Casimir-Périer resigned in January 1895. To the surprise of almost everyone, Faure was elected. He devoted much of his energy to consolidating the Franco-Russian alliance, which strengthened his political reputation. From the very beginning of the Dreyfus Affair, Faure was aware of the problems it raised. In February 1895, he revealed the existence of the 'secret file' to Dr Gibert who, like himself, was from Le Havre; Gibert repeated the information to Mathieu Dreyfus. But Faure was never willing to encourage a revision of the affair and his attitude became increasingly rigid. His sudden death, on 16 February 1899, broke the stalemate and opened the way for a new trial in Rennes. During his state funeral on 23 February, there were very extensive nationalist demonstrations (Déroulède led an attempted coup d'état).

FORZINETTI, Ferdinand (1839–1909)

Director of Cherche-Midi prison, where Alfred Dreyfus was jailed on 15 October 1894. Convinced from the start that Dreyfus was innocent, he took part in the first actions aimed at bringing about a revision, seconding Bernard-Lazare when he tried to publicize his pamphlet, in November 1896. Forzinetti was revoked on 18 November 1897; three days later, in *Le Figaro*, he published the story of Dreyfus's captivity, accusing du Paty de Clam of having tortured his prisoner. Though Forzinetti was summoned to Zola's trial on 11 February 1898, the presiding judge prevented Labori from questioning him and he was thus unable to testify.

GOBERT, Alfred (born 1848)

Graphologist with the Banque de France, appointed by the Garde des sceaux (Minister of Justice) on 9 October 1894, to appraise the bordereau. Gobert's report expressed doubt as to the identity of the handwriting. This led General Mercier to call on Alphonse Bertillon.

GOHIER, Urbain [DEGOULET, Urbain, known as] (1862–1951)

In 1884 he began writing for *Le Soleil*, a royalist paper founded by Edouard Hervé. In 1897 he moved to *L'Aurore*, where he led a resounding campaign in favour of Alfred Dreyfus. As of 1902, he began writing for a wide range of newspapers, from *Le Libertaire* to *La Libre parole*. He was a wily polemicist, denouncing the abuses of the Republic and criticizing the Church. Among his many books is *Leur République*, published in 1906; it is a ferocious attack on Zola and the Dreyfusards in general.

GONSE, Charles-Arthur (1838–1917)

In 1896 he was deputy chief of the General Staff and directly in charge of the Intelligence Bureau; as such he was closely involved in all of the intrigues in the Dreyfus Affair. As soon as Picquart began to harbour suspicions about the origin of the bordereau, Gonse blocked his way. He removed Picquart from his post as head of the Intelligence Bureau and covered up – or even advised – all of Henry's doings. After de Boisdeffre resigned, Gonse was transferred to reserve duty, on 1 October 1898.

HENRY, Joseph (1846–98)
A farmer's son. As a quartermaster sergeant in 1870, he took part in the Loire campaign and in October was promoted to second lieutenant. By 1874 he was a lieutenant and two years later he became aide-de-camp to General Miribel, then chief of the General Staff. He was assigned to the Intelligence Bureau in 1877 but was poorly thought of by Major Campionnet and was soon sent to Algeria. Later he served in Tonkin and in 1890 he was promoted to Major and Commandant d'armes at Péronne, France, where, in 1902, he married Berthe Bertincourt, daughter of an innkeeper. In January 1893 he entered the Intelligence Bureau, headed by Colonel Sandherr. Although Henry lacked professional experience, he had been imposed on the Bureau by General de Boisdeffre. He was hostile to Colonel Picquart when Picquart replaced Sandherr in July 1895 and was at the crux of the intrigues involved in the Dreyfus Affair. On 31 October 1896, he fabricated the document that came to be known as the 'Henry forgery'. In November 1897 he was promoted to Lieutenant-Colonel. On 30 August 1898, after Captain Cuignet had discovered the famous forgery, Henry was questioned by Godefroy Cavaignac, the Minister of War. Henry confessed and was taken to the Mont-Valérien prison. The next morning he was found dead in his cell, his throat slit with a razor that he was still holding in his hand. A huge crowd attended his funeral, at Pogny.

JAURES, Jean (1859–1914)
A farmer's son. In 1877 he began to attend the Collège Sainte-Barbe, in Paris, at the same time as Alfred Dreyfus. He won first place in the competitive examination to enter the Ecole normale supérieure, where Henri Bergson was a fellow student. Having passed the Agrégation in philosophy in 1881, he taught in Albi then, in 1883, became maître de conférences at the university in Toulouse. He wrote for the daily *La Dépêche* and in 1885 was elected Deputy from Castres. At first, he took positions close to those of Jules Ferry but he soon moved in the direction of socialism. Defeated in the 1889 elections, he became city councillor the following year. After the miners' strike in Carmaux, he agreed to become a candidate for Deputy from Carmaux. Elected in January 1903, he immediately became the socialist group's chief spokesman in the Chamber. On 19 January 1898, along with the other members of his group in the Parliament, he signed a manifesto hostile to any involvement by the socialists in the Dreyfus Affair; but three days later, in the Chamber, he denounced the government's attitude in the Affair, and in February he testified in favour of Zola at his trial. Defeated in the elections of May 1898, he became co-political director of *La Petite République* where, from 10 August to 20 September that same year, he published a series of articles entitled 'Les Preuves' which demolished the charges brought against Dreyfus. Elected Deputy from Carmaux again in 1902, he founded the daily *L'Humanité* in 1904. When the SFIO (Section française de l'internationale ouvrière) was created in 1905, Jaurès became the veritable leader of French socialism. On 31 July 1914, he was assassinated by Raoul Villain, a member of the Ligue des jeunes amis de l'Alsace-Lorraine.

JUDET, Ernest (1851–1943)
He taught at the lycée in Bastia (Corsica) in 1876 but was forced to retire in 1878 when he refused to be transferred to Châteauroux. He was an editor on the daily *Le National* beginning in 1879, and an unsuccessful candidate in the 1881 elections. He then wrote for *La France* and *La Nouvelle Presse*. In 1886, he began working with Hippolyte Marinoni's *Le Petit Journal* and three years later had become its de facto director. In that paper he led a violent campaign against Georges Clemenceau and was fiercely opposed to the revision of Dreyfus's trial. In May 1898, citing documents which Joseph Henry had tampered with, he published two libellous articles on Zola's father for which he was fined one

thousand francs on 3 August. On the same day, in response to further attacks, Zola brought suit against Judet for the use of forgeries. The case was dismissed and Judet then sued Zola for libel; Zola was acquitted in 1900. In 1905, Judet became the director of *L'Eclair*. He was a Germanophile and during World War I maintained clandestine contact with Baron von Romberg, the German ambassador in Switzerland. In June 1917 he was granted an audience with Pope Benedict XV. In December, sensing that he was under surveillance, he sold *L'Eclair* and fled to Switzerland. In 1919 he was found guilty of treason and in 1923 was convicted in absentia. He came back to France shortly thereafter and was acquitted.

LABORI, Fernand (1860–1917)
His father was a railway inspector in eastern France. In 1880 he entered the Paris law school and in 1884 he was admitted to the Bar. He became editor-in-chief of the *Gazette du Palais* and in 1893 stood for Deputy from Reims. Renown came in 1894, when he defended Auguste Vaillant, the anarchist. In 1897 he founded a literary review, *La Revue du Palais*, which, in November 1898, became *La Grande Revue*. In January 1898 he agreed to represent Lucie Dreyfus in the Esterhazy trial, then, after 'J'accuse' was published, to be Zola's lawyer. In July 1898 he was chosen to defend Colonel Picquart, and in January 1899 he represented Joseph Reinach when Berthe Henry, Colonel Henry's widow, brought suit against him. On 14 August 1899, during the Dreyfus trial in Rennes, Labori was shot and wounded in an assassination attempt. In the 1902 elections he was defeated as a candidate from Fontainebleau but in 1906 he was elected, as an independent. He consistently supported the first Clemenceau government, and his speeches in favour of the devolution of ecclesiastical property and the elimination of courts martial were famous. Elected president of the Bar in 1911, he was given a warm reception in England, the United States and Canada. In 1914 he defended Mme Joseph Caillaux after she killed Gaston Calmette, the director of *Le Figaro*.

LEBLOIS, Louis (1854–1928)
The son of a pastor, Georges-Louis Leblois, he and Georges Picquart were schoolmates. He studied law in Paris and became a member of the Bar in 1878, then deputy public prosecutor in Dijon in 1880. Appointed to Lille in 1885, he there made the acquaintance of Marcel Prévost, the novelist, with whom he remained very close. In 1890 he left the judiciary to act as a lawyer and settled in Paris. In June 1897, Picquart confided to Leblois what he had discovered; Leblois passed on this information to Scheurer-Kestner and threw himself into the battle for the revision of Dreyfus's trial. He was made to suffer the consequences of his involvement: on 24 February 1898, at the end of Zola's trial, Leblois was discharged from his functions as deputy mayor of the seventh arrondissement in Paris; on 22 March that same year, the association of barristers suspended him for six months; and on 12 July, Cavaignac lodged a complaint against him and Picquart at the same time. Leblois did not testify at the trial in Rennes, in 1899, but he continued his political combat. He supported Jaurès in April 1903, when it was decided to undertake a second revision to establish Dreyfus's innocence definitively; and when *L'Aurore* was in severe financial straits, Leblois contributed funds, thus fostering the development of Clemenceau's political career. Leblois devoted the last years of his life to working actively for various causes. His voluminous works on the Dreyfus Affair (*L'Affaire Dreyfus; L'iniquité, la réparation; Les principaux faits et les principaux documents*) were published posthumously.

LE MOUTON DE BOISDEFFRE, Charles (1839–1919)
He rose from Brigadier General in 1887 to Major General in 1892. In September 1893, he replaced General Miribel as head of the General Staff and in May 1894 was officially

made chief of the General Staff. Confronted with the developments of the Dreyfus Affair from the very beginning, he consistently covered up for his subordinates. He testified vehemently at Zola's trial (18 February 1898), intimidating the jury. On 31 August 1898, after the 'Henry forgery' was discovered, he resigned and the following year, he requested his transfer to reserve duty.

LOUBET, Emile (1838–1929)
With a doctorate in law, he was mayor of Montélimar and Deputy from the Drôme from 1876 to 1885. He joined the 'republican left' movement. Elected Senator, he became an influential member of the republican movement in the Senate. Appointed Prime Minister in 1892, he tried, a few months later, to hush up the Panama Canal scandal but was accused of dealing weakly with the 'chéquards' (government figures accused of having received bribes) and his government was overturned on 29 November. In January 1896 he was elected president of the Senate. Three years later he became the seventh President of the Third Republic; the Dreyfusards had supported his candidacy. On the evening of the day on which he was elected, the Ligue des patriotes organized a demonstration against him. In June 1899, at the Auteuil race track, he was struck and insulted. After pardoning Dreyfus, he called for an amnesty for all of the actions relating to the Affair. His term as president was marked by the anti-clerical policy of two Prime Ministers, Waldeck-Rousseau and Combes, by the World Fair in Paris in 1900, and by intense diplomatic activity. His state visits facilitated the rapprochement with Italy and the Entente cordiale. In 1906, at the end of his seven-year term, he retired to his estate near Montélimar.

MERCIER, Auguste (1833–1921)
Minister of War from December 1893 to January 1895. He was responsible for Dreyfus's conviction and never ceased to maintain that Dreyfus was guilty, particularly in the summer of 1899, during the hearings at the trial in Rennes, where he cleverly marshalled the anti-Dreyfusard forces. He was elected Senator in 1900. In 1906 he was still energetically opposed to the bill rehabilitating Dreyfus; it became law on 13 July of that year.

MERCIER DU PATY DE CLAM, Armand (1853–1916)
A graduate of Saint-Cyr and then of the Ecole d'Etat-Major, he was deputy chief of the third bureau at the Ministry of War when the Dreyfus Affair broke out. On 14 October 1894, as a criminal police officer, he was placed in charge of the preliminary investigation concerning Alfred Dreyfus. Endowed with an unbridled imagination, he lent himself to Col Henry's machinations. He was arrested on 1 June 1899, but his case was discharged for lack of evidence; in November 1905 he was given compulsory retirement. He resumed active service at the beginning of World War I and fought courageously at the head of his regiment. In September 1916 he died as the result of his wounds.

MIRBEAU, Alice (1849–1931)
Born Augustine-Alexandrine Toulet, she married a tools manufacturer named Jules Renard at the age of sixteen, in 1865. A widow at eighteen, using 'Alice Regnault' as a pseudonym, she began a career as would-be actress and kept woman. Renowned as a beauty, she managed her affairs astutely and within fifteen years acquired a large fortune. In 1881 she left the theatre. For some time she wrote the society columns in *Le Gaulois*, where she began a liaison with Octave Mirbeau; in 1887, they were married, in London. She wrote two novels: *Mademoiselle Pomme* (1886) and *La Famille Carmettes* (1888).

MIRBEAU, Octave (1848–1917)
Three years as a pupil in the Jesuits' school at Vannes, in Brittany, instilled in him a lasting hatred of priests and the nobility. Because his father, a doctor, opposed his wish for a literary career, he studied law in Paris from 1866 to 1868. Writing for *L'Illustration* and *L'Ordre*, he supported the Impressionists. For a time, after 16 May 1877 (when Mac-Mahon, President of the Republic, dismissed Jules Simon, the Prime Minister), he was the principal private secretary to the préfet of the Ariège district. He then returned to journalism, writing news items, articles on the 'Salons' and short fiction for *Le Gaulois*, *La France*, *Paris-Journal*, *Le Figaro*, *L'Echo de Paris*, *Le Journal* and *Le Matin*. In 1883 he held anti-Semitic views, but later, in *L'Aurore*, he expressed ardent support for the revision of Dreyfus's trial. Whereas he had been a Catholic and a monarchist, his views changed to such an extent that he became an apologist for anarchism and pacificism. He attacked conventional institutions and ideas and, above all, the powerfulness of the bourgeoisie. Among his novels were *L'Abbé Jules* (1888), an anti-clerical work which marked the beginning of his friendship with Edmond de Goncourt; *Sébastien Roch* (1890), *Le Jardin des supplices* (1899) and *Le Journal d'une femme de chambre* (1900).

MONOD, Gabriel (1844–1912)
A historian and professor, he was Director of the Ecole pratique des hautes études from 1897 to 1905. In an article published in *Le Temps* on 5 November 1897, he expressed his belief that Dreyfus was innocent, thus becoming the first of the intellectuals to make such a statement publicly.

PATY DE CLAM *see* MERCIER DU PATY DE CLAM

PELLIEUX, Georges-Gabriel de (1842–1900)
Military commander of the département of the Seine. After Mathieu Dreyfus had denounced Esterhazy, de Pellieux conducted two successive inquiries, the first administrative and the second judicial, concerning Esterhazy. He concluded that there were no grounds for accusing him. At Zola's trial, de Pellieux was rash enough to refer to the 'Henry forgery', thus revealing the first crack in the arguments for the defence constructed by the General Staff. General de Galliffet, Minister of War, dismissed de Pellieux in July 1899.

PICQUART, Georges (1854–1914)
He was born into an old family of magistrates and career soldiers from the province of Lorraine. Among his school friends was Louis Leblois. In 1872 he was accepted at Saint-Cyr and in 1874 he entered the Ecole d'Etat-Major. He first saw active duty in Africa, in 1878. From 1885 to 1888, he fought in the Tonkin war, and was promoted to Major when he returned to France. Appointed to the Ecole supérieure de guerre in 1890, he taught topography there until 1893; Alfred Dreyfus was one of his students. At that time he was an attaché on the general staff of General de Galliffet, who always thought highly of him. Intellectually gifted, and trusted by his superior officers, he was considered one of the French army's brightest hopes. In October–November 1894, he took part in the inquiry conducted within the General Staff concerning the bordereau but did not play a leading role in it; soon thereafter he attended Alfred Dreyfus's trial and military degradation. On 1 July 1895, he succeeded Colonel Sandherr as head of the Intelligence Bureau. Retracing his predecessor's investigation, he became convinced that Esterhazy was guilty but encountered the opposition of his superiors, who got him out of the way in October 1896 by sending him on inspection duty for an unspecified length of time, first in eastern France, then in Tunisia. Beginning in the autumn of 1897 he became more and more deeply involved in the battle surrounding

the Dreyfus Affair. As a result he was arrested for the first time on 13 January 1898. He was discharged, then imprisoned from 13 July that year until 9 June 1899. On 13 July 1906, he was reinstated in the army with the rank of Brigadier General; on 28 September he was promoted to Major General. In Clemenceau's first cabinet, Picquart was appointed Minister of War. When the Clemenceau government fell, Picquart was transferred to reserve duty. On 22 February 1910, he was put in charge of the second army corps, based in Amiens, where he died on 19 January 1914, as the result of a riding accident.

RAVARY, Alexandre-Alfred

He was the rapporteur to the first court martial (December 1894). On 4 December 1897, General Saussier, the military governor of Paris, put Ravary in charge of conducting the inquiry preceding Esterhazy's trial. He had the bordereau examined by experts and, upon completion of his inquiry on 31 December, concluded that the case should be dismissed for lack of evidence; his report absolved Esterhazy and severely criticized Picquart.

REINACH, Joseph (1856–1921)

The son of a banker of German origin, he studied law, then wrote for Gambetta's *La République française*. He became co-proprietor of that journal and led an outspoken campaign against General Boulanger. In 1885 he failed to be elected from the Seine-et-Oise, but was elected from Digne (Basses-Alpes) in 1889 and re-elected in 1893. During the Panama Canal affair, he paid back the sum of forty thousand francs which had been paid to him in settlement of family accounts by his father-in-law, Jacques de Reinach, who acted as financial adviser to Ferdinand de Lesseps. When Alfred Dreyfus was arrested in 1894, Joseph Reinach felt convinced that he was innocent and intervened with Casimir-Périer, the then President of the French Republic, asking that Dreyfus not be tried at a closed session. In 1897 he worked alongside Scheurer-Kestner to obtain a revision of Dreyfus's trial. His articles in *Le Siècle* aroused violent diatribes in the nationalist press. In May 1898, he lost his seat in the Chamber of Deputies, and in June he was stripped of his rank in the territorial army. Because of his revelations concerning Lt-Col Joseph Henry, Reinach was sued by Henry's widow. Defeated in the 1902 elections, he recovered his seat as Deputy from the Basses-Alpes in 1906. In 1901 he began to publish his monumental *Histoire de l'affaire Dreyfus*, in six volumes, plus a one-volume index. He also left important works on Gambetta and on World War I. In 1912 his son, Adolphe Reinach, married Marguerite Dreyfus, daughter of Mathieu Dreyfus. (Adolphe was killed in battle in 1914.)

ROZEROT, Jeanne (1867–1914)

She was of humble origin; her mother died when she was very young. In the spring of 1888 she was hired as linen maid at Médan, and her love affair with Zola began in December of that year. She had two children by Zola: Denise, born in 1889, and Jacques, born in 1891. In 1898, she and the children lived in Paris, in the rue du Havre, and spent the summer at Verneuil, near Médan, where Zola had been renting a country house for her since 1895.

SANDHERR, Jean (1846–97)

A graduate of Saint-Cyr and the Ecole de guerre; in 1891 he became head of the 'Statistics Section', the Intelligence Bureau of the War Ministry. Among his subordinates in 1894 was Major Joseph Henry. Sandherr fell ill, and was replaced by Picquart on 1 July 1895. Overcome by total paralysis, Sandherr died in May 1897.

SCHEURER-KESTNER, Auguste (1833–99)
He came from a Protestant family of industrialists with a republican tradition. In 1856 he married Céline Kestner, a young woman from Thann in Alsace, and began to work in his father-in-law's chemicals business. In 1862, during the Second Empire, he was sentenced to four months in prison for republican propaganda and served his sentence in Sainte-Pélagie, in Paris. After Alsace was invaded by the German armies in 1870, he offered his services to the government of national defence and was put in charge of the pyrotechnics installation in Sète. On 8 February 1871, he was elected representative from the département of Haut-Rhin in the National Assembly; then, on 2 July, he was elected Deputy from the Seine, in tribute to Alsace and Lorraine, which had both been annexed by Germany. In September 1875, he was made a life Senator. In 1879 his friend Gambetta, who had become president of the Chamber, made Scheurer-Kestner the political editor of *La République française*. In December 1883, he became the technical director of the Kestner factory, which was now an incorporated firm, and for the rest of his life he divided his time between his political responsibilities and his professional activities. In January 1895 he became vice-president of the Senate; the following month, Mathieu Dreyfus came to call on him, and Scheurer-Kestner began to gather information on the Dreyfus Affair. In July 1897, soon after Louis Leblois told him all he had learned from Picquart, Scheurer-Kestner began to campaign for Dreyfus's rehabilitation. On 7 December that year, he tried in vain to convince his colleagues in the Senate. On 13 January 1898, his bid for re-election as vice-president of the Senate failed. Already ill with throat cancer, he withdrew from the battle for revision. He died on the day on which Dreyfus was pardoned.

TRARIEUX, Ludovic (1840–1904)
He was called to the Bar in Bordeaux and was elected its president in 1877. Deputy from Bordeaux from 1879 to 1881, he was Senator from the Gironde from 1888 until his death. In 1893–4 he was rapporteur when three of the four 'lois scélérates' (villainous laws) were voted against the anarchists; in 1895 he was Minister of Justice (26 January to 1 November). Advocating the revision of Dreyfus's trial from 1897 on, he testified at Zola's trial in February 1898 and was one of the promoters of the Ligue française pour la défense des Droits de l'homme et du citoyen (League of the Rights of Man), whose statutes he drew up together with Paul Viollet. On 10 June 1898, he was elected president of the League.

VAUGHAN, Ernest (1841–1929)
He plied a number of trades before becoming director of a printing and dyeing plant near Rouen. A great admirer of Proudhon, he joined the First International in 1867, bringing his workers in with him. Arrested in April 1871 for having attended a meeting in favour of the Commune in Paris, he spent several weeks in prison, then took refuge in Brussels. There, with other exiles, he founded a section of the First International, and wrote for various newspapers. In 1880 he returned to France, where he wrote articles for a journal in Lyons, *L'Emancipation*; the following year he became manager of Henri Rochefort's *L'Intransigeant*. In 1888, he was made editor-in-chief of the *Petit Lyonnais*, whose columns he opened up to the socialists. In 1897 he founded *L'Aurore*. In 1903 he left the world of the press, becoming director of the 'Quinze-Vingts' hospital in Paris, a post he held until 1919. Later, he was administrator of Gustave Hervé's daily newpaper, *La Victoire*.

VIZETELLY, Ernest Alfred (1853–1922)
The son of Henry Vizetelly, Zola's English publisher, he studied at Eastbourne and in Paris. He became assistant manager of the Folies-Bergère, the famous Paris music hall

in the rue Richer, and it was there that he had his first conversation with Zola, in the course of the winter of 1877–8. With his wife, Marie Tissot, who was French, he returned to London in 1887, and there entered his father's publishing house. One of his first assignments was to revise and expurgate the English translation of *La Terre*, as a result of which he was fined £100 for an offence against public decency. In 1892, after his father went bankrupt, he translated Zola's *La Débâcle* into English for Chatto and Windus; the book sold so well that they were encouraged to publish other books by Zola, and Vizetelly became established as Zola's translator in England. In 1893, he was Zola's cicerone in London, and he helped Zola throughout his exile in 1898–9. He wrote *With Zola in England* (1899) and *Emile Zola, Novelist and Reformer* (1904), as well as several novels.

ZOLA, Alexandrine (1839–1925)

She was of working-class origins. Zola met her in 1865 and, after living together for several years, they were married in 1870. Authoritarian and considerate at the same time, and an accomplished housewife and hostess, she created a comfortable atmosphere that was propitious to Zola's work. The couple went through a serious crisis in 1891, when she discovered Zola's relationship with Jeanne; but the ties between husband and wife were re-established, strengthened by all the years and the difficult times they had shared. Alexandrine, who had no children, accepted Jeanne's children; she looked after them affectionately, much as an aunt or a grandmother might have done. After her husband's death, she recognized them and allowed them to bear the name 'Emile-Zola'.

Chronology

1894

20–25 September The Army's Intelligence Bureau ('Statistics Section'), headed by Colonel Sandherr, intercepts a letter – the 'bordereau' announcing the delivery to the Germans of documents concerning French national defence – addressed to von Schwartzkoppen, the German military attaché in Paris. At the request of General Mercier, Minister of War, an investigation is immediately carried out in the offices of the General Staff.

6 October Suspicions fall on Alfred Dreyfus, a probationary officer with the General Staff.

9 October The bordereau is submitted to Gobert, a handwriting expert, for analysis.

13 October Gobert hands in a report expressing doubt. Bertillon is then requested to analyse the bordereau. After an initial examination of it, Bertillon concludes that Dreyfus is guilty of having written it.

15 October Summoned to the War Ministry and subjected to rapid questioning, Dreyfus is arrested by Major du Paty de Clam, who has been put in charge of the investigation. Dreyfus is taken to the Cherche-Midi military prison in Paris.

18 October Du Paty de Clam begins to interrogate Dreyfus.

23 October Bertillon's official report is sent to Lépine, the Chief of Police.

29 October Two other handwriting experts, Charavay and Teysonnières, corroborate Bertillon's analysis.

31 October Du Paty hands in to the War Ministry his report on the investigation he has just carried out; it does not come to any specific conclusion.

1 November Dreyfus's name is publicly mentioned for the first time, in *La Libre Parole*.

3 November General Saussier, military governor of Paris, gives orders to open a judicial investigation, which is entrusted to Major d'Ormescheville.

19 December Dreyfus's trial begins before a court martial, in the Cherche-Midi prison. Dreyfus is defended by Edgar Demange. Proceedings take place behind closed doors (*à huis clos*).

20 December In the course of the second hearing of the trial, Major Henry, who represents the Intelligence Bureau, states his conviction that Dreyfus is guilty.

22 December By unanimous decision, the judges on the court martial sentence Dreyfus to deportation and imprisonment for life in some fortified place. By illegal means, they have had knowledge, prior to their deliberations, of a 'secret file' communicated to them by General Mercier; the documents in it are overwhelmingly against Dreyfus.

1895

5 January Captain Dreyfus is publicly subjected to military degradation in the main courtyard of the Ecole Militaire in Paris. The evening papers mention the condemned man's alleged confession to Captain Lebrun-Renaud.

17 January   Félix Faure is elected President of the Republic. That night, Dreyfus is taken from Paris to his place of detention.

7 February   Mathieu Dreyfus, brother of Alfred Dreyfus, goes to see Auguste Scheurer-Kestner, vice-president of the Senate (and Alsatian, like himself). He appeals to Scheurer-Kestner for help, but in vain.

12 March   The boat on which Dreyfus is being deported arrives in French Guiana.

13 April   Dreyfus is transferred to Devil's Island.

1 July   Major Picquart is appointed head of the Intelligence Bureau, replacing Colonel Sandherr, who is ill.

1896

1–2 March   The Intelligence Bureau comes into possession of a letter-telegram (later known as the 'petit bleu') written by von Schwartzkoppen and addressed to Major Esterhazy. Picquart decides to carry out an investigation concerning Esterhazy and soon becomes convinced that it was Esterhazy who actually wrote the bordereau.

5 August   Picquart voices his suspicions regarding Esterhazy to General de Boisdeffre, Chief of the General Staff. De Boisdeffre advises caution.

3 September   Picquart reports to General Gonse (Deputy Chief of the General Staff) on the results of his investigation concerning Esterhazy.

14 September   An article in *L'Eclair*, claiming to provide 'irrefutable proof' of Dreyfus's guilt, mentions for the first time that a secret file was communicated to the judges of the court martial.

16 September   Lucie Dreyfus petitions the Chamber of Deputies for a revision of her husband's trial.

27 October   Picquart's superior officers, who have decided to assign him to a post far removed from Paris, sign orders sending him on an inspection mission in eastern France.

31 October   Henry writes a letter (or has it written) which was supposedly sent by Panizzardi, the Italian military attaché, to von Schwartzkoppen, his German counterpart. It constitutes overwhelming evidence against Dreyfus. This is the document which is later to become known as the Henry forgery.

6 November   In Brussels, Bernard-Lazare publishes his first pamphlet on the Affair, entitled *Une erreur judiciaire. La vérité sur l'affaire Dreyfus (A miscarriage of justice. The truth about the Dreyfus Affair)*. In the course of the next few weeks, he tries to convince several leading figures in the world of letters or politics, including Zola. His efforts do not produce any result.

16 November   Picquart (who has had to leave his post as Head of the Intelligence Bureau) leaves Paris to carry out his mission in eastern France. The second edition of Bernard-Lazare's pamphlet is published by Stock, in Paris.

26 December   Gonse informs Picquart in writing that his mission has been extended and that he must leave for Tunisia.

1897

16 January   Picquart arrives in Tunisia.

21–29 June   While on leave in Paris, Picquart tells Leblois everything he has learned but swears him to secrecy; fearing that some machination against him is being prepared, Picquart gives him a 'general mandate to defend him'.

13 July   Leblois informs Scheurer-Kestner of what he has learned. Although Scheurer-Kestner has sworn to keep the secret, he decides to lead a campaign for Dreyfus's rehabilitation.

17 August   Esterhazy is placed in the non-active ranks on the grounds of 'temporary disabilities'.

16 October   During a meeting held at the War Ministry and attended by Gonse, Henry and du Paty, it is decided to warn Esterhazy of the accusations that will be levelled against him.

18 October   Esterhazy receives a warning through an anonymous letter (signed 'Espérance').

19 October   The first number of *L'Aurore*, a daily newspaper founded by Ernest Vaughan, is published. Among the editors are Georges Clemenceau, Urbain Gohier and Bernard-Lazare.

29 October   Scheurer-Kestner is received at the Elysée Palace by President Félix Faure.

30 October   Scheurer-Kestner has a long conversation with Billot (who is an old friend of his). Billot promises to launch an inquiry but asks Scheurer-Kestner to give him two weeks.

3 November   Scheurer-Kestner goes to see Méline, the Prime Minister (Président du Conseil).

5 November   In *Le Temps* (number dated 6 November), Gabriel Monod declares that Dreyfus is the victim of a miscarriage of justice.

6 November   One year after his first effort, Bernard-Lazare calls on Zola again. Bernard-Lazare is about to publish his second pamphlet, *Une erreur judiciaire. L'affaire Dreyfus* (Stock).

8 and 10 November   Louis Leblois pays visits to Zola, to talk to him about the Dreyfus file.

11 November   Mathieu Dreyfus has learned (thanks to a banker named Castro) who actually wrote the bordereau; he goes to see Scheurer-Kestner, who confirms to him that his information is accurate.

12 November   Mathieu Dreyfus, Leblois and Emmanuel Arène attend a meeting at Scheurer-Kestner's home.

13 November   Another meeting at Scheurer-Kestner's home. Zola is present, at Scheurer-Kestner's invitation, along with Leblois, Marcel Prévost, the novelist, and a lawyer named Sarrut.

15 November   In an open letter to 'a friend', published in *Le Temps* dated 16 November, Scheurer-Kestner declares that Dreyfus is innocent. Von Schwartzkoppen is recalled by his government (put in command of the 2d Regiment of Grenadiers of the Guard) and leaves Paris.

16 November   The morning papers publish a letter written to the Minister of War by Mathieu Dreyfus the previous day, accusing Esterhazy of having written the bordereau.

17 November   As a result of the accusation, an investigation is begun into Esterhazy's activities and is entrusted to General de Pellieux. Initially it is conducted through administrative channels (17 to 20 November); then it becomes a judicial investigation (21 November to 3 December).

25 November   Zola's first article in favour of the Dreyfusard cause, 'M. Scheurer-Kestner', appears in *Le Figaro*.

26 November   Picquart, recalled from Tunisia, arrives in Paris. He is questioned in connection with the investigation being led by de Pellieux.

1 December   Zola's campaign in *Le Figaro* continues with 'The Syndicate'.

3 December   De Pellieux hands in the conclusions of his investigation to General Saussier.

4 December   A new investigation concerning Esterhazy is entrusted to Major Ravary. Interpellation on the Affair in the Chamber of Deputies. Méline defends himself, stating that 'there is no Dreyfus Affair', 'there cannot be any Dreyfus Affair'.

5 December   Zola's third article in *Le Figaro* appears: 'The Minutes'.

7 December   In the Senate, Scheurer-Kestner interpellates the government.

14 December   Zola publishes *Letter to the Young People* (as a pamphlet, not as an article in *Le Figaro*).

26 December   Having examined the bordereau, the three handwriting experts, Belhomme, Varinard and Couard, hand in their conclusions to Ravary: it is not the work of Esterhazy.

1898

1 January   Ravary gives a report on the investigation to General Saussier; its conclusion is that the case should be dismissed for lack of evidence. Nonetheless, Saussier decides that Esterhazy should be tried.

7 January   Zola publishes *Letter to France* as a pamphlet. *Le Siècle* publishes the indictment against Dreyfus. At the same time, Bernard-Lazare publishes his third pamphlet, *Comment on condamne un innocent* (How an innocent man is convicted).

10 January   Esterhazy's trial begins at the Cherche-Midi prison. Within hours it is decided to hold the trial in closed session.

11 January   By unanimous decision, the court martial acquits Esterhazy.

13 January   Zola's 'J'accuse' ('Letter to M. Félix Faure, President of the Republic') is published in *L'Aurore*. In the Chamber, Albert de Mun interpellates the government. In the Senate, Scheurer-Kestner's term as Vice-President is not renewed. Early in the morning, Picquart is taken to the Mont-Valérien military prison and is placed under close arrest.

14 January   *L'Aurore* begins to publish a first 'protest' signed by a series of 'intellectuals' and calling for the revision of Dreyfus's trial. A second protest appears on 16 January.

18 January   Billot lodges a complaint against Zola and *L'Aurore*.

19 January   The *Manifeste du Prolétariat* is launched by the Socialist Deputies; it is opposed to any active involvement in the Dreyfus Affair. Jaurès signs it but very soon changes his mind.

20 January   Zola and Perrenx (manager of *L'Aurore*) are subpoenaed to appear in court.

21 January   Belhomme, Varinard and Couard, three handwriting experts, considering *J'accuse* libellous, have a writ served on Zola to appear before a magistrate's court.

7 February   Zola's trial opens at the Assize Court of the Seine.

11 and 12 February   Picquart testifies at the fifth and sixth hearings.

17 February   De Pellieux alludes to the 'Henry forgery' at the tenth hearing.

18 February   General de Boisdeffre testifies at the eleventh hearing; his assertions intimidate the jury.

21 February   Van Cassel, the prosecutor, makes his closing speech. Zola delivers his 'Statement to the Jury'. Labori begins his plea for the defence.

22 February   Zola's 'Statement to the Jury' is published in *L'Aurore*.

23 February   Zola is given the maximum sentence for libel: one year in prison and a fine of three thousand francs.

24–25 February   It is decided, at two meetings held at the homes of Trarieux and Scheurer-Kestner, to found the Ligue pour la défense des droits de l'homme et du citoyen.

26 February   By decree, Picquart is declared unfit for service on grounds of 'grave misconduct'. Zola appeals against the verdict of 23 February.

1 March   Zola's novel, *Paris*, is published.

9 March   Belhomme, Varinard and Couard, start proceedings against Zola before the ninth magistrate's court.

15 March   *Le Siècle* announces that a Committee is being formed to have a medal struck in Zola's honour (the Charpentier medal).

2 April   The Criminal Chamber of the Supreme Court of Appeal overturns the verdict of 23 February because of a legal technicality.

8 April   The judges of the court martial which acquitted Esterhazy bring a civil action against Zola.

8 to 22 May   Legislative elections: Jaurès and Reinach lose their seats in the Chamber of Deputies; Drumont is elected in Algiers.

23 May   Zola's trial opens in Versailles, at the Assize Court of Seine-et-Oise. Labori appeals, which suspends the proceedings. In *Le Petit Journal*, Judet publishes a libellous article about Zola's father.

24 May   Zola sues Judet for libel.

26 May   An election is held to choose a new member of the Académie française: not one vote is cast in favour of Zola. (Same result on 8 December, when another election takes place.)

15 June   Méline's government resigns.

16 June   The Supreme Court of Appeal rejects the appeal submitted by Labori on 23 May.

28 June   Brisson forms a Cabinet; Godefroy Cavaignac becomes Minister of War.

7 July   In a speech to the Chamber, Cavaignac asserts that he has irrefutable proof that Dreyfus is guilty. He specifically refers to three documents taken from the 'secret file'.

9 July   The libel suit by the three experts resumes. Zola receives a two-week suspended prison sentence and a fine of two thousand francs, and must also pay five thousand francs in damages to each of the experts. In a letter to the Prime Minister, Picquart challenges the validity of the proofs alleged by Cavaignac.

12 July   Cavaignac lodges a complaint against Picquart and Leblois. Esterhazy is arrested and imprisoned.

13 July   Picquart is arrested and imprisoned.

16 July   In *L'Aurore*, Zola publishes his 'Letter to Prime Minister Brisson'.

18 July   Zola's trial at the Assize Court in Versailles resumes. He is sentenced again. Zola leaves France that same evening for England so that the sentence cannot be served on him and become enforceable.

19 July   Labori appeals in the trial concerning the three experts. Zola stays at the Grosvenor Hotel, in London.

21 July   Beginning of a series of articles by Reinach, in *Le Siècle*, on 'the forgers'; they are aimed at du Paty du Clam and Esterhazy in particular.

22 July   Zola moves to the Oatlands Park Hotel, between Weybridge and Walton-on-Thames.

26 July   Zola is suspended from the Légion d'honneur.

1 August   He moves into 'Penn', a house near Weybridge.

3 August   Labori succeeds in obtaining a conviction for libel by the ninth magistrate's court against Ernest Judet and *Le Petit Journal*.

5 August   The Supreme Court of Appeal rejects the appeal by Zola and *L'Aurore* against the verdict in Versailles on 18 July.

8 August   Albert Fabre, the examining magistrate, begins to question Picquart.

10 August   The Chamber of Appeals before magistrates' courts stiffens the sentences in the trial of the three experts: Zola is sentenced to a month in prison and a fine of two thousand francs and must pay ten thousand francs in damages to each expert. Jaurès begins a series of articles entitled 'Les preuves' (Proof) in *La Petite République*.

11 August   Jeanne Rozerot and the children arrive at 'Penn'; they remain in England until 15 October.

12 August   Acceding to the request by Feuilloley, the prosecutor, the Chamber of Indictments decrees that the case against Esterhazy is to be dismissed. He is freed.

13 August   Captain Cuignet, an aide on Cavaignac's staff, examines the secret file and discovers the 'Henry forgery'.

25 August   Judge Fabre refers Picquart and Leblois to a magistrate's court.

27 August   Zola moves to 'Summerfield' (Addlestone). The Council of Inquiry in charge of ruling on the accusations brought against Esterhazy rules in favour of his discharge.

30 August   Colonel Henry admits to Cavaignac that he has committed forgery. He is arrested and taken to the fort at Mont-Valérien. General de Boisdeffre requests to be relieved from his duties.

31 August   Henry commits suicide in his cell at Mont-Valérien.

3 September   Cavaignac resigns from the government.

4 September   Esterhazy leaves France.

5 September   General Zurlinden becomes Minister of War.

17 September   Zurlinden resigns. He is replaced by General Chanoine.

20 September   Zurlinden (reinstated in his former functions as military governor of Paris) orders that inquiries be started against Picquart.

21 September   Picquart and Leblois appear before the eighth magistrate's court. The trial is postponed.

22 September   Picquart is taken to the Cherche-Midi prison.

10 October   Zola moves to Bailey's Hotel, Kensington, London.

11 October   In enactment of the verdict of 10 August, a distraint order is placed on the furniture and other belongings in Zola's home in the rue de Bruxelles and they are put up for auction. Eugène Fasquelle purchases a table for thirty-two thousand francs, which brings the sale to an end.

15 October   Zola moves to the Queen's Hotel in Upper Norwood, a London suburb.

25 October   The Brisson government falls. Alexandrine Zola arrives at Upper Norwood, where she remains until 5 December.

27 October   The Criminal Chamber of the Supreme Court of Appeal begins to examine the request for a revision of Dreyfus's trial.

29 October   The Criminal Chamber declares that the request is admissible and decides to conduct an investigation.

31 October   The Dupuy government is formed.

7 November   In an article in *Le Siècle*, Reinach accuses Henry outright of having acted in collusion with Esterhazy. (In the number dated 6 December, he reiterates the accusation and places himself at the disposal of the law and of Henry's widow.)

24 November   Zurlinden refers Picquart to the second Paris military jurisdiction.

25 November   *Le Siècle* and *L'Aurore* publish the first lists of signatures concerning the tribute to Picquart.

14 December   *La Libre Parole* opens a subscription in favour of Colonel Henry's widow, Berthe Henry, so that she can sue Reinach. (The subscription closes on 15 January 1899.)

22 December   Alexandrine Zola arrives at Upper Norwood for her second stay in England.

1899

3 January   Georges Clemenceau visits the Zolas at Upper Norwood.

6 January   Jules Quesnay de Beaurepaire, who presides over the Civil Chamber of the Supreme Court of Appeal and has accused the Criminal Chamber of having been partial towards Picquart, demands an inquiry.

8 January   Having received no reply from Charles Mazeau, first presiding judge of the Supreme Court of Appeal, Quesnay de Beaurepaire resigns.

12 January   Georges Lebret, the Garde des sceaux (Minister of Justice), instructs Mazeau to launch an inquiry into the facts pointed out by Quesnay de Beaurepaire.

21 January   Another distraint order and auction at Zola's home in Paris. Eugène Fasquelle buys a mirror and a table for two thousand five hundred francs.

27 January   Reinach's trial, at Berthe Henry's instigation, opens before the Assize Court. Labori defends Reinach and appeals.

30 January   Lebret introduces a bill in the Chamber of Deputies which would bestow on the three Chambers of the Supreme Court of Appeal, jointly, all power of decision with regard to a revision of Dreyfus's trial (this becomes the *loi de dessaisissement*, or law on change of jurisdiction).

9 February   The Criminal Chamber concludes its investigation concerning a revision.

10 February   The Chamber of Deputies passes the law on change of jurisdiction.

16 February   Félix Faure dies. He had been strongly opposed to a revision.

18 February   Emile Loubet is elected President of the Republic.

23 February   Félix Faure's funeral takes place. Déroulède leads an abortive attempt at a nationalist uprising.

27 February   Alexandrine Zola leaves Upper Norwood and returns to Paris.

1 March   The Senate passes the law on change of jurisdiction, which is promulgated the same day.

10 March   Jaurès visits Zola at Upper Norwood.

21 March   First plenary session of the Supreme Court of Appeal, all Chambers sitting jointly, with Charles Mazeau presiding. He has named Alexis Ballot-Beaupré as rapporteur.

27–28 March   Labori visits Zola at Upper Norwood.

29 March   Jeanne Rozerot and the children arrive in England to spend the Easter holidays. During that period Zola moves to the Crystal Palace Royal Hotel with them.

31 March   *Le Figaro* begins to publish the detailed proceedings of the investigation carried out by the Criminal Chamber.

8 April   Zola and Senator Ludovic Trarieux meet for discussions in London.

24 April   Hearings begin before the Supreme Court of Appeal; Captain Freystaetter appears. (He was one of the seven military judges at the trial in December 1894; since Henry's suicide, he has become convinced that Dreyfus is innocent.)

29 April   Final hearing before the Supreme Court of Appeal; Cuignet and du Paty de Clam are heard.

15 May   The first instalment of Zola's novel, *Fécondité*, appears in *L'Aurore*.

16 May   Clemenceau visits Zola in London again.

29 May   The Supreme Court of Appeal sits to hear Ballot-Beaupré's report.

1 June   Du Paty de Clam is arrested.

3 June   The Supreme Court of Appeal overturns the verdict of 1894 and rules that Dreyfus is to appear before another court martial.

5 June   Dreyfus is informed of the decree proclaiming the revision. Zola arrives in France. The Versailles sentence of 18 July 1898 is served upon him at his home in the rue de Bruxelles. Zola's article, 'Justice', appears in *L'Aurore*.

9 June   Zola challenges the Versailles verdict. Picquart is released from prison. Dreyfus leaves Devil's Island on board the cruiser *Sfax*.

12 June   The Dupuy government falls.

2 June   The Waldeck-Rousseau government 'of republican defence' is formed. The War portfolio goes to General de Galliffet, whose task it will be to persuade the army to accept the revision.

1 July   Dreyfus arrives in France and is taken to the military prison in Rennes.

18 July   *Le Matin* publishes a long article by Esterhazy, who gives his account of his role in the Affair. He acknowledges that he wrote the bordereau but states that he did so 'under dictation' and on orders from his superiors.

7 August   Dreyfus's trial by the court martial in Rennes begins. He is defended by Edgar Demange and Fernand Labori.

12 August   General Mercier testifies. In Paris, the police arrest a number of royalist and nationalist leaders, including Paul Déroulède. Jules Guérin, director of the newspaper called *L'Antijuif* (The Anti-Jew), barricades himself at the seat of the Grand-Occident de France in the rue Chabrol (episode called 'Fort Chabrol').

14 August   In Rennes, Labori is wounded in an assassination attempt.

31 August   Zola learns that he is summoned to appear in Versailles on 23 November.

8 September   Edgar Demange pleads for the defence (Labori has decided not to speak).

9 September   The Rennes trial ends, after twenty-five hearings: it finds Dreyfus guilty, once again, but with 'extenuating circumstances'.

12 September   Zola's article, 'The Fifth Act', appears in *L'Aurore*.

19 September   Dreyfus is pardoned by Emile Loubet, President of France. Scheurer-Kestner dies.

21 September   General de Galliffet sends the army an order in which he states, 'The incident is closed.'

22 September   Zola publishes his 'Letter to Madame Alfred Dreyfus' in *L'Aurore*.

4 October   The last instalment of *Fécondité* appears in *L'Aurore*. It is published in book form on 12 October, by Fasquelle.

23 November   The trial in Versailles is postponed to some unspecified date.

1900–1908

1 March 1900   An amnesty bill relating to all aspects of the Affair is laid before the Senate.

14 March 1900   Zola's testimony is heard by the Senate commission, as part of the debate over the amnesty bill.

29 May 1900   Zola publishes his 'Letter to the Senate' in *L'Aurore*.

18 December 1900   After several months of debate, the Chamber of Deputies passes the amnesty law.

22 December 1900   Zola publishes his 'Letter to M. Emile Loubet, President of the Republic', in *L'Aurore*.

24 December 1900   The Senate, in turn, passes the amnesty law.

1 February 1901   Zola publishes *La Vérité en marche*, which brings together all of the articles he wrote throughout the Dreyfus Affair.

29 September 1902   Zola dies at his Paris home, in the rue de Bruxelles.

5 October 1902   Zola's funeral takes place at the Montmartre cemetery in Paris. In his oration, Anatole France says, 'Let us envy him. His destiny and his heart reserved for him the most superb of fates: he was a moment in the conscience of mankind.'

26 November 1903   Dreyfus writes to the Minister of Justice requesting the revision of the trial in Rennes.

5 March 1904   The Criminal Chamber of the Supreme Court of Appeal declares his request admissible and orders an investigation.

19 November 1904   The investigation comes to an end.

12 July 1906   With all Chambers of the Supreme Court of Appeal sitting jointly, the Court revokes the verdict reached by the court martial in Rennes and declares that in reaching the verdict of guilty against Alfred Dreyfus, the court martial was 'in the wrong'.

13 July 1906   The Chamber of Deputies passes a law reinstating both Dreyfus and Picquart in the army, Dreyfus with the rank of squadron leader and Picquart with that of Brigadier General. On the same day, the Chamber passes another bill, asking that Zola's ashes be transferred to the Pantheon.

21 July 1906   Dreyfus is named Chevalier de la Légion d'honneur.

25 October 1906   Clemenceau becomes Prime Minister. He names Picquart Minister of War.

4 June 1908   During the official ceremony in which Zola's ashes are transferred to the Pantheon, a journalist named Louis Grégori fires two shots at Dreyfus, wounding him in the arm.

Bibliography

ARENDT, Hannah   *The Origins of Totalitarianism*, Harcourt Brace & Company, New York, 1973

BARRES, Maurice   *Scènes et doctrines du nationalisme*, F. Juven, Paris, 1902; Eds. du Trident, Paris, 1987

BARROWS, Susanna   *Distorting Mirrors: Visions of the Crowd in Late Nineteenth Century France*, Yale University Press, New Haven, 1981

BECKER, Colette (ed.)   *L'affaire Dreyfus: La Vérité en marche*, Garnier-Flammarion, Paris, 1969

BERNARD, Marc   *Zola par lui-même*, Editions du Seuil, Paris, 1952

BLUM, Antoinette   'Portrait of an Intellectual: Lucien Herr and the Dreyfus Affair', *Nineteenth-century French Studies*, Fall 1989, vol. 18, nos 1/2

BLUM, Antoinette   'Images of the Dreyfus Affair', *Jewish Quarterly*, Summer 1989, vol. 36, no. 2

BOUSSEL, Patrice   *L'affaire Dreyfus et la presse*, Armand Colin, Paris, 1960

BREDIN, Jean-Denis   *The Affair*, trans. by Jeffrey Mehlman, George Braziller, New York, 1986, and Sidgwick and Jackson, London, 1987 (*L'Affaire*, Julliard, Paris, 1983)

BREDIN, Jean-Denis   *Bernard Lazare*, Eds. de Fallois, Paris, 1992

BROGAN, D. W.   *France Under the Republic 1870–1939*, Harper & Bros., New York, 1940

BROMBERT, Victor   *The Intellectual Hero*, J. B. Lippincott, Philadelphia, 1961

BROWN, Frederick   *Zola: A Life*, Farrar Straus Giroux, New York, 1995

BURNS, Colin   'Zola in Exile', *French Studies*, vol. XVII, 1963

BURNS, Michael   *Rural Society and French Politics: Boulangism and the Dreyfus Affair*, Princeton University Press, Princeton, 1984

BURNS, Michael   *Dreyfus: A Family Affair, from the French Revolution to the Holocaust*, HarperCollins Publishers, New York, 1991

CAHM, Eric   'Péguy et le nationalisme français, de l'affaire Dreyfus à la Grande Guerre', *Cahiers de l'Amitié Charles Péguy*, Paris, 1972

CAHM, Eric   'Did the Dreyfus Affair Change France? The New Orientation of Research in the Centenary

	Year', *Modern and Contemporary France*,1995, vol. 3, no. 1
CAHM, Eric	'No End in Sight for Dreyfus Research: The Beginning of a Twelve-Year Centenary', *Modern and Contemporary France*, 1995, vol. 3, no. 2
CHAPMAN, Guy	*The Dreyfus Trials*, B.T. Batsford, London, 1972
CHARLE, Christophe	*Naissance des 'intellectuels': 1880–1900*, Editions de Minuit, Paris, 1990
CURTIS, Michael	*Three Against the Third Republic: Sorel, Barrès and Maurras*, Greenwood Press, London, 1977
DANSETTE, Adrien	*Histoire religieuse de la France contemporaine*, Flammarion, Paris, 1965
DATTA, Venita	'The Dreyfus Affair and Anti-Semitism: Jewish Identity at *La Revue Blanche*', *Historical Reflections*, Winter 1995, vol. 21, no. 1
DELMAIRE, Danielle	*Antisémitisme et catholiques dans le Nord pendant l'affaire Dreyfus*, Presses Universitaires de Lille, Lille, 1991
DELPORTE, Christian	'Images d'une guerre franco-française: la caricature au temps de l'affaire Dreyfus', *French Cultural Studies*, 1 June 1995, vol. 6, no. 2
DIANI, Marco	'Metamorphosis of Nationalism: Durkheim, Barrès and the Dreyfus Affair', *The Jerusalem Journal of International Relations*, 1 December 1991, vol. 13, no. 4
DOTY, Stewart	*From Cultural Rebellion to Counterrevolution: The Politics of Maurice Barrès*, Ohio University, Athens, Ohio, 1976
DREYFUS, Alfred	*Cinq annees de ma vie*, La Découverte, Paris, 1994
DREYFUS, Mathieu	*L'Affaire telle que je l'ai vécue*, Grasset, Paris, 1978
DRUMONT, Edouard	*La France juive*, 2 vols, Flammarion, Paris, 1885 and 1938
FELDMAN, Egal	*The Dreyfus Affair and the American Conscience*, Wayne State University Press, Detroit, 1981
FITCH, Nancy	'Mass Culture, Mass Parliamentary Politics and Modern Anti-Semitism: The Dreyfus Affair in Rural France', *The American Historical Review*, 1 February 1992, vol. 97, no. 1
FRIEDMAN, Lee Max	*Zola & the Dreyfus Case; his defense of liberty and its enduring significance*, Gordon Press, New York, 1973
GOLDBERG, Harvey	*Life of Jean Jaurès*, University of Wisconsin, Madison, 1962
GRIFFITHS, Richard	*The Use of Abuse: the Polemics of the Dreyfus Affair and Its Aftermath*, Berg, New York, 1991
GUILLEMIN, Henri	*L'énigme Esterhazy*, Gallimard, Paris, 1962
GUILLEMIN, Henri (ed.)	*J'accuse! La vérité en marche*, Eds. Complexe, Brussels, 1988
HALASZ, Nicholas	*Captain Dreyfus: the story of a mass hysteria*, Simon & Schuster, New York, 1955

HALEVY, Jean-Pierre   *Regards sur l'affaire Dreyfus/Daniel Halévy*, Editions
                               de Fallois, Paris, 1994

HERZOG, William   *From Dreyfus to Pétain*, Creative Age Press, New
                               York, 1947

HOFFMAN, Robert Louis   *More Than a Trial: the Struggle over Captain Dreyfus*,
                               Free Press, New York, 1980

HUTTON, Patrick   *The Cult of the Revolutionary Tradition: The Blanquists
                               in French Politics, 1864–1893*, University of Cali-
                               fornia Press, Berkeley, 1981

HYMAN, Paula   *From Dreyfus to Vichy: The Remaking of French Jewry,
                               1906–1939*, Columbia University Press, New York,
                               1979

JOHNSON, Douglas   *France and the Dreyfus Affair*, Walker, New York,
                               1967

JOSEPHSON, Matthew   *Zola and His Time: the history of his martial career in
                               letters, with an account of his circle of friends, his
                               remarkable enemies, cyclopean labors, public campaigns,
                               trials and ultimate glorification*, Macaulay, New York,
                               1928

KEDWARD, H. R.   *The Dreyfus Affair: Catalyst for Tensions in French
                               Society*, Longman, London, 1965

KLEEBLATT, Norman L. (ed.)   *The Dreyfus Affair: Art, Truth & Justice*, The Jewish
                               Museum, New York, and University of California
                               Press, Berkeley, 1987

LANOUX, Armand   *Bonjour, Monsieur Zola*, Amiot-Dumont, Paris, 1954

LARKIN, Maurice   *Church and State after the Dreyfus Affair: the Separation
                               Issue in France*, Macmillan, London, 1974

LEBLOND-ZOLA, Denise   *Emile Zola raconté par sa fille*, Grasset, Paris, 1986
                               (Fasquelle, 1931)

LEROY, Geraldi   *Les écrivains et l'affaire Dreyfus*, actes du colloque
                               organisé par le Centre Charles Péguy et l'Université
                               d'Orléans, octobre 1981, Presses Universitaires de
                               France, Paris, 1983

LEWIS, David L.   *Prisoners of Honor; The Dreyfus Affair*, William
                               Morrow & Co., New York, 1973

LINDEMANN, Albert S.   *The Jew Accused: three anti-Semitic affairs (Dreyfus,
                               Beilis, Frank), 1894–1915*, Cambridge University
                               Press, Cambridge, 1991

MARRUS, Michael   *The Politics of Assimilation: A Study of the French
                               Jewish Community at the Time of the Dreyfus Affair*,
                               Clarendon Press, Oxford, 1971

MAYEUR, Jean-Marie and   *The Third Republic from its Origins to the Great War
REBERIOUX, Madeleine   1871–1914*, trans. by J. R. Foster, Cambridge
                               University Press, 1984

MCMILLAN, James F.   *Dreyfus to De Gaulle: Politics and Society in France
                               1898–1969*, Edward Arnold, London, 1985

MITCHELL, Allan   'The Xenophobic Style: French Counterespionage
                               and the Emergence of the Dreyfus Affair', *Journal of
                               Modern History*, vol. 52, no. 3, September 1980

MITTERRAND, Henri — 'Emile Zola et "Le Rappel"', *Les cahiers naturalistes*, no. 15, 1960

MITTERRAND, Henri — *Zola journaliste de l'affaire Manet à l'affaire Dreyfus*, Armand Colin, Paris, 1962

NORD, Philip — *Paris Shopkeepers and the Politics of Resentment*, Princeton University Press, Princeton, 1986

NYE, Robert A. — *Crime, Madness and Politics in Modern France: the medical concept of national decline*, Princeton University Press, Princeton, 1984

PAGES, Alain — *Emile Zola, un intellectuel dans l'affaire Dreyfus*, Séguier, Paris, 1991

PORCH, Douglas — *The March to the Marne: the French Army 1870–1914*, Cambridge University Press, 1981

PROUST, Marcel — *Jean Santeuil* (chs V–IX), Gallimard, Paris, 1952

RALSTON, David B. — *The Army of the Republic*, MIT Press, Cambridge, Mass., 1967

REMOND, René — *The Right Wing in France from 1815 to De Gaulle*, trans. by James M. Laux, University of Pennsylvania Press, 1969

ROTH, Jack J. — *The Cult of Violence: Sorel and the Sorelians*, University of California Press, Berkeley, 1980

ROUSSO, Henry — *Le Syndrome de Vichy de 1944 à nos jours*, Eds. du Seuil, Paris, 1987

RUTKOFF, Peter M. — *Revanche and Revision: the Ligue des Patriotes and the Origins of the Radical Right in France, 1882–1900*, Ohio University, Athens, Ohio, 1981

SCHEURER-KESTNER, Auguste — *Mémoires d'un sénateur dreyfusard*, Bueb & Reumaux, Strasbourg, 1988

SILVERA, A. — *Daniel Halévy and his Times: A Gentleman Commoner in the Third Republic*, Cornell University Press, Ithaca, N. Y., 1966

SNYDER, Louis — *The Dreyfus Case: A Documentary History*, Rutgers University Press, New Brunswick, New Jersey, 1973

SONN, Richard D. — *Anarchism and Cultural Politics in Fin-de-Siècle France*, University of Nebraska Press, Lincoln, 1989

SOUCY, Robert — *Fascism in France: The Case of Maurice Barrès*, University of California Press, Berkeley, 1972

SPEIRS, Dorothy and SIGNORI, Dolores — *Emile Zola dans la presse parisienne 1882–1902*, University of Toronto Press, Toronto, 1985

STERNHELL, Zeev — *La droite révolutionnaire, 1881–1914: Les origines françaises du fascisme*, Editions du Seuil, Paris, 1978

STERNHELL, Zeev — *The Birth of Fascist Ideology*, trans. by David Maisel, Princeton University Press, 1994

SUTTON, Michael — *Nationalism, Positivism and Catholicism: The Politics of Charles Maurras and French Catholics 1890–1914*, Cambridge University Press, Cambridge, 1983

SWEETS, John F. — 'Hold that Pendulum! Redefining Fascism, Collaborationism and Resistance in France', *French Historical Studies*, vol. XV, no. 4 (Fall 1988)

TROYAT, Henri   *Emile Zola*, Flammarion, Paris, 1972

VIZETELLY, Ernest   *With Zola in England*, Chatto & Windus, London, 1899
VIZETELLY, Ernest   *Emile Zola, Novelist and Reformer*, John Lane, The Bodley Head, London, 1904

WEBER, Eugen   *Action Française; royalism and reaction in 20th Century France*, Stanford University Press, 1962
WEBER, Eugen   *France Fin de Siècle*, Harvard University Press, Cambridge, Mass., 1986
WILSON, N.   *Bernard Lazare: Antisemitism and the Problem of Jewish Identity in Late Nineteenth-century France*, Cambridge University Press, Cambridge, 1978
WILSON, Stephen   *Ideology and Experience: Antisemitism in France at the time of the Dreyfus Affair*, Fairleigh Dickinson University Press, Rutherford, New Jersey, 1982
WINOCK, Michel   *Edouard Drumont et Cie*, Editions du Seuil, Paris, 1982
WINOCK, Michel   *Nationalisme, antisémitisme et fascisme en France*, Editions du Seuil, Paris, 1990
WOHL, Robert   *The Generation of 1914*, Harvard University Press, Cambridge, Mass., 1979

Index